COURTING SCANDAL

The Rise and Fall of Jane Boleyn, Lady Rochford

JAMES TAFFE

Copyright © James Taffe

All rights reserved. No part of this publication may be reproduced, stored in a retrieval system, or transmitted, in any form or by any means, electronic, mechanical, photocopying, recording or otherwise, except as permitted by the UK Copyright, Designs and Patents Act 1988, without the prior permission of the author.

ISBN: 9798375083896

Taffe, James
    1. Jane Boleyn, Lady Rochford, courtier, d. 1542. 2. Great Britain—History—Henry VIII, 1509–1547—Biography. 3. Anne Boleyn, Queen, consort of Henry VIII, King of England, 1507–1536. 4. Henry VIII, King of England, 1491–1547. 5. Queens—Great Britain—Biography.

List of Illustrations:

Front Cover
Portrait of an Unknown Lady by Hans Holbein the Younger, c. 1532-43
A letter from Katherine Howard to Thomas Culpeper, 1541

Back Cover
Portrait of The Lady Parker by Hans Holbein the Younger, c. 1540-43
Jane Boleyn, Lady Rochford's signature, 1536

All images have been sourced from Wikimedia Commons.

For Mum

ACKNOWLEDGEMENTS

I would like to express my gratitude to Durham University, the Arts and Humanities Research Council, and the Northern Bridge Consortium for awarding me a Doctoral Studentship, and to University of Birmingham for the Edna Pearson Scholarship, without which, this book, based on my doctoral research, would not have been possible. I am particularly grateful to my supervisor, Dr Natalie Mears, for her support, training, advice, and patience throughout the last four years. I am grateful to Professor Glenn Richardson and Professor Christian Liddy for their comments and feedback on my thesis. I would also like to thank all of my friends and colleagues at Durham University, particularly Fergal, Rachel and Lily, who have always been so supportive, not least by sitting through many conference papers and in allowing me to discuss my research with them, often at length.

I am indebted to Paul John ('Mr. John'), Jane King, Dr Ceri Law, and Dr Jonathan Willis, from each of whom, as mentors at different, formative stages in my career, pupil to postgraduate, I have learnt so much. Their guidance, care, and enthusiasm for history, spanning nearly two decades, has been both inspiring and essential.

I would like to acknowledge the work and help of all of the staff in the The National Archives in Kew, The British Library in London, and at all other institutions, libraries and archives that I have visited to undertake research. I would also like to thank Dr Owen Emmerson for his support and encouragement, Dr Nikki Clark, Gareth Russell and Dr Sara Wolfson for sharing their unpublished theses – to Nikki in particular I am grateful for her advice, and for allowing me to vent my many frustrations while writing up my thesis.

I would like to thank Shahnaaz, Deepak, Jaspal, Lakshana, Jenny and Peter for their friendship over the years, but especially the last four years. After I relocated to Durham to study, they were sure to check in regularly, and were always encouraging. I am particularly grateful to Michael, for his love, support, and for helping to keep life in perspective. And to my Mum – I owe her everything, and without her I would not have made it this far.

CONTENTS

1	'My slaunder for ever shall be ryfe': Who was Jane Boleyn?	1
2	'Mistres Parker': Finding a foothold	6
3	'When she list to spit or do otherwise at her pleasure': Maid-of-Honour	13
4	'A glorified boudoir'?: Queenship	19
5	'For the establishment of good order': Ordinances and Perquisites	31
6	'The wicked wife': Marriage	40
7	'None but God can get him out of it': The Boleyn Ascendancy	48
8	'She would not damn her own soul on any consideration': Oath	59
9	'I loved you a great deal more than I made feign for': Intimacy	67
10	'Sythens I injoye their service they may have some porcion of my lyving': Advancement	76
11	'Preserve my courte inviolate': Piety and Pastime	84
12	'Poor banished creature': Exile	97
13	'...apon a certeyn tyme waytynge on your Grace at Honesdon': Jane and Princess Mary	103
14	'Certain other little follies': Arrest, Investigation, Trial	109

15	'Seche desyre as you have had to such tales hase browthe you to thys': The Fall of Anne Boleyn	119
16	'A power desolat wydow wythoute comffort': Widowhood	132
17	'No meet suit for any man to move such matters': Politics	137
18	'...sume of your speciall frendes nygh aboute the kynges highnes': Patron	145
19	'Those with the queen are guards and spies, not servants': Spy	153
20	'...you wyll com when my lade Rochforthe ys here': Bawd	163
21	'My lady of Rochford was the principal occasion of the queen's folly': The Fall of Katherine Howard	178
22	'wt goodly wordes and stedfast contenance': Execution	189
23	The Infamous Lady Rochford	199

| Notes | 202 |
| Bibliography | 242 |

1

'My slaunder for ever shall be ryfe'
WHO WAS JANE BOLEYN?

Jane Boleyn was a lady-in-waiting who served at the court of Henry VIII. She has been almost invariably described as a 'vicious', 'heartless', and most 'unnatural' woman for the betrayal of her husband, George Boleyn. Her intimate role in court intrigues sent not only her husband but two Tudor queens, Anne Boleyn and Katherine Howard, to the scaffold. For her involvement in the latter of these scandals Jane too lost her head.

On 13 February 1542, at about nine o'clock in the morning, Jane was executed at the Tower of London.[1] She had been convicted of treason by Act of Attainder for having 'falsely and traitorously aided and abetted' Katherine, Henry's fifth wife and queen, to commit adultery. The Act identified her as 'that bawde the Ladye Jane Rochforde', with 'bawd' meaning that she was an agent of sexual immorality and debauchery. Shortly after her arrest, the French ambassador Charles de Marillac made the curious remark that Jane 'all her life had the name to esteem her honour little, and has thus in her old age shown little amendment'.[2] Following her execution, Jane's name became synonymous with lust, depravity and moral decay. It is not difficult to imagine men and women at court exchanging, in hushed whispers, the sordid details of her crimes, each one in their turn scandalised by the legend of the infamous Lady Rochford. It was probably told as something of a cautionary tale, embellished and enlivened by popular gossip until it became difficult, for them, and now, for us, to tell the difference between fact and fiction.

Her conviction in 1542 would prove that Jane was morally bankrupt, dishonest and deceitful, leading many of her contemporaries to doubt the truth of the charges she laid against her husband, George, and sister-in-law, Anne, nearly six years earlier. In 1545, only a few years after Jane's death, Johannes

Sleidan, a Lutheran historian chronicling the Reformation, was sent on embassy to England where he was regaled with the sensational story of her betrayal. Sleidan remarked a decade later that Anne and George met their end 'through the false accusation of that errant strompet his wife, whiche afterwardes suffered therfore, accordynge to her desertes'.[3] Writing in around 1558, courtier George Cavendish, who knew Jane personally, lamented in her name:

> Beryng the name of an honest and chast wyfe;
> Where now my slaunder for ever shall be ryfe
> In every matter, both early and late,
> Called the woman of vice insaciatt.[4]

Here Cavendish casts doubt as to Jane's credibility; he, and her contemporaries, if Cavendish's verse was to resonate with them, must have felt that she, 'without respect of any wyfely truthe', had falsely accused Anne and George of incest. It was this betrayal, of a wife to her own husband, for which Jane would be remembered. John Foxe, an English historian and martyrologist, wrote in the 1576 and 1583 editions of his *Actes and Monuments* that 'it is reported of some, that this Lady Rochforde forged a false letter against her husband, and Queene Anne his sister, by the which they wer both cast away, which if it be so, the judgement of God then is here to be marked'.[5] In *Extracts from the Life of The Virtuous Christian and Renowned Queen Anne Boleigne* (c. 1605), George Wyatt, the grandson of Sir Thomas Wyatt, an English ambassador and poet who was accused alongside Anne and George in 1536, regarded Jane as a 'wicked wife' and 'the accuser of her own husband'. 'What she did', Wyatt wrote, 'was more to be rid of him than of true ground against him'.[6]

From the seventeenth through the eighteenth and nineteenth centuries, historians continued to set a judgmental tone in evaluating Jane. One historian described her as 'a Woman of no sort of Vertue', attributing to Jane an instrumental role in George and Anne's downfall. Casting her as the 'spiteful Wife', Jane 'carried many Stories to the King, or some about him, to persuade, that there was familiarity between the Queen and her Brother, beyond what so near a Relation could justifie'.[7] She had apparently 'outraged all decency' by testifying against her own husband.[8] Many speculated as to Jane's motives: 'whether out of any jealousie which she had of her husband, or out of some inveterate hatred which she had to the Queen, is not clearly known'.[9] Some doubted her credibility on moral grounds,[10] believing her to be quite capable of 'falsehood and artifices',[11] while others felt that she must have 'died unpitied' and 'unlamented by all',[12] finding justice in her conviction:

> But for the Lady Rochford, every body observed Gods Justice on her; who had the chief hand, both in Queen Anne Boleyns, and her own Husbands death and it now appearing so evidently what sort of Woman she was, it tended much to raise their Reputations again, in whose Fall, her spite and other Artifices had so great a hand. She had been a Lady of the Bed-Chamber to the last four Queens but now it was found how unworthy she was of that Trust.[13]

How far does tradition stand up to scrutiny? Deconstructing the myth and legend, and attempting to trace its origin, historians are now more objective and cautious in their handling of the evidence.[14] One author rather aptly described Jane as 'a bird of ill omen where English Queens were concerned';[15] another recognised her formidable presence at court later in life.[16] Some remained critical, regarding Jane as 'unhinged by malice',[17] or as a 'pathological meddler' who 'acted with unbelievable imbecility'.[18] Others have surely gone too far in reassessing and rehabilitating Jane's reputation. Representing Jane as 'a pariah of Tudor history' who has been 'thoroughly maligned', one biographer sought to vindicate her; indeed it seems rather they wanted us to sympathise with Jane, even to admire or like her.[19] This agenda is pursued relentlessly and distorts the evidence to excuse Jane as a 'scapegoat' at every turn in her career, reducing her to something of a victim of circumstances far beyond her control.[20]

Who was the real Jane Boleyn? What was she like? For how should we view her: as the vicious, spiteful, cruel, heartless, unnatural, abhorrent, malicious and murderously wicked wife of tradition, totally lacking in moral sense or scruples of conscience, or as the loyal, dutiful but hapless and blameless servant-woman of revision, naïve, unconscious and altogether oblivious to the nature of conspiracy, intrigue and court politics which governed the very world she lived in? Neither of these caricatures is wholly convincing.

Finding Jane can be difficult. There is not enough surviving source material to sustain a full biographical account: as one author dryly remarked, 'we know more about what she wore than what she thought'.[21] So much of what Jane saw, heard, thought, felt or did is lost to us, not least because she was a woman, and a servant, and no courtier, chronicler or ambassador would not have felt it worth their while to record it. Some relevant sources which we know did, at one time, exist, such as the journal of Anthony Anthony, or the letters that Jane wrote to her husband, are no longer extant, while others, like those mutilated in the fire at Ashburnham House in 1731, have been irreparably damaged. As a result, many accounts of Jane's life are necessarily punctuated with informed guesswork. She remains elusive, but it would be a mistake to operate on preconceptions, imagining what Jane must surely have been like. She cannot be judged according to her words, thoughts or feelings, of which there are few, but her actions: what she did, and why she did it. Jane's actions often at first appear to be totally lacking in reason or logic; indeed at times her behaviour is somewhat far-fetched and seems almost incomprehensible. Her motives have confounded historians for centuries; one even regarded Jane as 'strange'.[22] More often her actions are misinterpreted, misconstrued, or too hastily dismissed without due attention, in spite of the evidence we do have.

Consequently, this book concentrates, not, on her life, but on her career in the queen's household. Henry VIII married six times. Queens consort Catherine of Aragon, Anne Boleyn, Jane Seymour, Anne of Cleves, Katherine Howard, and Katherine Parr each had their own households, staffed with their own servants.[23] Examining Jane's career considers what it meant to be a woman in the court of a king, and in the service of a queen.[24] The queen's household comprised nearly half of the early Tudor court, and constituted the leading and largest group of women near to the English monarchy. How did Jane's experience at court differ from that of men? Were women at court doomed to domesticity, and the part they played fairly inconsequential, or could they have a meaningful role? What was the nature of Jane's relationship with the crown? How did she interact with her royal mistresses, and the wider court and kingdom? And what was the impact of Henry's marital instability on her career, which spanned two tumultuous decades, and saw Jane serve as many as five of his six queens? To know and understand Jane, we must take her back to the household in which she served and the court in which she lived. What emerges is not merely a story of service, but survival.

2

'Mistres Parker'
FINDING A FOOTHOLD

Jane began her career in the household of Henry VIII's first wife, Catherine of Aragon. Most of Catherine's attendants were chosen when she became queen. In the records of her coronation in 1509, at least twenty-one ladies and gentlewomen can be identified as her servants.[1] Jane was not among them. George Cavendish wrote that Jane had been 'brought uppe in the court' from a 'yong age', but she would have been far too young to serve the queen at her accession.[2] Although there is no record of exactly when Jane was first appointed as a Maid-of-Honour, there is evidence which indicates that she made her debut at the Field of Cloth of Gold, a diplomatic summit between England and France in 1520, where a 'mistres Parker' was noted as accompanying the queen.[3] It is likely that this was Jane, as both her father, Henry, and her mother, Alice, were in attendance. Jane does not appear in any household lists or exchequer accounts for the queen's household predating the summit, though these records are quite fragmentary. Certainly by 1522, Jane was at court, as on 4 March she participated in the Château Vert pageant.[4]

Positions in the royal household were highly coveted. Serving at court for most women was a chance to acquire status or a position better than they would otherwise have done strictly by birth or marriage. From the view of the English nobility and gentry, the queen's household provided additional opportunities to forge relationships with the crown. What recommended Jane in particular for royal service?

Was it her noble heritage? Jane was the daughter of Henry Parker, Baron Morley, a well-respected English peer, scholar, translator, and a descendant of the Lovell family, who married Alice St. John, Jane's mother and the daughter of Sir John St. John of Bletsoe. Throughout the medieval and early modern period, families like the Parkers or the St. Johns, with long traditions of royal service, were honoured with successive appointments to the households of kings and queens. Both of Jane's parents had built up a friendship with the crown serving in the household of the king's grandmother, Lady Margaret Beaufort.[5] Lady Margaret's accounts, dating from 1499 to 1509, reveal that she cared a great deal for Henry and Alice as her close attendants. She made payments towards Henry's education, and laid out a substantial sum of five hundred marks 'for redemyng of master Parkers landes' from Sir Edward Howard, his stepfather, to ensure that Henry kept some of the estate of his late father, Sir William Parker.[6] Lady Margaret covered 'thecxhibion', 'finding' or allowance, 'of maister Henry Parkere and his wyiff', varying from £9. 9s. 5d. to £26. 8s. 3d.,[7] and paid the wages of Henry's own servant, William Whitmore, at 6s. 8d. a quarter.[8]

There are innumerable entries in Lady Margaret's accounts for the making of Henry and Alice's clothes, such as gowns, kirtles, doublets, hose, coats, hats, bonnets, boots and shoes.[9] In 1507, both of Jane's parents were issued with several yards of French tawny, costing 36s. 3d., to line and make up their livery coats and gowns.[10] Rewards were also granted to Henry and Alice for their loyal and dutiful service.[11] Jane's father often went out on errands for Lady Margaret, riding to London or elsewhere 'by my ladyes commaundment', though it appears that he may have been rather clumsy as, in 1498, she paid 10s. for a surgeon 'for the helynge' of his leg, and in 1509, laid out a further 3s. 4d. 'for setting in' his arm, 'being oute of the joincte'.[12]

Lady Margaret's accounts indicate that she was fond of their children too.[13] Jane had a brother, Henry, and a sister, Margaret.[14] We do not know precisely when Jane was born, but we do know that her mother, Alice, gave birth in late 1502, when Lady Margaret sent 5s. in reward to her midwife, and again in early 1504, when the abbot of Peterborough was brought up for the 'crystenyng of master Parkers chylde'.[15] Upon the former occasion Lady Margaret even sent one of her attendants in haste to Sir John St John, Alice's father, with the good news of her safe delivery.[16] We do not know where Jane was born, or where she grew up. Hallingbury Place in Great Hallingbury, Essex, was the principal Morley residence, but there is no actual evidence to place a young Jane there.

From 1503 to 1508, Alice's nurse regularly received payments, in reward, varying from 20*d.* to as much as 20*s.* 'for kepyng of the chyld'.[17] This child could have been Henry or Margaret, but in a separate entry the woman is named as 'Jane Parkers norse'.[18] The Parker children did not live with their parents, but Lady Margaret covered the cost for the children to be brought up to see them, on one occasion, for instance, from Fotheringhay, in Northamptonshire, to Croydon, in London.[19] Fotheringhay may indeed be where Jane lived in her childhood, as in the summer of 1505, Lady Margaret laid out 5*d.* for 'mylk bought for yonge maistres Parkere by the way of Fodryngay'.[20] Jane would have been quite familiar with Elizabeth Massey, Lady Margaret's gentlewoman.[21] In 1508, the royal mistress paid 10*s.* 'to mastres Parkers norse for the borde of Jane Parker by the space of xiii wekes by mastres Masse'; another entry in 1509 noted 15*s.* 4*d.* to cover the expenses 'of maistres Parker[s] child[ren] leyng with maistres Massy'.[22]

Lady Margaret also covered the cost of clothes and other necessaries for the Parker children: in 1503 she laid out 6*d.* 'for a knytt cote for maister Parkers son', and later, 'ii payer of kidde shoys';[23] in 1508, bonnets were bought for 3*s.* 4*d.* for a 'lytell maistres Parker'[24] and, for 7*d.*, more explicitly, 'for Jane Parker'; a further 15*d.* was paid 'for makyng and lynyng of a cote', and 7½*d.* for a kirtle lined with white cotton 'for mastres Jane Parker'.[25] When her parents were issued with tawny for their livery in 1507, 'litell maistres Margett Parker' received 'a yerd and a quarter' of the same,[26] and later 14*d.* was spent 'to body and sleve' the 'yong master Parkers gowne' with tawny too.[27] Much like their parents, the Parker children were treated as dear members of Lady Margaret's household. On one occasion in 1509 she paid for their bread, ale, milk, butter and spices, as well as books and 'wacchyng candles', for burning before a shrine or altar; in 1508 she bought them almonds, treacle and 'candyth', or sugar candy. To a 'yonge maistres Parker', Jane, or Margaret, she gifted four puppets.[28] We do not know what Jane's childhood was like, but we can presume from the evidence in Lady Margaret's accounts that she was well-cared for.

Was Jane an accomplished musician, or deft with a needle? Did Jane, like Elizabeth Blount before her, excel in 'all goodly pastimes', to 'entertain with dancing, music, games, laughter, witticisms'?[29] Jane's father Henry acknowledged the virtues of female education, as he admired, in a later dedication to Princess Mary, her capability 'that rare doth happen to the woman sex' to 'read, write, and construe Latin, but furthermore translate any hard thing of the Latin into our English tongue'.[30] Presumably Jane learned to speak with grace and elegance, and to read and write.[31] There is one extant letter to which Jane signed her name (though we know that she wrote many more, which unfortunately, have not survived). Although the use of scribes and secretaries to compose letters was common, the fact that Jane had in her possession in 1536 three books, one of which, 'richly bound borded wt silver and gilt wt one clasp' was identified as a primer, containing prayers and psalms, suggests that she was literate.[32] Perhaps as a young girl Jane played on the 'payre of clarycordes', or clavichords, purchased for her mother, Alice, by her mistress Lady Margaret in 1502.[33]

Jane would have been taught to behave in a manner and decorum befitting her rank and status. All of the queen's servants had to be sincere, truthful, respectable, with good conversation, manners, morals and behaviour, have a pleasing temperament and demeanour, and be upright in mind, character and appearance, as opposed to sly, or deceitful.[34] 'Your ladyship knoweth the Court is full of pride, envy, indignation and mocking, scorning and derision', Honor, Lady Lisle was warned by her agent John Husee in 1537, shortly before the arrival of her daughters, Anne and Katharine. Husee promised her that the queen's ladies would 'exhort them to be sober, sad, wise, and discreet and lowly above all things, and to be obedient', as well as 'to serve God and to be virtuous, for that is much regarded, to serve God well and to be sober of tongue'.[35] In the contemporary *Il Libro del Cortegiano,* or *The Book of the Courtier* (1528), Baldassare Castiglione observed too that 'many faculties of the mind are as necessary to woman as to man' if they were 'to avoid affectation, to be naturally graceful in all her doings, to be mannerly, clever, prudent, not arrogant, not envious, not slanderous, not vain, not quarrelsome'.[36] Sewing luxury fabrics or embroidering fine shirts and wall hangings were as much a means of occupying a young girl's time and keeping idle hands busy as it was a practical skill. In his *Instruction of a Christian Woman* (1523), humanist scholar Juan Luis Vives urged that 'in the education of a woman the principal and, I might almost say, the only concern should be the preservation of chastity'.[37] Of course, conduct books were prescriptive, not descriptive. We can presume that Jane, as a maid, maintained her virtue, but her later 'mysgovernaunce' in allowing a young Katherine Howard, Henry VIII's fifth wife, to follow her 'carnall lust' and 'breke chastitie' had disastrous consequences for them both.[38]

Was it Jane's physical appearance and beauty which secured her appointment to the queen's household? Certainly for women who aspired to serve at court this was something of a prerequisite. Castiglione remarked that a woman at court 'lacks much who lacks beauty'.[39] Henry VII stressed that court ladies 'should be of gentle birth and beautiful, or at least that none of them should be ugly',[40] while Henry VIII remarked that the queen's maids-of-honour in particular 'showlde be fayre' and 'me[e]tt for the ro[o]me'.[41] Unfortunately, what Jane looked like remains a mystery, as there are no known portraits, nor are there any contemporary descriptions of her likeness.[42]

It must be asked not only what but *who* recommended Jane's appointment to the queen's household. Although the queen's lord chamberlain and vice-chamberlain might recommend an individual for royal service, the right to appoint them lay outside of their jurisdiction.[43] If there were many individuals who were all qualified and all vying for the same position, who held the power, or had the authority, to grant office? And how was their choice determined? It may have been Catherine of Aragon herself who chose Jane. Queens consort often appointed their own servants. Even Katherine Howard, who apparently 'did not see fit to spend her days in the sober administration of her house',[44] must have had a hand in retaining her childhood acquaintances from Lambeth and Horsham, like Francis Dereham, as her gentleman usher, and Katherine Tylney, as her chamberer. This was later used against her to secure her conviction in 1541. The indictment read that Katherine had 'traitorously retained' Dereham, a man with whom she had before led an 'abominable, base, carnal, voluptuous, and vicious life, like a common harlot', and Tylney, 'who was procuratrix between them and knew of their carnal life'.[45] Her attainder repeated the accusation. Katherine 'tooke most trayterouslye to her service the same person with whome she used that vicious lyef before, whose name was Fraunces Dereham', and 'calling also to her service in rowme of Chamberer a woman whiche was pryvie to her naughtie lief before'.[46] Of course, appointments, even those made by the queen herself, were subject to, and often required, the king's consent. When Katherine Parr was acting regent in England while the king was at war in France in 1544, she wrote to her husband directly to ask 'his pleasure as to accepting certain ladies into her chamber in lieu of some that are sick'. Henry was quite clear in that he felt the women his wife had chosen to replace them were themselves too weak and 'not be meete to serve'. 'You maye take them into your chamber to passe tyme… with you at playe', the king conceded, leaving it, on this occasion, to her 'owne choyse'.[47] The evidence suggests that queens shared in the custody of appointments to their households with the king, who, as their husband and sovereign, held ultimate authority.

By the late sixteenth and early seventeenth century in England, when an individual was sworn to serve in office, they were issued a warrant which, upon the payment of a fee, was enrolled on a patent roll in the Chancery, documenting their names and dating their entry into the household. No such records exist for the early Tudor period.[48] As a result, it is difficult to trace the process by which these appointments were made, or to know, more precisely, who made them.

Petitions for preferment to the queen's household are thus crucial. Petitioners and would-be servants vying for office would often solicit the queen or the king directly. In 1540, Katherine Howard received a letter from Joan Bulmer, an old acquaintance with whom she had served in the household of Agnes Tilney, Dowager Duchess of Norfolk: '…yt yst shewyd vnto me', Joan began, 'that god of hyse hyghe goodness hathe sent vnto the knowlege of the kyng a contrakt of a mattrymony that the quyne had mad wythe an nother before she came un to england and therapone theryse a lawfole devors had between them and as yt yst thoughte the kynge of hyse goodness wyl set you in the same honuar that she wase in.' The king's marriage to Anne of Cleves had been annulled on 9 July, and within a few weeks of receiving Joan's letter, Katherine married Henry and became queen. Finding herself to be in 'the moost mesary of the world and moost wrechyd lyf meny mo ways then I cane expres', Joan wrote in some haste and urged Katherine to remember 'the unfaynyd love that my hart hathe alwayes borne toward you', before petitioning her directly for preferment to her household. 'I besyche you to stay some rome for me what you shal thynke best yourself, for the nerar I ware to you the glader I wold be'.[49] Others appealed to those near to the crown whom they could trust were in a position to advance their suit. Upon Anne Boleyn's coronation in the summer of 1533, the merchant Stephen Vaughan heard that the new queen was in need of a silkwoman to 'prepayre, furnysshe and tryme her grace withe suche things as her grace shall accustome to vse and were'. He recommended his wife, Margery, for the position in a letter to Thomas Cromwell, the king's secretary: 'Yow know what she canne do. I suppose no woman can better trymme her grace.'[50] Margery even 'devysed certeyne works for the Quene her grace, whiche although she dyd bryng vnto her grace to be seyn was neyther seyn ne her good wyll and hymble seruyse knowen'. Her husband wrote again to Cromwell a month later: 'Your pleasure maye be to have her in remembrance with her grace, who in her facultie I dare well saye can serue her better then any woman in the Realme.'[51] Eventually Margery was appointed as the queen's silkwoman, probably at Cromwell's suit, if not by Anne herself when Margery's 'works' were eventually brought to her attention.

If a similar petition was sent on Jane's behalf to secure her appointment to the queen's household, it has not survived. We cannot now know precisely what or who recommended Jane, but much can be inferred from the fact that she was actually appointed to serve, and did secure an advantageous marriage. An illiterate, or unattractive girl who could not sew, weave, sing, dance or even play a musical instrument was quite unremarkable, and would not have been fit to serve in the court of a king or in the chambers of a queen. Nor would an unchaste girl lacking in practical skills or the most basic of genteel accomplishments make an attractive bride.

3

'When she list to spit or do otherwise at her pleasure'
MAID-OF-HONOUR

The queen's household comprised many departments and rested on a broad stratum of servants. As a Maid-of-Honour, and later, as a Lady of the Privy Chamber, Jane was part of the *domus regis magnificencie*, 'Chamber', or household above-stairs, which was responsible for attending upon the queen's person and performing menial or routine tasks on her behalf, such as making her bed, waiting on her at table, dressing or undressing her, or standing guard in her chambers. Everything in and of the queen's household 'above-stairs' was facilitated by the operation 'below-stairs', the *domus providencie*, or 'Household', which fulfilled the day-to-day administering of various provisions to the Chamber, like food, drink, light and fuel, for warmth, security and shelter.[1]

Like the king's household, the queen's household was a rigidly-constructed hierarchy in which servants like Jane held a fixed position, clearly defined and formally circumscribed by their office. Office, the title, rank and position held by a servant, determined the role that they performed and their place in the institutional, hierarchical chain of command. What the queen's servants did, how much they were paid, where and what they ate, how many horses they had stabling for, how many beds they were given to accommodate their own servants, what perquisites or 'fees' they were entitled to, what room or chamber they served in, and even what they wore, all corresponded with their office.

Such offices became increasingly defined throughout the Tudor period. Reflecting the king's concern for privacy, the 1490s saw the development of the 'Privy Chamber', a significant innovation for the English royal household under Henry VII, which became more clearly defined and fully developed under Henry VIII.[2] Previously the architectural structure of royal residences mirrored the bi-partite division of a household above-stairs ('Chamber') and below-stairs ('Household'). By the end of the fifteenth century, there had developed a third, autonomous department, the 'Privy Chamber', which functioned by 'not admitting', or restricting access, to the king.[3] Simultaneously, there developed, alongside the king's side, on the queen's side, her own Privy Chamber.[4] Some time in around 1529, when Wolsey went to Bridewell to visit Catherine of Aragon, he, 'being in the chamber of presence', waited until the queen 'came out of her privy chamber'. 'If it please you,' the cardinal advised Catherine, 'to go into your privy chamber, we will show you the cause of our coming', to which the queen replied, 'My lord, if you have any thing to say, speak it openly'. The ensuing conversation was recorded in detail by George Cavendish, Wolsey's servant, until Catherine took the cardinal 'by the hand and led him into her privy chamber', where they 'were in long communication' and during which Cavendish remained 'in the other chamber'. There Cavendish and the rest of the servants 'might sometime hear the queen speak very loud, but what it was we could not understand'.[5]

Institutionally, the queen's household was administered alongside the king's household, and the queen's servants were to be governed by the same ordinances as his own.[6] The author of the *Black Book of the Household of Edward IV* stated briefly in c. 1471 that:

> We fynde of old recordes and new both, that for the quene's seruyse, wich must be nygh like vnto the king, and for her ladyes and other worshipfull men and jentylwomen, theire seruices and lyuerez after as hit accordith to high and lowe degree aftyr the maner as hit is to the kinges household maynie.[7]

The households of queens were firmly integrated with, and in many ways treated as an extension of, the king's household. Unlike the king's household, the queen's household was headed – at least, figuratively – not by the sovereign, but the wife of the sovereign, a woman. This meant that many of her servants necessarily had to be women. Ordinances did not, however, provide specifically for the offices held by women on the queen's side until the 'Orders and Regulations of the Government of the Queen's Household' were drawn up for

Henrietta Maria of France in 1627, the first set of ordinances for the household of a queen consort of England.[8] It is likely that the ordinances of 1627 formalised what was already in practice for the households of early Tudor queens consort. Even when Mary I or Elizabeth I were on the throne as queens regnant, no further distinction was made, or felt necessary, between the responsibilities of male servants who served the king, and their female counterparts, who served the queen.[9] That these servants were on the queen's side and not the king's side, or indeed that these servants were themselves women was, in many ways, inconsequential. Offices were created, developed and defined by men, and for men, but few adaptations were felt necessary to accommodate women. The duties, tasks and functions of these women may thus be ascertained by identifying which male offices in the king's Chamber and Privy Chamber are absent from those of his queens, namely the Gentlemen of the Privy Chamber, Grooms of the Privy Chamber, the Groom of the Stool, and the Esquires for the Body, who, it is no coincidence, were the most intimate of the king's servants.

Ladies and Gentlewomen of the queen's Privy Chamber were responsible for her personal, intimate and everyday service. The queen's Privy chamber was a set of two or three smaller rooms, yet more restricted from the court, where the queen retreated and relaxed in private, and in 'quiet, rest, comfort and preservation' of her health. Adjacent to the Privy chamber and the innermost of her privy lodgings was the queen's bedchamber, where the queen slept, at which time her gentlewomen would 'lie on the pallet within' the Privy chamber, and presumably would wake the queen if necessary and draw the curtains come morning.[10] Ladies and Gentlewomen of the Privy chamber undertook the same duties as the king's Gentlemen of the Privy Chamber, attending specifically to the queen's 'bodily' needs. They would dress and undress her, wash and bathe her, and wait on her, with none other presuming to touch her body, and without being 'too homely or bold advanceing themselves thereunto, otherwise than to their roomes doth apperteyne'.[11] We can presume that it was also these women who, on occasion, helped style the queen's hair and apply her make up.

There is no record of any servants in the households of Henry VII or Henry VIII's queens bearing the title 'Groom of the Stool', though it is likely that one of the Ladies or Gentlewomen of the Privy Chamber fulfilled this role and attended to the queen in 'other privey places', when she used the lavatory, privy or 'close stool'. Chamberers were the female equivalent of Grooms of the Privy Chamber, in that they were responsible for making the queen's bed, cleaning and arranging her bed linens, wardrobe and lodgings, preserving and maintaining her Privy chamber and bedchamber in a 'pure, clean, wholesome and meet' condition.[12] They were to 'wayte and give their attendaunce at all tymes' the queen was present in her Privy chamber, ready to receive at the door bread, ale, wine or anything else that was fetched by her gentleman usher, or relate messages as and when they were delivered by her page. When the queen was to lie in her Privy chamber, these women 'everie night prepared and made ready' the pallets on which the queen's gentlewomen would sleep, 'and the fires made up, and lights ordered, afore they shall depart to their lodgeings'.[13]

The queen's Privy Chamber staff often had charge of petty cash, sometimes acting, *ex officio*, as keepers of her 'privy purse', handling the varied personal expenses of their mistress.[14] A queen's expenditure covered the costs incurred for paying the wages of her household, handing out rewards, distributing alms, repaying gambling debts, and the purchasing of jewels and fine materials.[15] They were also responsible for handling her clothes, jewels, plate, linens and furnishings, and often sourced and carried to the queen miscellaneous items, for instance, fennell, rosewater and 'fyne perfumes', to keep her chambers sensually pleasing.[16]

Outside of the Privy Chamber, there were Ladies in Presence, or 'Great Ladies', and Maids-of-Honour, like Jane, who attended upon the queen in her Presence chamber. Like the king's Esquires for the Body,[17] the queen's maids-of-honour were 'to come into the Presence Chamber before eleven of the clock, and to goe to prayers, and after prayers attend untill the Queene bee sett at dynner'.[18] When the queen dined publicly, she sat on a throne in her Presence chamber under a canopy, situated directly opposite the entrance, and strictly no other 'no manner of whatsoever degree he [or she] be of' was permitted to go beneath the 'cloth of estate'.[19] After the queen had her dinner, maids-of-honour were to return to the Presence chamber, 'there to remaine untill supper time', or 'for some reasonable time, especially when any ambassador hath audience'.[20]

Maids-of-honour were also thought to be fit companions for a queen, accompanying her whenever she left her chambers, and carrying her train behind her. These young girls were supervised and chaperoned by a Mother of the Maids, who ensured that they behaved in a sober and virtuous manner.

The presence of her ladies and gentlewomen servants is what distinguished the queen's side from the king's side, as the king's household was essentially male in composition, and historically, households were predominantly male institutions. It is a popular misconception, however, that the queen's household was exclusively, or even predominantly, female. Only her most intimate servants necessarily had to be women.

The queen's Chamber was headed by her Lord Chamberlain and Vice-chamberlain, who were in charge of administering the rest of her servants by distributing lodgings, keeping strict attendance records and arbitrating disputes.[21] Gentlemen Ushers were to oversee the queen's yeomen, grooms and pages, ensuring that they were 'redie to do all such service' and 'to maintaine them in the right of theire places'.[22] Yeomen Ushers and Yeomen of the Chamber stood guard at the entry to her chambers and kept a watchful eye 'in case they shall perceive any person to be there, not meete nor convenient to be therein'.[23] Grooms of the Chamber were responsible for maintenance, ensuring that all rooms were 'pure, clean, wholesome and meet' and kept 'in right perfect maner'. This meant they had to 'take good heede' that all furnishings, floors and windows were 'kept cleane from dust, filthe, and cobwebbes'.[24] The Groom Porter was in charge of provisions 'as it hath been accustomed to be deliuerid'.[25] Pages of the Chamber had to be 'redie at all tymes' to 'wayte uppon' the chambers,[26] and like the Messenger, was often 'sente in message', to convey letters or run errands, sometimes 'oute of courte'.[27]

Queens consort had their own Carvers, Cupbearers, Sewers and Gentlemen Waiters, who served them 'at houres and tyme of dyner and souper'. The sewer would 'fetch the seruice', 'setteth and dyrecteth' the meal and wait on their royal master or mistress at table, while the carver would be brought forward to cut the meat and, 'with the accustomed reverences', would 'see the meate honourably served to the board'. A cupbearer would take the cup, covered, pour out a few drops into the cover to taste it for himself as to prevent their mistress being poisoned, before handing it to them.[28] Yeomen, Grooms and Pages of the Wardrobe of the Robes and of the Beds were responsible for the keeping, repairing and transport of her clothing, mattresses, bed-linen and coverlets 'saufly and clenly, that no stranger shall touche it'.[29] The Physician and Apothecary cared for the physical and mental health of their mistress, though they were chiefly in attendance when she fell ill, or if she was pregnant.[30] Confessors were responsible for her spiritual welfare, hearing her confession for the preservation of her soul, and often provided her with counsel, whereas her Almoner distributed her alms and her Chaplains held religious services such as 'mattines, masses, and other devotions' for the queen and her servants.[31] The Chancellor liaised with the queen's councillors, while the Secretary handled her correspondence.[32] And finally, queens had a Master of the Horse, who was in charge of her Stable, and a Receiver-General, who accounted for her income and expenditure.[33]

Rarely in the evidence do we see the queen's servants actually undertaking the responsibilities of their office, as few would have felt it worth their while to record them. There are, however, occasional glimpses into the practical life of the household. At a banquet for the coronation of Anne Boleyn in 1533, Elizabeth Browne, Countess of Worcester and the new queen's lady-in-waiting, stood beside her chair and 'did hold a fine cloth before the Queen's face when she list to spit or do otherwise at her pleasure'.[34] Such was the nature of royal service in the Tudor period. Jane too would undertake duties which were sometimes degrading or demeaning, onerous or laborious, and yet the role she performed, exalted, humble or menial, was always honourable, and could prove to be both rewarding and profitable.

4

'A glorified boudoir'?
QUEENSHIP

Predominantly concerned with the early Tudor court as the administrative centre of government, historians have focused their attentions on the king's side, not the queen's side, and as such, on the careers of men, not of women, who, it was clearly felt, held no political significance.[1] This is reflected in the debate concerning the nature of the 'Privy Chamber'.[2] Whereas the king's Privy Chamber became involved in national administration, governed in the localities, embarked on diplomatic missions and undertook financial and secretarial duties, such as obtaining the king's signature, or in operating the dry stamp, a queen's Privy Chamber, when the sovereign was a woman, apparently became a 'glorified boudoir'.[3] Its significance under Mary I was 'neutralised', and her women were lacking in ambitions to form a 'petticoat government'.[4] The Privy Chamber under Elizabeth I, we are told, 'retreated into mere domesticity', suffering a 'sudden and catastrophic decline', as her most intimate servants were necessarily women.[5]

Although Jane's role was formally circumscribed by the office she held, this does not mean that she was doomed to domesticity. All of the queen's servants were sworn by oath to be loyal and faithful to their mistress, to obey her in *everything*. The Eltham ordinances of 1526 provided for servants to 'give their continuall and diligent attendance' and 'have a vigilant and reverent respect and eye' for the queen, so that, merely by her 'looke or countenance' they 'may know what lacketh', to know and act on her pleasure 'to be had or done'.[6] The nature of service was thus determined, and in a sense, negotiated, between mistress and servant. What mattered was not necessarily what they were doing, but their ability or capacity to do it, and to do it well – to achieve whatsoever their queen commanded or desired. The multiplicity, or complexity, of her demands, was interminable, and varied greatly depending on her personality, ambitions, and interaction with her household. As Jane's career would testify, nothing was outside of the scope of their activity, as the queen's servants were drawn in to the personal and political affairs of their mistress, and could be employed to meet the needs and responsibilities of the crown, sometimes engaging in matters more *ad hoc* or further afield, in the wider court and kingdom, whatsoever they may be.

Unlike the king's household, the queen's household was headed, not, by the sovereign, but the wife of the sovereign, a woman. Queens consort did not govern; their ladies and gentlewomen functioned for the practice, construction and display of queenship – but what did this involve?

As queen, Catherine of Aragon would undertake roles which were no different from that of any other married woman in this period, though on a much grander scale. Her first and foremost duty was to give birth to a male heir. A queen's Privy Chamber and its servants functioned to protect her modesty, her dignity, and most importantly, the integrity of the crown. Ensuring the legitimacy of heirs was paramount. A queen's body was sacred, and she had to guard her chastity, or risk compromising the purity of the true and royal bloodline.[7] The lack of a male heir was a source of anxiety, and apprehension, and as a result, a queen's physical attractiveness, character, demeanour, morality, health and fertility, were all scrutinised by court and kingdom.

Catherine fell pregnant within weeks of marrying the king. Henry wrote cheerfully to her father with the news on 1 November 1509: 'Your daughter, her Serene Highness the Queen, our dearest consort, has conceived in her womb a living child and is right heavy'.[8] Unfortunately Catherine miscarried a few months later.[9] Her belly remained swollen, however, and this led her physician to speculate that she 'remained pregnant of another child'.[10] He was mistaken; Catherine was menstruating, though disastrously, the delusion was sustained, and the queen withdrew from court for her confinement.[11] But there was no labour, and it soon became apparent to those who were privy to the matter that the queen was not actually pregnant. Luis Caroz, the Imperial ambassador, later commented that the king's councillors were 'vexed and angry at this mistake', blaming chiefly her bedchamber women for leading the queen 'to understand that she was pregnant whilst she was not'.[12] An unnamed Spanish woman may have been somewhat responsible, as she had assured Catherine's confessor and confidante, Diego Fernández, that she was with child, having ascertained as such from some 'secret signs' exhibited in the queen.[13] Catherine remained in confinement until her swelling disappeared. Her pregnancies in the first seven years of her marriage, ending in either miscarriage, stillbirth, or premature death, gave rise to rumours that she was unable to conceive, though she became pregnant again in the spring of 1515, and on 18 February 1516 delivered a healthy baby girl, Mary, 'a fayre prynces', at Greenwich Palace.[14] Three days later, at the nearby Church of the Observant Friars, Mary was baptised. Elizabeth Howard, Catherine's lady-in-waiting, carried the baby in her arms from the queen's bedchamber to her outer apartments, to be honoured by members of the English nobility who had gathered for a glimpse of the princess.[15] Shortly after her delivery, William, Lord Mountjoy, Catherine's lord chamberlain, had 'gyven thanks and praysings to almyghty god' and marked the occasion with processions and bonfires.[16]

Catherine would not again conceive a child after Jane's arrival at court some time in around 1520. Jane would, however, undertake the responsibilities of caring for the queen in childbirth when attending upon Catherine's successors, Anne Boleyn and Jane Seymour. The protocol for royal childbirth was outlined in *The Ryalle Booke*, or the ordinances of 1493, and when Anne became pregnant in 1533, William Mountjoy sent a copy of these ordinances to Thomas Cromwell for Anne's lord chamberlain, Thomas, Lord Burgh:

> I do sende vnto youe certaine remembraunces of thyngs necessary to be provyded ageinst the Quenys grace takethe hyr chambre wherof I had experyence the tyme I dyd occupye the Rome. Hit may please you the same may be delyveryd vnto my Lorde hyr Chamberlaine for it was his desyer moche to have information therof.[17]

The Ryalle Booke of 1493 observed that, when a queen was heavily pregnant, some time between four and six weeks before the birth, she was to be taken 'to hir chamber where sche schall be delyvryd'. 'When it plessithe the Quene to take hir chambre', she was escorted, in solemn procession with lords and ladies of the court, to the Chapel Royal to hear mass, and then to her Presence Chamber, where she, 'stondyng or sittinge at his plessure', would 'take spice and wyne vnder the clothe of estat'.[18] The queen was then escorted to her bedchamber, richly adorned with tapestries and pillows for the occasion, at which time all the men would 'take ther leve off the quene' and 'all the ladys and gentylwomen' were 'to go in with her and after that no man to come into hir chamber save women and they to be made all maner off offecers'.[19] Men were no longer admitted to be in her presence, and women were to undertake all of their duties. Even after giving birth, queens remained in seclusion, surrounded only by her female attendants, as it was customary to 'lie in' for up to forty days after the delivery until her 'churching', or purification, after labour. We cannot know now exactly what role Jane played at the birth of Princess Elizabeth, or Prince Edward, though we can presume that all of the queen's women in attendance, responsible for the safe delivery of the heir, would have ensured her comfort; Thomas Cromwell, however, bitterly remarked that Jane Seymour's death, shortly after she gave birth, was caused 'by the neglect of those about her who suffered her to take cold and eat such things as her fantasy in sickness called for'.[20]

The importance of royal marriages, fertility, and the health, illness and death of queens, with their implications for dynastic security, or insecurity, cannot be overstated, but it is now clear that the responsibilities of queen consorts amounted to more than the birth of male heirs. As Catherine of Aragon's maid-of-honour, Jane frequently accompanied the queen from palace to palace, and participated in the crowded court agenda of pageants, masques, banquets, feasts, jousts and tournaments. Henry VIII's court had an unprecedented veneer of luxury and extravagance that consciously perpetuated majesty and grandeur. The Tudor court was a stage, and the eyes of many visitors from throughout the kingdom and further afield were fixed upon kings, queens, princes, princesses, and those who attended upon them.[21]

At the Field of Cloth of Gold, a diplomatic summit between England and France which took place from 7 to 24 June, 1520, Jane, along with the rest of the queen's household, functioned for display and magnificence.[22] 'A Memoriall of such things as be requisite', drafted in preparation for the summit, accounted for the presence of both queens and their ladies and gentlewomen:

> ...the Kyngs Hyghnesse with hys Nobles, and the Qwene with her Ladyes and Jentylwemen, schall mete with the Frensche Kyng and hys Qwene, with thayr Nobles, Ladies and Gentilwemen, at the said place on horseback, and after embracyng of each other familierly, and the Qwenys to do semblablely for theyr parties, the said Kyngs, Qwenys, and thays traynes, forthwith to repayre to Calais in such goode order.[23]

Both kings were determined to achieve parity in numbers, though exceptions may have been made for women, whose attendance at the summit was greatly welcomed, even encouraged. Francis I was especially anxious to avoid either entourage exceeding the other,[24] though Sir Richard Wingfield, the English ambassador, reassured him, later remarking to Henry, 'I never sawe your highnes encombryd or fynde defaulte with over grete presse of Ladyes'.[25]

A few months prior to the summit, Wingfield reported that 'great search is made to bring to the meeting the fairest ladies that may be found' to accompany the French queen, Claude, remarking that Catherine must 'bring such in her band that the visage of England, which hath always had the prize'.[26] Henry 'wrote letters of summons to all suche lordes, ladies, gentlemen and Gentlewomen as he felt should give their attendaunce on hym and the quene'.[27] As a member of Catherine's household, it was Jane's duty to attend, and to absent oneself without good reason could incur the displeasure of her sovereign. Her physical appearance and presence constituted 'queenliness', the feminine expression of queenship, and her body was appropriated in its construction. In this, clothing, the wearing of costly jewels and rich garments, was materially, and culturally, significant.[28] Dressing the queen and her attendants required the utmost attention to detail. The accounts of Elis Hilton, Catherine's yeoman of the robes, reveal that she laid out vast sums – as much as £710, 3s. 1½d. from April to May 1520 alone – indicating that the queen took care in outfitting her household appropriately.[29] Jane had approximately two or three months to put herself 'in a redines after the moste costliest fashion', and neither she, nor the rest of the queen's ladies and gentlewomen, would disappoint. On 5 June, Jane travelled with king Henry and queen Catherine from Calais to their royal lodgings, the portable palace, or castle, at Guînes. Adorned with cloth of gold, the queen rode through the town on horseback and in procession 'with her trayne of ladies', in full view of attendees.[30] At a banquet held on 10 June, Catherine's gentlewomen were 'richlie appareled in cloth of gould velvet and silkes after the most gorgeous fashion'.[31] As the chronicler Edward Hall remarked, 'To tell you the apparel of the ladies, their riche attyres, their sumptuous Iuelles, their diuersities of beauties… I assure you ten mennes wittes can scarce declare it.'[32]

For Jane, the wearing of rich clothes and jewels reflected and perpetuated the magnificence of her mistress, accentuating her status as queen. Extensive and occasionally detailed reports by foreign ambassadors in attendance concentrated on their physical appearance, though such accounts could be distorted by their own prejudices or tastes, and they did not hesitate in their scrutiny. Soardino, the Mantuan ambassador to France, was unlikely to be neutral in observing that Catherine's ladies 'were ornamented in the English fashion, but were not richly clad'. Claude, on the other hand, was 'accompanied by forty ladies of high rank, richly dressed and with jewels'.[33] Whereas the English ladies were on this occasion described as 'well-dressed but ugly', at a masque on 24 June, the French ladies were 'richly attired', all 'dressed in the Italian fashion with velvet caps, round which were feathers'.[34] This contrast is reiterated by an anonymous report, which described Catherine's women as 'handsome and well arrayed', though again, compared them unfavourably with the French ladies, 'all dressed in crimson velvet, their sleeves lined with cloth of gold, a beautiful fashion, which the English is not'.[35] Not all of the attendees were impressed with the attire of the French ladies. Polydore Vergil felt it was 'singularly unfit for the chaste', and regretted that many of the English ladies in attendance had taken up the fashion, 'abandoning for the most part the far more modest costume of their forebears.'[36] Mirroring the rivalry of the kings Henry and Francis, there was much comparison, and competition, between the queens and their women, with one observer remarking yet more plainly that they were 'all vieing with each other in beauty and ornamented apparel'.[37]

Certainly her contemporaries focused their reports on Jane's physical appearance and attire, but there is evidence that she was engaged in the summit in ways which were more than merely decorative. Her hospitality and sociability in facilitating interactions at both formal and informal gatherings in the queen's chambers required grace and gaiety. As Castiglione observed, 'in her ways, manners, words, gestures and bearing, a woman ought to be very unlike a man; for just as it befits him to show a certain stout and sturdy manliness, so it is becoming in a woman to have a soft and dainty tenderness with an air of womanly sweetness in her every movement'.[38] Unlike Jane, who, as a young maid, was new to court life, Catherine's ladies and gentlewomen were accomplished, and well-rehearsed, in welcoming and entertaining guests, as they did on many occasions in the queen's chambers in England. The queen and her servants would often host, entertain, and occasionally dine with the king, courtiers and councillors, and receive foreign ambassadors and dignitaries, whose reports are punctuated with references of being taken by the king through 'to the Queen's chamber'. In 1510, at Richmond, 'diuerse straugers' and 'Ambassadours of Spaygne' dined with Henry, and after supper, the king 'willed them to go into the Quenes chamber', where they were received by Catherine, her ladies and her gentlewomen servants.[39] In 1517, Sebastian Giustinian reported that an Imperial ambassador was taken by the king 'into the Queen's chamber', where Henry 'made her and all those ladies pay him as much honor as if he had been a sovereign, giving him amusements of every description'.[40] Giustinian's secretary, Nicolas Sagudino, wrote that, after the banquet, the king and his guests 'betook themselves into another hall' to 'the damsels of the most serene Queen', who danced with them.[41] When Catherine received the king in her apartments at Havering in 1519, she and her servants 'purveyed all thynges in the moste liberallest maner: and especially she made to the kyng suche a sumpteous banket', to such 'greate prayse' that 'the kyng thanked her hartely'.[42] This hospitality strengthened social and political bonds between the queen and visitors to her household. At a banquet held at the Field of Cloth of Gold on 10 June, 1520, Francis I was reportedly 'received in the most courteous manner possible'.[43] 'When that dinner was doune', Francis

> passed the tyme in the banqueting chamber with dauncing among the ladies first erre that he dide daunce he went from one ende of the chamber to thother on both sides and with his capp in his hand and

kissed the ladies and gentilweomen one after an other…saving iiii or fyve that were ould and not faire standing together'.[44]

Apparently the king of France had forgotten his manners! How Jane and the rest of the queen's attendants reacted to this faux pas cannot now be known, though we can imagine that these women quite often had to bite their tongue to keep up appearances. They dined again with Francis in the queen's chambers two weeks later, on which occasion the king staged a masque. Ladies and gentlewomen were 'apparaled in masking clothes with vizers on their faces gorgiouslie beseene', and they all 'danced to the sound of fifes'.[45] Upon his departure, Francis crossed paths with Henry, and the two kings embraced, declaring 'What cheer?'[46] Clearly the queens' ladies and gentlewomen created an amicable, relaxed environment for 'pleasaunt' pastime and diplomatic conciliation.

Such occasions facilitated close interaction between the English and the French courts, so that they 'shall se and conuerse together familiarly, to the ende that it may engender betwene them an amitie more firme and stable, for that cause and that more suerly and agreably they may bee together'.[47] It was reported that 'there was very great abundance of good cheer, and vast pomp',[48] as 'the Frenchmen' were 'making merry with the English women', and 'the Englishmen with the French women'.[49] Surely aiding in the merriment were the stores of wine and beer flowing freely at the summit. The Mantuan ambassador Soardino observed that, 'in the long hall were prepared two large cupboards of silver-gilt vases, constantly used by persons drinking, and the Englishwomen never gave those bowls and flasks any rest'.[50] At a tournament held at Guînes on 11 June, in the midst of the summit, one of the queen's ladies 'took a large flask of wine, and putting it to her lips, drank freely, and then passed it to her companions, who did the like and emptied it'. 'Not content with this, they drank out of large cups, which, during the joust', it was observed, 'circulated more than twenty times amongst the French lords and those English ladies'! The Mantuan ambassador stood aghast, remarking a few days later that these ladies 'were neither very handsome nor very graceful'.[51] It may be that this unflattering report of the queen's attendants drinking freely, and without ceremony, hardly perpetuated an image of virtue, or magnificence. Yet as the French lords too were partaking in the merriment, a more nuanced reading of the evidence suggests that these women were engaging in the 'performance' of familiarity required of diplomacy, embracing fully the spirit of the summit, a celebration of peace. The chronicler Hall regarded only their 'good behaviour from day to day since the first metyng'.[52] The bishop John Fisher, whose account survives in a sermon preached shortly after the summit, was in attendance on the queen's side, and as such was an eyewitness to all these festivities. Though Fisher condemned the cost, extravagance and wastefulness of the summit, of the 'fayre ladyes' he testified only to their 'sumptuouse and gorgeous apparell', and their active participation in 'suche daunsynges, suche armonyes, suche dalyaunce, and so many pleasaunt pastymes'.[53] That neither Hall nor Fisher made mention of any disorder by the women suggests that their behaviour was seen, at least by the English camp, in good cheer. By their beauty, charm, gaiety, and, occasionally drunken, diplomacy, these women fostered friendship and goodwill, or at least, eased tensions and deflected attention from irreconcilable differences between the two countries.[54]

As their contemporary Castiglione observed, no man at court could 'be graceful or pleasing or brave, or perform any gallant feat of chivalry, unless moved by the society and by the love and pleasure of ladies'.[55] At an ennoblement ceremony held at Lambeth on 2 February 1514, 'the Queen and the ladies' were in attendance to bear witness, and 'stood there as they might see all the order of their creations'.[56] The queen's ladies and gentlewomen were an integral element of a chivalric court culture.[57] At the jousts celebrating the king and queen's coronation in 1509, it was observed that their many 'feats' were done 'for the loue of ladies',[58] while at a tournament held at Greenwich in 1512, the queen and her ladies introduced the king and his men before they 'ran their courses'.[59] At the Field of Cloth of Gold in 1520, in preparation for the 'justes, torneys and other feats of armes', a number of 'galleries withdrawyng places, tents, pavilions, and other things necessarie' were built 'for the Quenes ladies, nobles, and all other comers, as shall reasorte to see the said feats'.[60] Here the two queens exchanged greetings and began 'talking and amusing themselves, surrounded by great personages and their favourite ladies'.[61] When it began to rain, both Henry and Francis 'ascended the ladies' stages and too amused themselves'.[62] Again, there were jousts on 15 June, and though neither queen was present, both English and French ladies attended. Both kings reportedly 'passed the time partly on horseback, and partly with the ladies'.[63] In the words of chronicler Hall, it was only 'after salutacions' were 'made to the Quenes being by their stages', and 'the reuerence done to the Quenes and their ladies', that 'the kynges had their speres redy.'[64] 'For love of them', it was observed, 'each of the jousters endeavoured to display his valour and prowess, in order to find more favour with his sweetheart'.[65] If the presence of women on these occasions was meant to elevate the competitive spirit and encourage the men in their feats, certainly this was achieved, though it may have amounted to a spontaneous wrestling match and some ungentlemanly behaviour between Henry and Francis.[66]

In addition to the jousts, pageants and masques too were staged with chivalric themes. Predating Jane's arrival, in 1510, Henry and twelve of his men 'came sodainly in a mornyng, into the Quenes Chambre' at Westminster, 'all appareled in shorte cotes… with hodes on their heddes, and hosen of the same, euery one of them, his bowe and arrows, and a sworde and a buckler, like out lawes, or Robyn Hodes men', before 'certeine danses and pastime' were made. Amusingly, the queen and her ladies were 'abashed, aswell for the straunge sight, as also for their sodain commyng'.[67] During a pageant held in 1511, a few riotous and unwelcome guests 'ranne to the pagent, and rent, tare, and spoyled' it, even 'to the kyng, and stripped hym into his hosen and dublet', while 'the ladies likewyse were spoyled'. After this 'the kyng with the quene and the ladyes returned to his chamber, where they had a great banket, and all these hurtes were turned to laughyng and game… and so this triumphe ended with myrthe and gladnes'.[68] In 1518, twelve 'ladyes disguysed' with twelve 'knightes disguysed' together 'daunced at one tyme and after they had daunced, they put of their viziers, & then they were all knowne', and all the company 'had high chere' until two o'clock in the morning.[69]

Henry VIII's enthusiasm for such festivities and merriment at court saw an increase in the frequency in which these events were staged. At Shrovetide, on 4 March 1522, Jane participated in the mock siege of Château Vert at York Place.

Château Vert, or 'Castle of Virtue', was a masque in which the queen's ladies and gentlewomen performed a carefully-rehearsed dance in elaborate costume. Jane was cast as one of the many abstract qualities, or 'virtues', deemed to fit the mistress of chivalric tradition: Beauty, Honour, Perseverance, Kindness, Constancy, Bounty, Mercy and Pity.[70] The chronicler Hall recorded it in exquisite detail:

> ...this castle was kept with ladies of straunge names, the first *Beautie*, the second *Honor*, the third *Perseveraunce*, the fourth *Kyndnes*, the fifth *Constance*, the sixte *Bountie*, the seventhe *Mercie*, and the eight *Pitie*: these eight ladies had Millian gounes of white sattin, every Lady had her name embraudered with golde, on their heddes calles, and Millein bonettes of gold, with jwelles. Under nethe the basse fortresse of the castle were other eight ladies, whose names were, *Dangier*, *Disdain*, *Gelousie*, *Unkyndenes*, *Scorne*, *Malebouche*, *Straungenes* [...] then entered eight Lordes in clothe of golde cappes and all, and great mantell clokes of blewe sattin, these lordes were named. *Amorus*, *Noblenes*, *Youth*, *Attendance*, *Loyaltie*, *Pleasure*, *Gentlenes*, and *Libertie*, the kyng was chief of this compaignie [...] the lordes toke the ladies of honor as prisoners by the handes, and brought them doune, and daunced together verie pleasauntly, which much pleased the straungers, and when thei had daunced their fill then all these disvisered themselfes and wer knowen...[71]

If, as many historians have remarked, Anne Boleyn's role as Perseverance proved to be rather apt, Jane's role as Constancy would prove to be rather inapt, as she would hardly show herself to be faithful or dependable throughout her career in the queen's household; not only would Jane betray her own husband, she eventually would be convicted and herself die a traitor to the crown.[72]

'No court, however great it be,' Castiglione remarked, 'can have in it adornment or splendour or gaiety, without ladies'.[73] A court was not a court without its women, as was clear when Catherine of Aragon and her ladies and gentlewomen were exiled. 'All men sayde that there was no myrthe' at the Christmas festivities held at Greenwich in 1531, 'because the Queene and the Ladies were absent'.[74] Such festivities were not merely trivial or peripheral events, staged for the merriment of all those involved. Through spectacle, splendour and regality there was sustained an elaborate court culture which reaffirmed, for the king, his right to rule, and for its participants, their status as members of the royal entourage, or *familia*.[75] Serving as a maid-of-honour to the queen, Jane was one of the many jewels in the king's crown.

Jane performed her duties for the projection of the queen's majesty and magnificence, by maintaining her in regal state, ensuring that she always ate, slept, dressed, and was in every place treated and honoured like a queen, often in elaborate ceremony. As she accompanied the queen, rode on horseback in procession, dined and danced with kings, engaged in the chivalric culture of the jousts, or kept up conversation and merriment with visitors, Jane demonstrated her importance both practically and culturally, and the power of her presence, visually, materially, and diplomatically, even while performing roles which were intrinsically, and essentially, domestic.

5

'For the establishment of good order'
ORDINANCES AND PERQUISITES

Life in the queen's household was governed by a set of articles, or 'ordinances'. When Cardinal Wolsey was tasked with economising and improving the efficiency of Henry VIII's household, ostensibly 'for the establishment of good order, and reformation of sundry errours and misuses', the result was the Eltham ordinances of 1526.[1] Such ordinances described the manner in which the household was to be conducted, addressing concerns with security, cleanliness, cost and waste, incompetency, idleness and laziness, and riotous or unlawful behaviour, like petty thievery, or violence.[2] As one of the queen's maid-of-honour, Jane had to abide by the household's strict rules and regulations. They were to be set in 'a booke', which was signed by the king's hand.[3] Upon being sworn in, probably some time in around 1520, Jane was first brought in to the countinghouse, where the aforementioned 'booke' was kept, and each ordinance was read aloud to her by the queen's lord chamberlain, William Blount, Baron Mountjoy, and her vice-chamberlain, Sir Edward Darrell, so that Jane could not excuse herself later 'by ignoraunce or for lacke of knowlege'.[4] Jane had to be dressed 'clenlye and decentlye' at all times; to 'abstayne from vicious lyving blasphemy' and 'sweryng'; to not be 'pickars of quarelles nor sowers of discorde & sedicion', or 'fighte nor brawle nor give occacion so to do'. During dinner, supper, or when the queen had withdrawn and retired to her bedchamber for the night, Jane had to 'kepe scilence', and was warned sternly not to be too raucous. Jane was forbidden too from participating in 'vnlawfull geemes as dyce, cardes and suche other prohibited by ye Kinges Lawes', and was warned not to 'pike nor breake lokes nor dors of anny house of office nor chambr within the said house'.[5] She would have been wise to observe carefully the rest of the queen's maids, who would be her immediate and constant companions, and from whom she would learn how to conduct herself while at court.

How far Jane's day to day life was actually governed, or restricted, by these rules is difficult to discern. Such ordinances reveal only how it was understood that Jane ought to behave, but not necessarily how she did. In theory, Jane had to adhere strictly to the rules or risk being punished. Punishments varied from the docking of wages, to being reprimanded by the lord chamberlain. But how often were these enforced? William Cecil, Baron Burghley, tasked with reforming the royal household, urged in 1576 that servants had to believe that they acted 'vppon payne of suche ponishement... or els all our labors shalbe in vayne'.[6] The queen's lord and vice-chamberlains were meant 'to serche and ouersee' her chambers and punish her servants 'for ony offence or outrage'.[7] Yet it is clear that some ordinances could and were often broken without fear of sanction. Records indicate that gambling, seemingly prohibited, was one of the king's most frequent pastimes. Between 1529 and 1532, George Boleyn, Lord Rochford, by then Jane's husband, was regularly paid out of the king's privy purse for money owed to him, often 'for a wager'.[8] Other ordinances, however, if broken, could not, and, for Jane, would not, go unpunished. In most circumstances, queens could dismiss servants as and when they felt it was necessary. In 1510, when Francisca de Cáceres, Catherine of Aragon's gentlewoman, was caught acting as an informant – or a gossip – for the resident Imperial ambassador, Luis Caroz, she was 'forbidden to enter the Palace' by the queen.[9] Caroz reported that Cáceres had been put out of the queen's service and that Catherine refused to see her. 'She is so perilous a woman that it shall be dangerous', the queen later remarked, 'I have no more charge of her'.[10] Jane herself was in violation of the ordinance which warned servants not to be 'pickars of quarelles nor sowers of discorde and sedicion' when, in 1534, she conspired to provoke, 'through quarrelling or otherwise', a young woman to withdraw from court, and when caught, Jane herself was banished.[11]

Notwithstanding this, few were punished so severely as to be deprived of their office, or banished from court. Deconstructing the queen's household, and breaking down its composition, reveals that the period from 1487 to 1527 was, for its servants, characterised by stability in office. Records may be fragmentary, but those which do survive indicate that serving the queen in this period could mean a sustained, lasting career. Of the 74 men and women of 'the Quenes chambr' who can be identified as attending upon Catherine of Aragon at her coronation on 24 June 1509, 43 of them remained in her service for at least ten, some even twenty years or more. An additional 41 men and women who were appointed shortly after Catherine's coronation had the same longevity in their careers serving the queen.[12] Foremost among them were William Blount, Baron Mountjoy, her lord chamberlain, who had served Catherine for 21 years, Maria de Salinas, Lady Willoughby, 32 years, Francis Phillip, her sewer, 26 years, Elizabeth Stafford, Duchess of Norfolk, 22 years, and Jorge de Athequa, Bishop of Llandaff, her confessor, 21 years, all of whom were her intimate servants, and thus could expect to remain in her household for as long as she was queen.

Men and women left the service of the king or queen if they grew too old, or became unwell. All servants had to be in good health, to have the strength and vigor to meet the often strenuous demands of royal service. The Eltham ordinances of 1526 stated that servants who were 'found impotent, sicklie, unable or unmeete persons' had to be discharged, though not to be 'left without some competent living'.[13] Offices could be made vacant when the servant who held it became sick, or worse, if they died. In 1517, 'there came a plague of sickenes, called the Swetyng sickenes', which was 'so feruent and infeccious' that 'many died in the kynges Courte'.[14] All servants in the royal household were routinely discharged upon the death of their master or mistress. When Elizabeth of York died in 1503, Henry VII broke up her household. Some of them were granted annuities, or pensions,[15] but many of the queen's servants retained their offices. More than six years lapsed between the death of Elizabeth and the crowning of her successor, Catherine, yet Henry VIII appointed at least 29 of his mother's servants to the household of his first wife.[16] To serve their queen was to serve their sovereign. Their loyal and enduring attendance kept them in office, providing a marked sense of continuity and stability between reigns.

All of the queen's servants had to be paid and provided for. Queens consort were endowed with sufficient income and revenue for their own expenditure, specifically to meet the 'greate Costes Expences and Charges' which she was to 'susteyne and bere in her Chambre'.[17] When Anne Basset was appointed to the queen's household in 1537, John Husee warned her mother that 'the Queen will be at no more cost with her but wages and livery';[18] months later he reiterated that 'the Queen will give her *but* £10 a year'.[19] Records kept by Griffith Richards, Catherine of Aragon's receiver-general, indicate that the queen was responsible for much of the costs incurred in maintaining her household. From 1525 to 1530, Richards noted her expenses, among them the 'fees and wages of knights, ladies, maids, and lawyers', with totals varying from £789. 4s. 10d. in 1525-26 to as much as £902. 12s. 6½d. in 1529-30.[20] Like the king's servants, the queen's servants received an annual salary which was paid monthly, quarterly or yearly, corresponding to their office: the queen's lord chamberlain was paid £40 a year, whereas his deputy, the vice-chamberlain, received only £26. 13s. 4d; Jane, as a maid-of-honour, was paid £10 per annum, whereas the queen's chamberers received £6. 13s. 14d.[21]

In addition to her wages, Jane was given her own lodgings in royal palaces. She was also entitled to stabling for one horse, and a bed for one of her own servants.[22] Certainly later Jane had her own maidservant, though we know nothing about her, only that she was known to her contemporaries in the 1530s as 'my Lady of Rochford's woman'.[23] Jane was also permitted to eat and drink in the queen's chambers.[24] The English court ate three meals a day.[25] A queen could take her meals in the Privy chamber, or occasionally, if she was entertaining, her Presence chamber. When Catherine of Aragon dined in private, it is likely that Jane sat with the rest of the queen's maids and ate in the Great Hall. Occasionally Jane may have taken her meals in their own rooms, though ordinances forbade the practice of dining in dark corners, or 'secret places', as this inevitably led to increased expenditure and saw the 'good order' of the palace 'greatly impaired'.[26] The Eltham ordinances of 1526 prescribed that Jane and the rest of the queen's maids would have been served

> among them for their Bouch in the morning, one chet lofe, one manchette, one gallon of ale; for afternoon, one manchette, one gallon of ale; for after supper one chet lofe, one manchette, two gallons of ale, dim' pitcher of wyne; and from the last day of October unto the first day of Aprill, three lynckes by the weeke, by the day six sises, one pound white

lights, six talshides, six faggots... amounting by the yeare to the sume of xxiiiil. xixs. xd.[27]

Jane also had a right to 'bouche of court', or to retrieve rations of food and drink, such as bread, ale and wine, as well as fuel and candles, provided for at the expense of the crown. Had Jane survived the scandal in 1541 and somehow retained her position until she quietly and comfortably retired from court, she would have been a likely candidate for an 'annuity', or pension, as the king often gave recognition to those who demonstrated their enduring commitment to the crown. In 1519, Margaret Bourchier, Lady Bryan, received £50 'and one tun of Gascon wine yearly' for attending upon the queen, Catherine of Aragon, for over a decade.[28] Similarly Catherine's gentlewoman, Elizabeth Saxby, was granted £20,[29] whereas Elizabeth Wolveden and Alice Davy both received an annuity of £10.[30] Even after Blanche Twyford had disobeyed the king's orders by refusing to swear a new oath to Catherine as 'Princess Dowager' in 1534, Henry, some years later, acknowledged 'her long and painful service', and rewarded her with an annuity of £66., 13s., 4d.[31]

While serving at court, Jane wore the queen's livery. 'Livery' was the clothing, or uniform, worn by men and women to mark them publicly as servants of the queen's household. It was issued to the queen's servants *en masse* at coronations and royal funerals.[32] For the coronation of Anne Boleyn in 1533, her ladies and gentlewomen were granted 'livereies of silke and scarlet'.[33] When a queen died, her servants dressed 'in suche most sadde and symplest clothyng that they had' until their 'mourning' livery could be made.[34] At the funeral procession for Jane Seymour in 1537, it was observed that

> all the Ladyes and gentlewomen did put of their sumptuous Appareill and token on them thabbytt of mornyng — levyng of their bonnettes richly appareled and toke white kerchers to appareill their heddes which attyrement is callyd parrys heddes with white kerchers coueryng over their sholders so knelyng abowt the said herse.[35]

Were the crimson satin sleeves or black damaske gowns and kirtles later detailed in the inventories for Jane's possessions worn on these grand occasions?

Livery was otherwise issued as and when it was required by the queen's servants. It was the responsibility of the queen herself to ensure that her servants were appropriately attired. A book kept by Richard Justice, Catherine's groom of the robes, itemised entries for livery to be distributed to the queen's servants from 1515 to 1517, such as 'a gowne of tawne velvet' for Maria de Salinas, Catherine's maid-of-honour, 'iii yerds blake for a nyght gown' for Isabel de Vargas, her chamberer, and 'vii yerds' of 'blake velvet' for Roger Radclif, her gentleman usher.[36] Warrants, bearing the king's signature, indicate that Henry often approved provisions for livery to clothe his queens' servants. One such warrant in 1511, orders that Margaret Penyngton, Elizabeth Colyns and Elizabeth Lysle, the queen's chamberers, were to be delivered gowns of damask furred with pure miniver and edged with 'letewes'.[37]

Livery was often embroidered with the queen's heraldric badge or motto. Spanish emblems of pomegranates and sheaves of arrows were sewn into Catherine of Aragon's livery. John Glynn, Catherine's yeoman, was given a green velvet gown with sleeves lined with cloth of gold, 'of the Spaynysh faccion', and Agnes, Duchess of Norfolk, received a gown of crimson velvet with 'spaynesh slevys' lined with 'grene clothe of gold of damaske'.[38] A servant's livery could even be fashioned to make pointed, politically-charged statements. Anne Boleyn had her livery embroidered with the motto, 'Ainsi sera, groigne qui groigne' ('What will be, will be, grumble who may'), in reaction to murmurs at court against the king's 'Great Matter'. Shortly after the king married Anne in 1533, Catherine of Aragon provocatively had her servants 'arrayed entirely in new apparel', embroidered with the letters 'H' for Henry and 'K' for Katherine.[39] The livery that Jane wore strengthened her identification with, and ties to, her mistress, whose presence and authority was represented wherever she went.

All of the queen's servants had to be 'apparelled according to their degrees'.[40] Livery worn by the queen's servants had to meet specific expectations, or customs. When Anne Basset was appointed to the queen's household, her mother, Lady Lisle, received notice from her agent in London, Husee, urging that she ensure that her daughter was properly attired. Anne 'must have such apparel' as 'a bonnet of velvet and a frontlet of the same';[41] Husee reiterated that 'she must have a bonnet or ij, with frontlets and an edge of pearl, and a gown of black satin, and another of velvet'; 'she must have cloth for smocks and sleeves, for there is fault founden that their smocks are too coarse'[42] and 'she must have against the Queen's churching a new satin gown, and against Christmas a new gown of lion tawny velvet'.[43] Anne wrote to her mother insisting that she send her 'an edge of pearl'.[44] Within a few weeks, Anne repeated that she 'must needs have her pearl, as shortly as is possible',[45] and again less than two weeks later, 'if you would send me an edge of pearl... I shall be much bound to you'.[46] The pearls were soon conveyed to Anne, yet she complained still that 'six score are not enough'. 'Indeed they are not to be worn in the Queen's service', she complained, 'unless they can be set full'.[47] Lady Lisle received another letter a day later, informing her that Anne 'saith that the vj score pearls which she hath received be all rags, and too few to serve'.[48] The urgency with which Anne requested the pearls indicates the importance of proper attire for the queen's servants.

Wages were modest, if not meagre considering the expenses Jane would have laid out serving at court.[49] There were, however, nonmonetary perquisites that could be accrued to supplement her income. Whereas gentlemen ushers received a tip for preparing the queen's lodgings in advance of her coming when her household was itinerant, and grooms and pages regularly received rewards if they ran an errand, her ladies and gentlewomen often kept articles of clothing taken from the Great Wardrobe.[50] The Revels accounts recorded in great detail the various ornate gowns, bonnets, hoods, frontlets, garments, ribbons, satins, cloths and jewels commissioned for ladies who were participating in court festivities, and often specify that performers 'kept their corresponding articles of attire' as payments in kind. In one entry, the author of the account, Richard Gibson, explicitly states that '24 yds of fine yellow satin' for 'the 8 ladies' garments', and the '8 cauls of Venice gold for the ladies' heads' remained 'with the French queen, the countess of Devonshire, Mistress Boleyn, Mistress Karre, Mistress Parker, Mistress Browne, Mistress Danet'.[51] These accounts correspond with the mock siege of Château Vert at York Place on 4 March 1522. The 'Mistress Parker' here, of course, is Jane. She kept the attire – a rich gown of white or yellow satin[52] with 'her name embraudered with golde' and a matching gold bonnet adorned 'with jwelles' – probably in recognition of her performance as Constancy in the pageant.[53] Inventories for Jane's possessions taken in 1536, and again in 1541-1542, when her goods were confiscated, indicate that, by the end of her career, she had accumulated a rather elaborate wardrobe.[54] Her fine clothes, jewels and other rich adornments exemplified her noble rank and her status as one of the queen's women.

Although she was entitled to wages, livery, accommodation, 'bouche of court' and other nonmonetary perquisites, perhaps the greatest advantage of all for Jane in serving as one of the queen's maids-of-honour was that she was strategically well-placed to secure an advantageous marriage. Her residence at court, itself a marriage market and a major site for negotiating matrimonial alliances and the exchange of wealth and property, functioned as a sort of prestigious 'finishing school'. It was for this above all that parents of young, unmarried girls belonging to noble families were anxious, and often went to extraordinary lengths, to secure for their daughters a place in the queen's household. Marriage was crucial to the progression of Jane's 'career' both as a woman, into wifehood, and as a servant, in the royal household. Her status as a maid-of-honour to the queen could only ever be temporary; in order to qualify as either a Lady or a Gentlewoman of the Privy Chamber, Jane had to contract a good marriage, preferably to one of the king's gentlemen, who had the most success in placing their wives at court.

Crucially, attending upon the queen facilitated her access to, and contact with, the king's most eligible courtiers. All royal residences had a king's side and a queen's side. John Norris, Henry's gentleman usher, drew up instructions in c. 1545 for preparing the king and queen's lodgings, in which he observed that, when 'the kinge and the Quenes lodginges shalbe made', queens were to 'have as many Chambers as the kinge hathe'.[55] An inventory taken at Hampton Court in 1547 illustrates the layout of the queen's apartments, comprising a 'with drawinge chambre on the Quenes syde', followed by 'the privey chambre' and 'the kinges bedchambre on the Quenes syde', leading to the 'Quenes galorie'; and from there 'the Quenes bedchambre', a second 'with drawing chambr on the Quens syd', another 'privey chambre', and finally, the 'privey Galorie'.[56] The queen's chambers are where Jane lived and served for much of her time at court.

The queen's side was established separately and distinct from, but adjacent to, the king's side, often 'mirroring' its structural layout, and both of their servants were accommodated in close quarters, occupying physical space – quite literally – under the same roof. At a banquet held at Greenwich on 7 July 1517, Giustinian observed that 'the ladies, indeed, sat alternately, that is to say, a gentleman and then a lady',[57] while at a banquet held by the king at Beaulieu on 4 September 1519, there once again 'sat a Ladie and a Lorde' who 'were plenteously served'.[58] Jane's participation in the elaborate court culture situated her at the centre of its medieval tradition of chivalric pursuits, or 'courtly love'. She may have flirtatiously exchanged letters and tokens with men in the same manner that maids Elizabeth Blount and Elizabeth Carew did with the king and Charles Brandon, Duke of Suffolk, in 1514, leading Suffolk to remind Henry 'to [tell my]sstres Blount and mysstres Carru [the] next tyme yt I wreth un to them [or se]nd them tokones thay schall odar [wre]th to me or send me tokones agayen'.[59] At the mock siege of Château Vert in 1522, for instance, Jane performed as an object of desire and rescue, before 'the lordes toke the ladies of honor as prisoners by the handes, and brought them doune, and daunced together verie pleasauntly'. It was in this context that Jane could and would be courted and flattered for her affection.[60] She was in an unparalleled position to attract the attention of men at court.[61] And some time in around the early 1520s, it was the attentions of one man in particular whom Jane attracted: George Boleyn.

6

'The wicked wife'
MARRIAGE

Jane Parker married George Boleyn in around 1525. Virtually nothing can be recovered as to the state of their marriage, but most historians have speculated that it was an unhappy one;[1] that their marriage was a failure, and that by 1536 the two of them were estranged, either because George was promiscuous, and Jane grew jealous of the attention he would show to other women, among them his own sister, Anne,[2] or on account of George's alleged homosexuality.[3]

Let us consider first the circumstances surrounding their marriage. It is unlikely that it was a love match. A marriage between a nobleman and woman in Tudor England was foremost a contract, pursued much like a business proposition, with little or no regard for the emotional sentiments of the individuals concerned. For any English noble or genteel family, such as the Parkers, or the Boleyns, a love match was entirely out of the question. In 1534, when it was disclosed that a widowed Mary Boleyn had secretly married William Stafford, a major mésalliance with a man beneath her station whose prospects were few, her family were furious, and even had her banished from court. Ostracised, her situation thereafter grew desperate. Mary was forced to admit that she 'did not well to be so hasty nor so bold' and had to solicit Thomas Cromwell to intervene with the king on her behalf.[4] To avoid a similar fate, Jane and George were under real pressure to contract a good marriage. As a marriage contract might secure property, wealth, social prestige or political favour, reaffirm status, grant protection, broaden and strengthen networks, or forge familial or even factional alliances, it required shrewd negotiation, and any prospective match would be scrutinised.

What recommended George as a match for Jane? He was a talented musician, and a poet, accomplished in courtly skills, literature and verse. Cavendish's *Metrical Visions*, lamenting in George's name, acknowledged his virtues, among them grace, elegance, intelligence and wit:

> God gave me grace, dame Nature did hir part,
> Endewed me with gyfts of natural qualities:
> Dame Eloquence also taughte me the arte
> In meter and verse to make pleasaunt dities,
> And fortune preferred me to high dignyties
> In such abondance, that combred was my witt,
> To render God thanks that me eche whitt.[5]

Like Jane, it was regarded as George's good fortune that he was well-born and introduced to the court at a young age. He was the only surviving son of Sir Thomas Boleyn, Earl of Wiltshire and Ormond, and Lady Elizabeth Howard. His father was a knight of good lineage, an excellent linguist and a statesman who built his career in financial administration and diplomatic negotiation. Thomas served the sovereign with unremitting zeal. Henry felt him to be competent and capable as a diplomat, but also regarded him as a close friend and companion. George participated in a masque at the 1514-15 revels,[6] and by 1516, with Thomas as his father and patron, he had been appointed as one of Henry's pages. In 1522, George was in receipt of joint grants made out to his father, and to him as his heir apparent, for offices in the manors and parks of Tonbridge, Brasted and Penshurst, which had belonged to the executed Duke of Buckingham.[7]

Negotiations for a match between Jane, an accomplished maid-of-honour to the queen, and George, a charismatic young courtier with a promising future as a 'boon companion' of the king, probably began in late 1524. The marriage was contracted by Jane's father, Henry, Lord Morley, and George's father, Sir Thomas Boleyn, solidifying an already kindred alliance between the two neighbouring families in Essex.[8] In late 1526, shortly after the marriage was contracted, Sir Thomas received the substantial sum of £33 6s. 8d. from a servant of Morley's, which may indicate that the two fathers had come to some sort of an agreement as to its value, and negotiations in this case were not in vain.[9] It was certainly not unusual for the parents of young, unmarried girls to negotiate marriages on their behalf: Jane's father would later contract the marriage between her sister, Margaret, and Sir John Shelton, whose uncle was none other than Sir Thomas Boleyn.

Part of the negotiation or custom in marriage-making was the condition that a noblewoman be invested with a dowry, an inheritance of parental property or wealth for the groom as a provision of financial stability. The more prestigious those involved in the match were, the higher they could demand in negotiation. As one of the queen's maids-of-honour, Jane had royal patronage. Both Henry and Catherine were often intimately involved in arranging and providing for their servants in marriage. In 1509 the king wrote to the queen's father, Ferdinand of Aragon, on behalf of Inez de Venegas, her maid-of-honour, begging for his favour in Inez's marriage to the queen's lord chamberlain, William Mountjoy.[10] In 1511, the queen gave Anne Weston, one of her gentlewomen, a dowry of two-hundred marks when she married another of her servants, Ralph Verney.[11] In 1516, Catherine negotiated a prestigious match between Maria de Salinas, and William Willoughby, Baron Willoughby, providing her maid with a dowry of eleven-hundred marks 'in tender consideration of the long and right acceptable service to her grace done by the said Mary Salinas to her singular contentation and pleasure'.[12] In 1525, Catherine wrote to Wolsey, soliciting him to obtain consent and confirm the jointure of Elizabeth Dannet, one of her maids, for her marriage: 'the goodness of my woman causeth me to make all this haste, trusting that she shall have a good husband and a sure living'.[13] The queen was clear in that the king had already spoken with 'Arondell, the heyre', or Sir John Arundell, the eldest son and heir of Sir John Arundell and Eleanor Grey, 'for a marriage to be had between him and one of my maids'.[14] Similarly Henry had urged a 'Mr Broke', probably Thomas Broke, his yeoman usher, 'not to marry without his advice, as he is intended for one of the Queen's maidens'.[15]

When the time came for the marriage between Jane and George to be contracted, it was Henry who would act as their patron, indicating that they were firmly in the king's favour. In 1524, Henry granted George the manor of

Grimston in Norfolk, previously owned by Sir Thomas Lovell, the former Chancellor of the Exchequer who had died months earlier, as an early wedding present.[16] Jane was invested with a handsome dowry of 2000 marks, amounting to £1333 6s. 8d., which was no small sum. A portion of this was generously provided for by the king, presumably when her father could not alone meet the amount set in negotiation with the Boleyn family; Morley's annual income was around £233 6s. 8d.[17] 'The King's Highness and my Lord my father paid great sums of money for my jointure to the Earl of Wiltshire', Jane would later recall, 'to the sum of 2000 marks'.[18] Perhaps a hard bargain, but it seems Morley was committed to forging an alliance with his neighbours.

It is plausible that the marriage between Jane and George was contracted purely for advantage, without any concern for the emotional sentiments of those involved. Without knowing the exact circumstances of how they first met, or any details of their courtship, a love match cannot be ruled out. They served the crown in close quarters. One could quite easily have caught the other's eye at a masque or banquet. And of course, many couples are known to have developed feelings of love and affection for one another after their marriage was contracted for advantage.[19]

We have no exact date or place at which Jane and George were married, because the ceremony itself was not documented, but it took place no later than 1525, as by early 1526 she was known publicly as 'hys wyfe'.[20] What was their marriage like? It lasted for just over a decade, and it was childless. Although they had no acknowledged children, George Boleyn, Dean of Lichfield (d. 1603) was said to have been their son. This George named Henry Carey, Baron Hunsdon, the son of Mary Boleyn, as an executor of his will, and in that will referred to Sir William Knollys, Mary's grandson, as his kinsman. However there is no record of Jane ever being pregnant, celebrating a birth, or taking an absence from court to do so.[21] We do not know if the marriage was even consummated. While Jane remained childless, it may have caused tensions between the couple, but this does not necessarily mean that their marriage was unhappy. Certainly in the eyes of their contemporaries, it may have been considered a failure, and it was Jane alone who, as a woman, was held responsible for the preservation of her husband's patrilineage.[22] We know Sir Thomas Boleyn felt that the match between Jane and his only son to be unsuccessful on account of it not producing an heir. Her father-in-law later made scornful remarks as to her childlessness.

George spent a considerable amount of time away from court as an ambassador in France on diplomatic missions for the king, particularly in the early 1530s as he tried to secure Francis I's support for Henry's new marriage and the break with Rome.[23] We might speculate that, as they spent much their married life apart, Jane may have been left feeling distant, and lonely. On the other hand, it does appear that, at least in 1533, while George was on embassy, husband and wife were in the habit of writing letters to one another when they were apart. Jane kept George up to date on the goings-on back at court. None of their correspondence has survived, but we know that they sent letters because Sir Edward Baynton acknowledged as much in a report to George: Baynton wrote only briefly regarding news of the Dukes of Norfolk and Suffolk because 'the matier doeth probably appere in a letre by my lady your wife, or els by sum other, I am sure, that hath advertised hym by their letters'.[24] If we cannot prove a close companionship, it is reasonable to suggest that Jane and George, at least, had a working partnership.

A French manuscript, 'Les Lamentations de Matheolus', containing a satirical poem entitled 'Les Tourmens de Mariage', or 'The Torments of Marriage', bears the inscription 'Thys boke ys myn, George Boleyn'. As the title suggests it is a rather cynical satire attacking the institution of marriage, and George's inscription is dated as 1526, only a year after his marriage to Jane was first contracted. Was George having early doubts about the match? Did he regret his union with Jane? Perhaps George identified with the author, who in the satire lamented 'the great sadness of his soul', and dated 'the beginning of all his torments' to the day he was wed?[25] No more plausible is this than the suggestion that the manuscript was probably a wedding gift from a kinsman with a very dry sense of humour.[26] What, if anything, at all, can be inferred from George's possession of the manuscript? One author has speculated that George was homosexual. It is their contention that if Jane, in May 1536, 'were told that he had committed buggery with a male friend, she could have felt dishonored enough by the perceived insult to her womanhood to be receptive to the charge that he had engaged in other illicit sexual acts'.[27] The logic here is unclear, almost absurd.[28] On what evidence? The claim is based largely on the fact that the manuscript 'Les Tourmens de Mariage' also bears the signature of a 'Marc S', identified as Mark Smeaton, a court musician with whom George was supposed to have been very intimate. 'Such volumes were expensive and normally changed hands only in the form of gifts', and if the two were intimate friends then perhaps Smeaton came to be in possession of the book when George gave it to him.[29] But there is no evidence to substantiate this theory. They may have shared the manuscript and an interest in music. We know they frequented the same court circles. The identification of 'Marc S' as Smeaton is reasonable, though to some remains 'fairly contentious'.[30] Further evidence of George's homosexuality is apparently found in a statement he made on the scaffold, in which he remarks that he was a 'miserable sinner, who have grievously and often times offended', and as such deserved death 'for more and worse shame and dishonor than hath ever been heardof before'.[31] Homosexuality in the sixteenth century was both illegal and considered unnatural and an act against God. George did refrain from specifying exactly the nature of his crimes, which, it is felt, 'is consistent with the suggestion that he was guilty of sexual acts, including buggery, which were considered unnatural'.[32] As intriguing as it might be, the theory that George was homosexual is altogether unfounded.

Less absurd is the notion that George was promiscuous. Cavendish accuses him of 'unlawfull lechery'. The particular nature of this lechery cannot now be construed, and Cavendish only specified 'women', 'wydowes' and 'maydens' as the objects of his 'bestyall' living. Cavendish, who served Cardinal Wolsey as a gentleman usher until his master's death in 1530, was a natural enemy of the Boleyns, and might have exaggerated George's licentiousness:

> My lyfe not chaste, my lyvyng bestyall;
> I forced wydowes, maydens I did deflower.
> All was oon to me, I spared none at all,
> My appetite was all women to devoure,
> My study was both day and hower,
> My onleafull lechery how I might it fulfill,
> Sparyng no woman to have on hyr my wyll.[33]

Cavendish's portrayal of the courtier, in spite of any supposed hostility or ill-feeling he may have held for the Boleyns, otherwise seems fair, balanced and well-informed. Surely it had to have struck a chord with his audience, and as such this verse indicates that George publicly had the reputation of a libertine, and a womaniser.[34] If George was unfaithful, Jane was prudent enough to, again, at least publicly, tolerate his indiscretions. In private, she could have been hurt, perhaps jealous, or at least, embarrassed. She may even have berated him for his philandering. There were limits to what a wife might be expected to endure, and it is not difficult to see how George's womanising would have put a strain on their marriage, not least if, at its most extreme, it went so far as to involve his own sister, Anne Boleyn. If Jane began to suspect that her own husband was committing incest, it would have been quite enough to shatter any illusions of marital bliss. Jane is often thought to have been particularly jealous of his relationship with his sister, but rather than seeing the queen as a rival for her husband's affections, the evidence suggests that the two women were quite close (of which, more later).

The significance of all this is that, if their marriage was unhappy, if Jane was unhappy, it could explain why, in 1536, she provided evidence against her own husband. One near-contemporary author, George Wyatt, later claimed that 'what she did was more to be rid of him than of true ground against him'. Jane is described as 'the wicked wife, accuser of her own husband, even to the seeking of his blood', tying her involvement in his downfall directly to the state of their marriage.[35] Although Wyatt sought to vindicate Anne, his account should not be disregarded too hastily; his source was one of the queen's own attendants, who could quite plausibly have been a witness to the troubled marriage of Jane and George while they both resided at court.

More useful is a mutilated letter dated 4 May 1536, suggesting that, shortly following George's arrest on suspicion of treason, Jane sent to ask after her husband in the Tower, to 'se how he dyd', and moreover, promised that 'she wold humly sut unto the kyngs hy[nes]… for hyr husband'.[36] This is one of, if not the only surviving testament to the nature of their relationship. Jane appears to show her husband pity, and compassion, but how do we reconcile her promise to petition the king on behalf of her husband with her furnishing of the prosecution's case with evidence which, true or false, was incriminating enough to secure his conviction? Was Jane insincere in promising to petition the king? Was she twisting the knife, providing him with false hope? It is unconvincing to find 'malice' in Jane's promise.[37] What would she have to gain? George, who 'gaf hyr thanks', surely thought that she was sincere.[38] If her husband was to be acquitted and released from the Tower, her prospects were better with him than without him. George would have been her last remaining tie to the court. Alternatively, if her husband was convicted and executed for treason, she would be left a penniless widow with few prospects and only her jointure to rely upon. It was customary that the property of a convicted criminal would be confiscated: all their possessions, including all land, estates and personal property that they had carefully accumulated as a couple, would consequently be seized by the crown.[39] With this in mind, Jane promised to petition the king. As we shall see, it is entirely possible that Jane did not yet know how serious the charges were, and might well have believed that there was still a chance for mercy. She may also have been showing her husband pity and compassion if only to keep up appearances as his dutiful and devoted wife. Following George's death, Jane was outwardly mournful, a 'wydowe in blake' in the words of Cavendish; the inventory of Jane's possessions taken in 1542 indicates that she continued to predominantly (if not exclusively) wear black in her final years.[40]

Here the intention was to establish or explain Jane's motives in 1536, by determining whether the marriage of this ill-fated couple was happy, or unhappy. Yet none of the evidence provides any actual insight into the state of their marriage. The use of 'may', 'if' and 'perhaps' cannot be overstated. Their relationship, from the date at around which their union was contracted in 1525 through until George's arrest in 1536, made little to no impression on the surviving source material. What we do know, and what we can prove about their marriage, is very little, and much of it depends on how any one person interprets what is, for the most part, inconsequential evidence. The question which arises, then, is not one of love, but of loyalty, and as we shall see, throughout the 1520s and much of the 1530s, Jane would show herself to be fully committed to the Boleyn ascendancy.

7

'None but God can get him out of it'
THE BOLEYN ASCENDANCY

Jane served Catherine of Aragon until at least 1525, when she married George Boleyn. Upon securing a good marriage, maids-of-honour usually retired to their husband's estates. Jane's whereabouts in these years are nowhere recorded, but it is possible that she left court for Grimston, Norfolk, to manage household accounts, administer George's local affairs, and raise their prospective children.[1] Some women left their husband's estates for extended periods of time to continue in their vocation as royal servants, and in doing so 'modified the pattern of wifehood'.[2] Not all maids-of-honour left the queen's service when they married. John Husee reported in 1537 that Margery Horsman, one of the queen's maids, 'shall be married, but as far as I can learn she shall keep her old room still'.[3] After marrying Sir Michael Lyster, Margery continued to serve the queen in her household as one of her gentlewomen. It is thus possible Jane remained in Catherine's service, but we cannot be certain.

What Jane would find is that, as George's wife, her future – her fate – was inextricably tied to that of her husband. Her identity as the young 'Mistress Parker', one of the queen's fair maidens, was no more. Although her own name disappears altogether from court records until 1532, Jane survives in grants concerning George, as 'hys wyfe'. His fortune would be her fortune, as would his misfortune. In around 1525, George had been appointed to serve as a Gentleman of the king's Privy Chamber, a prestigious office which entitled both he and his wife to reside at court. But when Wolsey instituted the Eltham ordinances of 1526 and reshuffled the Privy Chamber, George was unseated from his new position after a mere six months. Those who were to be 'discharged out of the kynges preve chambre' were compensated. George was granted 'provysyon' in the sum of £20 a year for 'hy[m a]nd hys wyfe to lyve therapon'.[4] He was also appointed as a royal cupbearer, to serve intermittently 'when [the] Kyng dynyth [o]wt'.[5] Consequently, George and Jane might have been forced to retire to Grimston, as the ordinances did not provide for servants 'in extraordinary' (or their wives) to reside at court. Exceptions were made, however, as the young couple were named among those privileged few who were entitled 'to have lodging in the King's house when they repair to it'.[6]

George and Jane were in royal favour, but for how long? Fortune was fickle, as was the mind of their sovereign. Serving only on the periphery of the royal household, their position at court was still somewhat precarious. That was, until Henry became infatuated with George's sister, Anne Boleyn. Some time in 1527 or 1528, Anne began receiving love letters from the king.[7] Henry claimed he had been 'stricken with the dart of love', declaring himself her 'loyal and most assured Servant'.[8] Jean du Bellay, the French ambassador, regarded Henry to have been so enamoured with her by 1528 that 'none but God can get him out of it'.[9] Henry's courtship of Anne coincided with a marked progression in her brother's career. In 1528 alone, George was appointed as an Esquire of the Body, Master of the King's Buckhounds and Keeper of the Palace of Beaulieu in Essex. By 1529, George had been knighted, granted the chief stewardship of Beaulieu, and began serving as a diplomat in France.[10] He was even reinstated in his former office as a gentleman of the king's Privy Chamber, and was one of Henry's regular 'boon companions' with whom he played bowls and tennis, hunted, and gambled on dice and card games.[11] What is more, Anne's father Sir Thomas Boleyn was created Earl of Wiltshire and Ormonde, which saw George inherit the courtesy title of 'Viscount Rochford' and Jane, as his wife, the title of 'Viscountess Rochford'. In these early years of the Boleyn ascendancy at court, Jane may well have been reinstated to (or indeed, perhaps, never left) the household of the queen, Catherine of Aragon. Jane did receive a New Year gift from Catherine in 1528, as 'Jane Bollen'. She was listed among many of other gentlewomen in service of the queen, but there are others in the same list who were merely lodged at court with their husbands serving the king.[12]

Simultaneously, Henry came to doubt the validity of his marriage to Catherine, and embarked on his 'Great Matter'. His conviction was that it was invalid, that it had always been invalid, should never have been permitted and, now, had to be annulled. Henry and Catherine, in spite of private tensions, remained publicly gracious, 'as if there had never been any dispute'. At this early stage, even the queen 'strenuously' maintained that the king, her husband, was acting on his conscience, 'and not from any wanton appetite'.[13] Anne was sent home to Hever in September 1528, and Henry resided conspicuously with Catherine, apparently to keep up appearances of good faith for Cardinal Campeggio, who was due to arrive at court.[14] Henry wrote to Anne, assuring her that Wolsey had arranged a lodging for her to be nearer to him.[15] This could not have been very subtle, as by December, du Bellay reported that the king had placed her 'in a very fine lodging, which he has prepared for her close by his own'.[16]

The amorous attentions of the king for his queen's maid were far from discreet, and there were many who felt that Henry was led, not, by his consicence, but by passion. Upon learning that Henry was seeking an annulment, 'the Quenes ladies, gentlewomen, and servauntes' murmured, if indiscreetly, that a woman 'called Anne Bulleyne' had 'so entised the kyng, and brought him in such amours, that only for her sake and occasion, he would be divorsed from his Quene'. The chronicler Edward Hall regarded this as 'foolishe communicacion', and 'contrary to the truth',[17] yet we know, in hindsight, that this was more than the mere gossip of women. In August 1527, the king applied for a dispensation allowing him to marry again, specifically a woman with whom he contracted 'first degree of affinity' through sexual intercourse, that is, the sister of a previous mistress, namely Mary Boleyn.[18] Anne herself was consulted and kept informed of proceedings for the divorce. Edward Fox was sent to Rome in 1528 with a new proposal for the king's Great Matter. When he returned in May, Fox was received at Greenwich by the king, who sent him to Anne's chamber. Fox informed Anne, and then Henry, that his discussion with the Pope had been promising, and there in Anne's chamber they both questioned him 'at great length'.[19] Clearly Anne was no mistress. She was a queen-in-waiting.

Lying at the heart of the king's Great Matter, the queen's household became a matter of royal policy. Loyalties, and/ or allegiances, in the queen's household, were managed, or manipulated by the king, to create one queen, and simultaneously, dethrone the other. Anne's unpopularity in England, even at court, was problematic for Henry.[20] Her reputation as the king's mistress, a seductress, the 'other woman' who had usurped England's rightful queen, was incompatible with queenship. The creation of her household addressed this, first, by appointing men and women to serve Anne who were firmly aligned with her and the king, pledging their loyalty and fidelity by oath, and second, by legitimising Anne as queen-in-waiting, surrounded by an attendant staff befitting her new status. Anne's household served, often, quite literally, to legitimise her as Henry's queen. 'I see they mean to accustom the people *by degrees* to endure her', du Bellay remarked in 1528.[21] Eustace Chapuys too observed that Henry was 'very watchful of the countenance of the people, and begs the lords to go and visit and make their court to the new Queen'.[22]

Precisely when Jane left Catherine's household, and began serving Anne, is unclear, but surely she had jumped ship by 1531, when Anne was reportedly 'preparing her state royal by degrees', appointing various men and women to attend upon her as her own servants.[23] She was treated 'more like a queen than a simple maid'.[24] By 1532, Anne was 'lodged where the Queen used to be' and was 'accompanied by almost as many ladies as if she were Queen'.[25] Thus a rival household emerged, and, with Henry acknowledging Anne as his queen, hers was the one that mattered. 'Greater court is now paid to her every day than has been to the Queen for a long time', du Bellay reported in 1528.[26] Foreign ambassadors, dignitaries and other visitors to the court were received in Anne's chambers, and petitioners, like Honor Grenville, Lady Lisle, now aggressively courted Anne, and her servants, with letters, tokens and gifts for their favour.[27]

On the other hand, from 1529 to 1531, Henry scarcely saw Catherine, and kept himself distant,[28] before he exiled her to The More in Hertfordshire, where the queen and her household were 'scantily visited'.[29] Exile had severe consequences for the queen's servants, as they were ostracised from king and court. Her servants could no longer hope to gain from the rewards accrued in royal service. Richard Wood, Catherine's page, is said to have 'sustained great losses without recompense'.[30] Mario Savorgnano, who visited the queen in her exile, observed that 'she had some thirty maids-of-honour standing round the table, and about fifty who performed its service', but that they were 'not so much visited as heretofore'.[31] Catherine's household-in-exile must have feared that their careers were all but over. Few men and women now aspired to serve her. Thomas, Lord Vaux, who had been dispatched by Henry to administer Catherine's household, remarked in 1533 that he would 'rather die in some other of the King's service than continue here much longer'.[32] Sir Richard Baker refused an appointment to serve Catherine, and 'loath now to serve anybody but the King'.[33]

Nor did Catherine's household receive a gift from the king at the celebrations for New Year. In the gift roll for 1532, Catherine and her servants are conspicuous by their absence.[34] Chapuys reported on 4 January 1532 that the king 'used to send New Year's presents to the ladies of the Queen', and although 'this custom, hitherto' had been 'faithfully observed', he noted that 'this has not been done this year'.[35] What is more, Chapuys reported that Henry explicitly forbade courtiers and councillors from sending the queen and her household any gifts of their own.[36] On the other hand, Anne and her ladies and gentlewomen, with Jane, 'the Lady Rocheford', all received gifts, and engaged in the 'queenly' ritual of New Year gift exchange on 1 January 1532. It must have been clear that the more viable and promising career was with Anne. Jane gave the king 'two velvet and two satin caps, two being trimmed with gold buttons', while Henry closed the exchange by giving Jane a gilt goblet.[37] Gift-giving was often indicative of who was, and indeed, who was not, in favour. The New Year gift rolls indicate that Jane both gave and received gifts consistently from 1528 through 1534, at which time she presented the king with a fine shirt embroidered with silver ('a shirte with a collor of siluer worke').[38]

Jane would accompany her sister-in-law in 1532 when she and the king visited Calais to meet with Francis I, granting Anne recognition as Henry's wife on an international stage.[39] This recognition was unlikely to come from Spain, as Charles V would approve of neither a rejection of the Pope's authority nor that of his aunt, Catherine, as queen, and further to that her daughter Mary as Princess. Henry had therefore hoped to secure Francis' backing in his Great Matter. Preparations were made in the months prior to their departure. On 1 September, Anne was created Marquess of Pembroke in an elaborate ceremony at Windsor Castle,[40] and in addition to the '20 rubies and 2 diamonds reserved' and purposefully 'delyvered by the Kinges hyghnes' to his goldsmith at the beginning of October, Henry commissioned further 'costly dresses' and rich 'ornaments' for Anne to wear for the occasion.[41] The king felt that Anne should look like a queen, and to this end ordered Thomas, Duke of Norfolk to retrieve certain jewels in Catherine's possession. Catherine was understandably stubborn to this request, however, and apparently refused because 'it was against her conscience to give her jewels to adorn a person who is the scandal of Christendom'.[42] Henry was 'vexed' and 'astonished' at her stubbornness. No one detail could or would be taken for granted, from the jewels adorning Anne's neck, to the ladies in her entourage. The king could not risk a show or even a hint of falsity and dissidence in the royal party. Mary Tudor, the king's sister, who had previously served as queen consort of France, was notably absent, but she had already once let slip her hostility towards her brother's new amour. That Jane was chosen to attend suggests that she left no doubt as to her allegiance.

Jane boarded *The Swallow* on 11 October and set sail at around five o'clock in the morning, before arriving in Calais, where the royal party were 'honorably received with procession' by an array of knights and soldiers amidst the 'great peal of guns' in salute.[43] While Henry and Francis conducted 'with great cheer' their various interviews at the French court in Boulogne,[44] back in Calais, Anne and her ladies anxiously awaited their return. Together they carefully rehearsed Anne's debut, which finally took place on 25 October, at a banquet held by Henry in Francis' honour, where Jane, 'gorgeously apparelled' in a gold dress with crimson satin, an ornamented silver sash and a full-face visor to conceal her identity, appeared alongside her sister-in-law:

> After supper came in the Marchiones of Penbroke, with. vii. ladies in Maskyng apparel, of straunge fashion, made of clothe of gold, compassed with Crimosyn Tinsell Satin, owned with Clothe of Siluer, liyng lose and knit with laces of Gold: these ladies were brought into the chamber, with foure damoselles appareled in Crimosin satlyn, with Tabardes of fine Cipres: the lady Marques tooke the Frenche Kyng, and the Countes of Darby, toke the Kyng of Nauerr, and euery Lady toke a lorde, and in daunsyng the kyng of Englande, toke awaie the ladies visers, so that there

the ladies beauties were shewed, and after they had daunsed a while they ceased, and the French Kyng talked with the Marchiones of Penbroke a space, and then he toke his leaue of the ladies.[45]

Although Jane is not explicitly named by chronicler Hall as one of the seven 'ladies in Maskyng apparel', Wynkyn de Worde's *The Maner of the tryumphe of Caleys and Bulleyn*, informed by an eyewitness in the royal party and printed in London a few days later, confirms that a 'lady Rocheford' was among those in attendance.[46] And thus Jane resumed the responsibilities and socio-political functions of her former role in Catherine's household, but now, for the practice, construction and display of Anne's queenship.

From 1527 to 1532, Anne's 'rival' household grew out of necessity, as the king saw fit. It became fully established when, frustrated by the deadlock in his Great Matter, Henry took the radical step of breaking with Rome, making him independent of the papacy and rejecting the Pope's authority in favour of his own. Henry and Anne were married in secret at a private ceremony on 25 January 1533. Anticipating that she would shortly be queen, a priest approached Anne and expressed his desire to serve in her household as one of her chaplains, to whom she advised that 'he must wait a little until she had celebrated her marriage with the King'.[47] It is unlikely he had to wait too long, as it was reported, Henry, 'perceiuyng his newe wife Quene Anne, to bee greate with childe, caused all officers necessary, to bee appoynted to her'.[48] As Hall observed, 'the Courte was greatly replenished with lordes, knightes, and with ladies and gentlewomen, to a great nomber, with all solace and pleasure'.[49] By the spring of 1533, with her household established, Anne was a queen lacking only a crown. Now that she was pregnant, the king 'appoynted the daie of her Coronacion'.[50]

Anne's rise to queenship inspired feverish loyalty. Some time in May 1533, in the days before Anne's coronation, Thomas Burgh, her lord chamberlain, seized the barge of queen Catherine, and 'mutilated' her coat of arms. He, 'rather ignominiously', had it 'torn off and cut to pieces'. When Chapuys learned of this, he informed Cromwell, and advised that by 'the tearing off of her escutcheon from her Royal barge' the king and his council risked upsetting the Emperor, Charles V. It appeared to have been done almost out of spite, as 'there were in the river many others equally fit for the Lady's service'. Cromwell apparently 'knew nothing about that', though he was surely feigning ignorance. As was the king, who claimed that he was 'grieved to hear that the Queen's arms had been removed from her barge'. For his part, Burgh was, we are told, 'severely reprimanded'. Had Burgh acted excitedly, perhaps rather too hastily, in a fit of loyalty for his new mistress? Was it Anne herself who gave the order? As an outraged Chapuys observed, 'the Lady has unscrupulously made use of it at this coronation of hers, and appropriated it for her own use'.[51]

Honor, Lady Lisle, was one of the women who accompanied Anne as one of her ladies when she and the king met with Francis I in 1532. She was also in Anne's entourage at her coronation in 1533. Now residing in Calais, some distance from the court, Lady Lisle appeared to be quite anxious to keep up this affinity with the new queen and her household, and thus in 1535, she requested a kirtle in the style of the queen's livery. For this, Lisle's agent, Husee, approached George Taylor, the queen's receiver-general, who approved the request.[52] A month later, Husee wrote again to his mistress: 'Your Ladyship may be assured of having your kirtle of the Queen's livery before Midsummer. Mr. Taylor will not forget you…'[53] Perhaps Taylor had forgotten Lady Lisle after all, as several months later, in December, her agent resorted to visiting the queen's chambers himself for it: 'I have been five times within these six days for the kirtle the Queen gave you, but am always put off.'[54] Outwardly a servant's livery was a visual, symbolic representation of their identity as a servant to the queen at court and in the wider kingdom, conferring upon them social status, a mark of the protection they were assured, and the royal favour which they enjoyed. Evidently Lady Lisle was quite determined to wear the queen's livery, as she sent her servant, Thomas Warley, to retrieve it: 'I have been attendant at the Court for the kirtle which your ladyship have long looked for', Warley reported the following year. Eventually, her persistence paid off, and Lady Lisle received the kirtle she so desired.[55]

Anne Boleyn's accession led to the sudden and conspicuous promotion at court of men and women with ties to the new queen. Whereas some appointments were made in response to pressure by petition, others gave way to pressure unspoken, as there were servants who felt they had rightful a claim to office. At the crucial turn of Anne's rise to queenship, many such crown or 'civil' servants were already tied, or 'bound', to the household of Catherine of Aragon. Satisfying these lineages, retaining and rewarding such servants, might otherwise have proven to be a burden.[56] On this occasion, Anne and Henry were somewhat relieved of the usual constraints and appointed whomsoever they wished to serve the new queen. This was something of an exception, however, as the households of the rest of Henry's queens ran nearly consecutively, and they each, in turn, inherited servants from their predecessor's establishment.

Like the king's household, the queen's household was a complex network of overlapping familial, social, political and religious affiliations and obligations. From the view of the queen herself, appointments were of utmost interest, as they had the potential to create, maintain and branch her networks throughout the wider court and kingdom. No one appointment would have been made unconsciously or have been lacking in real significance. Henry's queens retained servants with whom they had pre-existing ties, and whose interests were thus likely aligned with their own. Perhaps as a gesture towards ensuring their comfort, the queen's kinsmen and women were the first to be appointed to serve.[57] English-born queens (Anne Boleyn, Jane Seymour, Katherine Howard, Katherine Parr) fulfilled familial or dynastic ambitions by advancing her kinsmen and women. In the household of Anne Boleyn, Elizabeth Howard, Countess of Wiltshire, her mother, Mary Boleyn, Lady Carey, her sister, Dorothy Howard, Countess of Derby, Anne Boleyn, Lady Shelton, and Elizabeth Wood, Lady Boleyn, her aunts, were all appointed as ladies in her Chamber and Privy Chamber, whereas Sir James Boleyn, her uncle, became her Chancellor. As the wife of the new queen's brother, Jane was surely in no doubt of her place. More distant relatives in the Parker, Tylney and Howard families, like Alice Parker, Lady Morley, Jane's mother, Agnes Tylney, Dowager Duchess of Norfolk, Anne's step-grandmother, Sir Phillip Tylney, and Margaret Gamage, who later married William Howard, found preferment too.[58]

Familial alliances between the Boleyns and other noble and genteel families strengthened their claim, and these were honoured with prestigious appointments near the crown. A cross-section of prominent local families in Norfolk and its neighbouring counties in the East and South-East of England, like the Sheltons, Gainsfords and the Ashleys, who had geographical ties to the queen and were firmly aligned with the Boleyns, were too represented in the queen's household. Sir John Shelton the younger, became her sewer, and his sisters Mary and Madge Shelton, were her maids-of-honour, as did Anne Gainsford, who served the queen alongside of her father Sir John Gainsford, her would-be husband Sir George Zouche, and Mary Zouche, his kinswoman. George Taylor, Anne's receiver-general, was the nephew of George Gainsford. Jane Ashley became her maid-of-honour, Rafe Ashley, her gentleman usher, John Ashley, her sewer, and Thomas Ashley too attended upon the queen.[59]

Service not only created but reinforced ties of obligation, and a queen's household formed the core of her support. To command service from within, and draw upon the loyalty of those who were sworn to them, queens had to rely on their servants to establish themselves securely, reaffirm their status, and, in crisis, for emotional comfort, even political backing. Queens, sharing in the custody of appointments with the king, might surround themselves as far as possible with men and women whom they knew well, liked and cared for, could trust and confide in and whom they felt would serve them loyally and faithfully. Friends, confidantes and companions of the queen could also be appointed to serve in her household. Anne chose Bridget Wiltshire, Lady Wingfield, Anne Savage, Lady Berkeley, and Margery Horsman. Queens patronised and promoted men and women who shared in her religious convictions to serve in her household. Anne appointed many known 'evangelicals': Nicholas Shaxton was her almoner, and Hugh Latimer, William Betts, Matthew Parker and William Latymer all served as the queen's chaplains.

All of Henry's queens built a network of support and obligation with their households at its core – though, infiltrating this network, it was the king who ultimately had charge of administering and appointing the new queen's household. Servants appointed by the queen were far outnumbered, and their presence at court overwhelmed, by servants who were more closely affiliated with the king. Henry could appoint whomsoever he wished to serve his wives. For the household of Anne Boleyn, the king chose many men who had previously served in his own household. Thomas Burgh, Baron Burgh, her lord chamberlain, served as one of the king's spears, and Sir Edward Baynton, who had served the king as a squire of the body, was now Anne's vice-chamberlain (and his wife, Isabel Legh, Lady Baynton, was also appointed to serve the new queen). Sir William Coffin was a gentleman of the king's Privy Chamber before becoming the queen's master of the horse (at which time, his wife, Margaret Coffin, née Dymoke, became her gentlewoman), whereas William Oxenbridge served the king as a page before advancing to serve Anne as a groom porter. Henry Webbe and Richard Dauncy, her gentleman ushers, Edward Floyd, yeoman of the robes, William Smith, yeoman of the chamber, Richard Bartlett, her physician, John Uvedale, her secretary, and Sir Thomas da la Lynde can all be traced to the king's household before serving on the queen's side. The wives, sisters and daughters of Henry's own courtiers and councillors, such as Elizabeth Browne, Countess of Worcester, sister of Sir Anthony Browne, gentleman of the king's Privy Chamber, Elizabeth Cheney, Lady Vaux, the wife of Thomas, Lord Vaux, Elizabeth Hill, Anne's chamberer and the wife of Richard Hill, Sergeant of the king's Wine Cellar, and Elizabeth Holland, maid-of-honour and mistress of Thomas Howard, Duke of Norfolk, also found preferment. What is more, the king's family, like his niece, Lady Margaret Douglas, and his daughter-in-law, Mary, Duchess of Richmond, wife of Henry, Duke of Richmond, the king's illegitimate son, and even his mistresses, Jane Seymour and an unnamed 'damsel' later identified by Chapuys, attended upon the new queen.[60]

8

'She would not damn her own soul on any consideration'
OATH

Upon her appointment to the new queen's household, Jane, as one of Anne's servants, was obliged by the swearing of an oath to her mistress. In a ceremony administered by Anne's lord chamberlain, Thomas, Lord Burgh, a great number of men and women were sworn in, pledging their fidelity and allegiance to their mistress, as her loyal and faithful servants, to obey her in everything.[1] Great sanctity was placed on the sworn word. An oath was a sacred and irrevocable act of faith, binding on their conscience, even citing God to witness the truth, sincerity and integrity of their statement. They were highly regarded, and would not have been taken lightly.[2] Evidence for the 'taking' of an oath, however, is non-existent. When Anne Basset was appointed to the queen's household in 1537, her mother's agent Husee could only report that she had been 'sworn the Queen's maid'.[3] As such, oaths are insufficient as evidence of loyalty. Were they taken seriously, passively, or rather too hastily? Was it seen merely as a formality, and somewhat burdensome, or was it treated with urgency, as a matter of conscience? Did it invoke emotion, or was it merely routine? By the time Jane was sworn in to serve Henry's fifth wife, Katherine Howard, this ceremony would have been all too familiar. She must have been well-rehearsed in, and we can expect, growing weary of, the rhetoric of the oath. The affective language invoked positive virtues – to be 'loyal', 'faithful', 'good', 'true' – which could engender feeling in the individual taking the oath, like a sense of duty, and commitment. Where this rhetoric found meaning was in relationships, and the experience of such emotions shared between mistress and servant.

Traditionally, servants were retained by a master or a mistress, with their allegiance sworn to them, and strictly no other. In 1519, Sir William Bulmer, 'beyng the kynges seruaunt sworne', was summoned to the Star Chamber for 'diuerse riottes, misdemeanors and offences'.[4] Upon learning that Bulmer had 'refused the kynges seruice' and was retained by Edward Stafford, Duke of Buckingham, Henry, who presided over the trial in person, was enraged, exclaiming 'that he would none of his seruauntes should hang on another mannes sleue'.[5] The reason for this is, again, obvious. To guard against multiple or conflicting allegiances, the oath sworn by the king's servants was explicit in that they must 'be reteyned to no manner a person but onlie to the kinge highnes'.[6] Unlike the king's servants, the queen's servants were sworn to the queen *and* to the king. The oath sworn by Catherine of Aragon's servants does not survive, but in a report written on 10 October 1533, the king's servant, Thomas Bedyll, observed that 'those who appertain to the chamber were sworn to king Henry and queen Katharine'.[7] It is likely that this oath was similar, if not identical, in its language and purpose, to that which was sworn by servants in the household of Princess Mary in 1525, which is extant, and illustrates that her servants too were sworn to the king:

> Ye shalbe true and faithful vnto the Kinge our Soveraigne lord kinge Henry the eight and vnto his heires and successor kings of England And ye shalbe failhfull and true vnto my lady princesse grace.[8]

It has been suggested that the proviso here was 'to clarify a point which would otherwise be in doubt': to whom did Mary's servants owe their loyalty first?[9] By 1544, the oath sworn by servants to Katherine Parr bound them to 'our sayde soveraine Ladie the Quene', to 'withstonde every and anny person or persones of what condicion state or degre they be of that woll attempte or entende vnto the contrarie *except our soveraine Lorde the Kyngs moste royall Majestie*'.[10] The phrasing of this oath suggests that careful attention was taken to guard or protect against multiple or conflicting allegiances. It was explicit that the crown was sacrosanct. The king, as their sovereign, embodied order, commanded respect, and ought to be obeyed. Loyalty was due first to Henry, as the divinely-appointed sovereign, who had royal prerogative and retained ultimate authority, and the queen's servants, as his subjects, were obliged to obey and to serve *the king* in everything.[11]

Yet the potential for multiple, or conflicting, allegiances, remained. Catherine of Aragon's household was altogether fractured on 8 April 1533, when the queen and her servants were visited by the king's commissioners, led by Thomas Howard, Duke of Norfolk, who informed them that Henry and Anne, who was 'greate with childe', had married in a secret ceremony on 25 January.[12] Strict instructions were sent from the king to be declared to Catherine and her household by William Mountjoy, her lord chamberlain, Griffith Richards, her receiver-general, Sir Robert Dymoke, her chancellor, and John Tyrrell, her sewer, urging that he 'would not allow her henceforth to call herself Queen', and that her servants had to take a new oath and be sworn to her as 'Princess Dowager'.[13] On 5 July, Henry issued a proclamation which declared that his marriage to Catherine was illegitimate, and that she 'may not for the future have or use the name, style, or title, or dignity of Queen of this realm, nor be in any guise reputed, taken, or inscribed by the name of Queen of this realm, but by the name, style, title, and dignity of Princess Dowager'. This proclamation specifically forbade her servants to address her as queen, 'under pain of incurring the penalties and provisions comprised in' the Statute of Praemunire.[14] In addition to the king's concerns over Catherine's status, Henry 'felt himself so much aggrieved at the expense of her allowance', and begrudged 'the expense of keeping so many houses'.[15] Henry warned Catherine, who might rethink her obstinacy if it was her servants who would be at risk, that he would 'be compelled to punish' those who refused to comply.[16] 'He would not defray her expenses, nor the wages of her servants', even if Catherine's own income 'would not suffice for her attendants a quarter of the year'.[17] Yet Catherine, who was convinced that Henry acted not 'by a scruple of conscience, but only by mere passion',[18] stubbornly refused, maintaining that she was his true wife.[19] It was, she felt, Anne 'who has put him in this perverse and wicked temper'.[20] Chapuys remarked on 15 April that if 'there was nothing left for her and her servants to live upon, she would willingly go about the world begging alms for the love of God'.[21] 'Though she was grieved at the illtreatment of her servants',

Catherine insisted that 'she would not damn her own soul on any consideration'.[22]

And nor would her servants. Thomas, Lord Vaux, wrote to the Duke of Norfolk from Ampthill, to inform him that, although he and Mountjoy had warned her servants that they must now serve Catherine as 'Princess Dowager', they outright refused a new oath.[23] Thomas Bedyll reported on 10 October 1533 'that sundry persons in this house of the lady Princess Dowager will not desist from calling her Queen'. 'All women, priests, and ministers of the Princess's chamber, as sewers, ushers, and such other, who fetch any manner of service for her,' Bedyll observed, 'call for the same in the name of Queen, for so she has commanded them'.[24] This was corroborated by Mountjoy, who wrote that 'the gentlewomen, both of her privy chamber and others' could not 'discharge their consciences to call her Princess as they were sworn to her as Queen'.[25] Such reports indicate that, notwithstanding the king's orders, the queen's servants regarded highly the command of their mistress. Refusing the new oath, Catherine's servants effectively became the embodiment of her will.

Reflecting the king's control of the institution, servants who refused his orders were regarded as unfit to serve, and were necessarily discharged. When Charles Brandon, Duke of Suffolk, arrived at Buckden, near Huntingdon, on 18 December 1533, to 'brake all the ordre of the Quenes Courte', he recommended 'that seche as wer about her' who had shown themselves loyal, encouraging Catherine in her resistance, 'should be put from her'.[26] Her servants were so reluctant to take a new oath that Suffolk was 'in despair of having any one of them sworn'.[27] 'In their conscience', Suffolk observed, they 'were sworn to her as Queen, and they think the second oath would be perjury'.[28] 'Some saied thei were sworne to her as Quene, and otherwise thei would not serue', Suffolk wrote, and thus he 'had great difficulty in inducing servants to be sworn'.[29] A few days later, they 'proceeded to take away her chamberlain, chancellor, almoner, master of the horse, and other chief officers', and 'almost all the rest of her servants and ladies'.[30]

The household-in-exile kept up their resistance. Jorge de Athequa, Bishop of Llandaff, Catherine's confessor, Dr. Miguel de la Sa, her physician, John Sotha and Philippe Doganaghte, her apothecaries, Anthony Rocke and Bastian

Hennyocke, gentleman waiters, all refused to swear a new oath. As did eight of her gentlewomen, Elizabeth Darrell, Elizabeth Fynes, Elizabeth Otwell, Elizabeth Lawrence, Emma Browne, Margery Otwell, Dorothy Wheler and Blanche Twyforde.[31] Chapuys reported on 29 May 1534 that 'certain maids who had likewise refused the oath had been shut up in a chamber, and that her confessor, physician and apothecary were forbidden to leave the house, and four other servants were put in prison'.[32] Around a month later, the king 'sent messengers to her to make the ladies about her swear, with instructions in case of refusal to bring them away prisoners'. 'This the commissioners would have performed altogether', Chapuys observed, 'if it had not been for the difficulty of taking so many ladies away against their will'.[33] For the king, the matter was quite straightforward. The queen's servants had broken the oath they had sworn to him as their master or sovereign.

Yet, it is clear that the medieval, feudal system, by which an oath could 'bind' a servant to their master or mistress, was fundamentally outdated. The oath implied loyalty, but it did not guarantee it.[34] Catherine's servants forfeited their careers when they refused to swear a new oath to their mistress as Princess Dowager. This, they did, not, as such reports suggest, because of the oath they had previously sworn to Catherine as queen – that they might have obeyed their sovereign if not for this oath is implausible, as they had sworn to serve him too.[35] Crucially, these servants refused a new oath because their mistress 'herself protests against it, and her household *regard less the King's commandment*'.[36] Certainly the oath sworn by the queen's servants was invoked for its power to legitimise their resistance,[37] but this oath alone could not and did not 'bind', or oblige, servants, to be loyal and faithful, to be 'good'.

Confronted with the question of their allegiance, many of the queen's servants would defy their sovereign out of obligation to their mistress. William Mountjoy refused the king's orders to deliver the names of servants who were loyal to the queen. 'It shall not lie in me to accomplish the King's pleasure herein', Mountjoy informed Cromwell, and begged, 'without the King's displeasure', to be discharged, 'if it be thought by the King that any other can serve him in this room'.[38] He felt that, though Catherine's servants 'never ceased to call her by the name of Queen', they did 'bere their trewe hertes servyce and allegyaunce to the Kynges grace'.[39] This was the conflict dealt with by many of the queen's servants who found themselves in an unenviable position. Mountjoy was anxious not to upset the king, yet would not betray his mistress, and as such was forced to resign. It is surely significant that Mountjoy began his career as Henry VIII's tutor, and was likely appointed as lord chamberlain by the king in 1512, yet after 21 years of serving Catherine, he was, perhaps unsurprisingly, loyal to her.

Clearly it was not the oath they had sworn but their relationship with the queen, built and developed over time, some over two, nearly three decades, which fostered loyalty, familiarity, intimacy, and trust between Catherine and her servants. Maria de Salinas, Lady Willoughby, whom Catherine was known to have loved 'more than any other mortal',[40] served for 32 years before being discharged by the king. 'Even a Spanish lady who has remained with her all her life, and has served her at her own expense', Chapuys reported, 'is forbidden to see her'.[41] María wrote to Cromwell on 30 December 1535 for the king to grant her request to visit Catherine in her exile. 'I heard that my mistress is very sore sick again. I pray you remember me, for you promised to labor with the King to get me licence to go to her,' she wrote, 'before God send for her'.[42] Even María was careful in addressing Cromwell and Henry, appealing to their 'goodness'. Whereas she maintained her devotion to Catherine, she did not refer to her as queen in the letter, only 'my mistress'.[43] She knew well that it was pragmatic to remain, if only outwardly, loyal to the crown. In any case neither Cromwell nor the king granted her petition, which was, perhaps, indicative of her fall from favour. A few days later, María arrived at Kimbolton, without a licence, and forced her way through to be with her mistress shortly before her death.[44]

Servants could be more outspoken in their loyalty to the queen, which often brought them into opposition against the king. Whereas previously, there was stability in loyalty, servants who were intimate with and trusted by the queen, and who rallied behind her in support, now did so at the risk of incurring the king's indignation.[45] When Catherine, 'under constraint', was 'compelled under oath', to write a letter to her nephew 'at the King's dictation' requesting that the original papal bull be sent to England, she asked one of her chaplains, Thomas Abel, to deliver the letter to Charles V.[46] Upon his arrival, Abel handed the

Emperor the letter but urged him, on Catherine's behalf, to ignore it, and 'in nowise give up the brief, notwithstanding that the Queen's letter earnestly requests it'.[47] Abel was later arrested and taken to the Tower for encouraging Catherine to be obstinate. At least two more ladies, who were 'most devoted to the Queen, and in whom she found more comfort and consolation than in any others', were discharged.[48] Many of Catherine's servants demonstrated their loyalty to her by their words, and their actions, which, again, put them at great risk. Elizabeth Stafford, Duchess of Norfolk, urged the queen to be 'of good courage', promising to 'remain faithful to her',[49] and even smuggled to her mistress, secreted within an orange, letters from Gregory Casale, the English ambassador in Rome. She was discharged from her service in 1531 'because she spoke too freely, and declared herself more than they liked for the Queen'.[50] Likewise Catherine's physicians, Dr. Ferdinand de Victoria and Dr. Miguel de la Sa, 'divers times helped to close and seal letters from her to the Emperor and to Rome'; her apothecary, John Sotha, carried letters from Catherine to her daughter, Princess Mary; her page, John Wheler, communicated 'any matter by mouth' for the queen, and 'bore her tokens'; the queen's footmen, Lancelot and Bastian, conveyed letters to Chapuys, while Griffith Richards, her receiver-general, sent her 'learned men at Rome'. All of these attendants were, in turn, discharged from Catherine's household.[51]

The Duke of Suffolk acknowledged in his report on 19 December 1533 that, in swearing Catherine's household to a new oath, there were a few servants who did, 'after some exhortations', comply with the order, and were now 'sworn to accomplish the King's pleasure'.[52] Upon learning this, Catherine 'sodainly in a fury... departed from hym, into her priuie Chamber and shutte the doore'. Those 'that remaigned to serue her', and 'were sworne to serue her as a Princes Dowager, and not as Quene', were 'vtterly refused' by her. Catherine 'affirmed that she would not have any others', and 'by her wilfulness may feign herself sick, and keep her bed, or refuse to put on her clothes'.[53] 'She has refused to eat or drink anything that her new servants bring her', Chapuys reported a month later, observing that 'the little food she takes in this time of tribulation is prepared by her maids-in-waiting within her own bedroom'.[54] 'She will not regard them as her servants', Catherine protested, 'but only her guards, as she is a prisoner'.[55] She maintained that if her servants 'took any further oath than they has done to her she would never trust them again', and later asked that she have only a few servants but that they 'shall take no oath but to the King and to her, and none other woman'.[56] Catherine refused the service of those whom she felt were not loyal, reiterating again that an oath sworn only promised loyalty, it did not guarantee it. By the time Catherine had fallen ill, few of her own servants remained. It was observed that 'those with the Queen are guards and spies, not servants, for they have sworn in favor of Anne, not to call her highness Queen, nor serve her with royal state'.[57] By complying with the king's orders, these 'guards and spies' remained loyal to their sovereign, and what is more, remained in service.

Servants were neither strictly loyal to the queen, nor to the king. Upon marrying the king, queens were merely figureheads of their own households, and control of the institution remained firmly in the hands of the sovereign. But control, or more specifically, command, of the servants *within* that household, required loyalty, which had to be won. Perhaps Catherine had won Jane's affection like she had so many others in her household. Unfortunately, we know nothing of the relationship between Jane and Catherine. We do know that Jane had served in the queen's household for at least five years, and potentially, a few years after her marriage to George. As we shall see, Jane's friendship with Catherine's daughter, Princess Mary, indicates that she may have been torn between two factions. If she continued to serve Catherine into the late 1520s, she will eventually have had to turn her back on and abandon her former mistress. Quietly, Jane may have struggled with such a decision, but there was surely too great a risk of ostracising herself. If Jane was close with Catherine, no doubt she prioritised political ambition over her personal convictions. In the late 1520s and early 1530s, pragmatically, and perhaps, inevitably, her future lay with the Boleyns. As a Boleyn herself, she will have been expected to support Anne's rise to queenship; it was also in her interests politically to see her snare the crown. Catherine's household was a sinking ship that Jane had unknowingly escaped when she married George and became almost inextricably aligned with his family. Many of Catherine's servants forfeited their careers for their mistress – would Anne command the same loyalty from her household?

9

'I loved you a great deal more than I made feign for'
INTIMACY

On 1 June 1533, Anne Boleyn was crowned Queen of England. Her coronation was an extraordinary occasion, at which large crowds gathered, anxious to catch a glimpse of their new queen. Preparations for the event anticipated the presence of 'a great number of ladies and gentlewomen on palfreys dressed according to their estates'.[1] Reflecting the importance of her appearance in projecting the queen's magnificence, Henry himself wrote a letter of summons to 'the right dere and welbeloved' Anne, Lady Cobham in 1533, having appointed her 'amongs other' to attend 'the Coronacion of our derest wif the Lady Anne our Quene, as to her astate and dignitie doth appertain'. 'Trusting that for the lyveraies and ordering of your said women aswell in their apparel as in their horsses', the king wrote, 'ye woll in suche wise provide for them as unto your honor and that solemnpnite apperteineth', ensuring that she, and all of her own servants, were properly attired for the occasion.[2] Most surviving accounts of the coronation observed that there were indeed many 'ladies and gentlewomen in chariots and on horseback'; some 'richly garnished' in 'crimson velvet and cloth of gold', others 'in robes of scarlett furred with ermins and rounde cronettes of golde on their heades'.[3] 'Livereis of silke and skarlet' were distributed to all of the women who had been appointed to serve in Anne's household. Jane, or 'the ladi Rochforde', was granted twelve yards of crimson velvet and one yard of tawny cloth of gold to border her livery gown.[4]

Thomas Cranmer, Archbishop of Canterbury, who anointed and crowned the new queen at her coronation, witnessed that after Anne 'cam iiij. riche charettes, one of them emptie and iij. other furnysshed with diuerse auncient old lades; and after them cam a great trayne of other Lades and gyntillwomen'.[5] Jane held a prominent place at the front of the procession, riding side-saddle on horseback, almost immediately behind the queen. This may be indicative of a close relationship between them. Other ladies of a similar rank to Jane were two, some three chariots behind. Traditionally, Jane has been characterised as hostile towards Anne, and their relationship fraught with tension.[6] Yet there is evidence that the two women were, at least initially, on good terms. We do not know exactly how or when Jane and Anne first met, but both of them served as maids-of-honour in the household of Catherine of Aragon. They performed together in the mock siege of Château Vert at York Place in 1522, and it is plausible that the two young girls struck up a friendship while serving in the queen's chambers. Perhaps it was Anne who first introduced Jane to her brother George, whom Jane would marry in 1525, making them sisters-in-law and strengthening their bond with ties of kinship. This bond was strengthened further as Anne became queen and Jane became her loyal and faithful servant. Now that Anne was queen, Jane was formally reinstated as a member of the royal *familia*. Her patience, like Anne's, had paid off. In what office or capacity Jane served her sister-in-law is nowhere recorded, but it is likely that she was a Lady of the Privy Chamber.

This office, however, merely laid the foundation for Jane's career; it was her intimacy and interaction with the queen, her mistress, which built and sustained it. Office conferred status, measured authority, and denoted rank and precedence in the hierarchy of the queen's household. But this order was, inevitably, circumvented by the queen, and those to whom she did, or did not, show her favour; those to whom she did, or did not, grant access, and those whom she did, or did not, trust.

It is not difficult to conceive of when or where Jane might have had the opportunity to interact with the queen. All of the queen's Chamber and Privy Chamber staff had access to their mistress. 'Nearness', or proximity, was crucial in determining when and where they interacted outside of performing their regular duties, tasks and functions. The measure of access varied from servant to servant, corresponding to the office they held, and thus the 'chamber' to which they were sworn. The significance of the development of the 'Privy Chamber' is that it created a hierarchy of space in the queen's chambers, with access carefully regulated and controlled.[7] A useful distinction can be made between the 'inward' chambers and 'outward' chambers of the queen's side: the 'outward' chambers, where virtually all of the queen's Chamber servants, and occasionally visitors, moved without restriction, were the Presence and Guard chambers, whereas the 'inward chambers', the space 'from the door of the privy chamber onwards', constituted the queen's Privy chamber and bedchamber, and any additional rooms, lodgings or galleries built on this side of the palace, access to which was restricted to servants of the Privy Chamber and a privileged few granted entry by the queen herself.[8]

Establishing the measure of access which Jane could claim is relatively straightforward. More difficult is determining how she interacted with the queen. All of the queen's servants had to know their place and act with deference towards their mistress. The Eltham ordinances of 1526 declared that servants had to 'be of good towardnesse, likelyhood, behaviour, demeanour' and 'be humbly reverent, sober, discreete, and serviceable, in all their doeings'.[9] Ordinances for the household of Princess Mary in 1525 instructed the

> lades gentlewomen and maydens being about her persone and also her chambers with others attendant vpon herr… vse themselves sadlei, honorable, vertuously and discreetly in words, countenance, gesture, behavior and deed with humility, reverence, lowliness, due and requisite, so as of them proceed no manner of example of evill or vnfiltinge manners or conditions, but rather all good and godly behauior.[10]

Interactions between a royal mistress and her servants were ritualised, and potentially constrained, by custom and protocol, with ordinances dictating how far, and in what manner they could behave. What is missing is what occurred in between. Ordinances did not govern their every word or gesture. Nor was access strictly formal, and institutional, measured physically, and in terms of proximity. It was informal, and could be measured emotionally, or psychologically, and perhaps more sensitively, in terms of intimacy, and trust. How far servants could 'access' the queen was determined by the personality, and character, of the queen herself, as mistress of the household.

Relationships, between queens and their servants, or the ways in which they interacted, and were 'bound' to one another, were crucial. To reconstruct them with some meaning, these relationships must be interpreted in the context of their roles as 'mistress' and 'servant'.

Near-contemporary accounts on Anne Boleyn provide a view of the interactions between the queen and her household. Such accounts were informed by the testimony of the men and women who attended upon her. In the *Actes and Monuments* (1563-1583), the English martyrologist John Foxe attributed his description of Anne to 'the chiefe and principall of her waiting maides about her', and 'especially the Duches of Richmond', Mary Howard, Anne's cousin and lady-in-waiting, as well as her silkwoman, Joan Wilkinson.[11] Mary Howard, the Duchess of Richmond, was Anne's first cousin and a notable patroness of Protestant reformers, even lodging Foxe at Mountjoy House in London. George Wyatt's *Life of The Virtuous Christian and Renowned Queen Anne Boleigne* was informed by 'a lady, that first attended on her both before and after she was queen, with whose house and mine there was then kindred and strict alliance'. The lady in question has been identified as Anne Gainsford, who was the queen's maid-of-honour, although her testimony was likely taken second-hand, and probably shared through a relation, as she is known to have died before Wyatt was even born.[12] Wyatt also claimed to have been informed by 'a lady of noble birth, living in those times, and well acquainted with the persons that most this concerneth, from whom I am myself descended'.[13] What made their accounts so compelling – and what makes them compelling today – is that, as the women who knew and served the queen, their testimony is invaluable. We must be cautious, however, in using this evidence, as the testimony of Anne's servants could have been distorted, if not by their own biases, memory or hindsight, then by those who conveyed the information in their accounts second or third-hand.[14]

In *A briefe treatise or cronickille of the moste vertuous ladye Anne Bulleyne late quene of England* (c. 1564), William Latymer testifies to Anne's queenship and her relationship with her household. Latymer related all as he 'did heare, see and certaynly know' as one of her 'ordinarie chappellaynes', and further to that claimed to 'atteyne to the knowledge of' those 'whoo did attende her highnes in dyverse kyndes of service' to corroborate his account, namely Thomas, Lord Burgh, Anne's lord chamberlain, Sir Edward Baynton, her vice-chamberlain, Sir

James Boleyn, her uncle and chancellor, and John Uvedale, her secretary. Although Latymer was determinedly one-sided in exaggerating Anne's pious and 'godly' rule, his account more accurately represents the idyllic, or 'good' mistress. Sixteenth- and seventeenth-century representations of women, and patriarchy in contemporary texts, like conduct and polemical literature, provide further social, political and gendered context to the relationships between queens and their servants. Christine de Pizan's *Le Trésor de la Cité des Dames*, or *Treasure of the City of Ladies* (1405), a conduct book for women, is particularly useful, as it consists in part of advice specifically for queens consort and women attending at court.[15] It reflects what contemporaries thought of, and how they understood, the role and expectations of queens, their ladies, gentlewomen and maids.[16] To explain how and why queens and their servants interacted as they did, Latymer's *Cronickille*, and others, like Pizan's *Le Trésor*, provide a framework to interpret this evidence and reconstruct the relationship between them.

If, institutionally, the queen's household remained firmly integrated with, and was treated as an extension of, the king's household, it still had its own identity, separate from the king's side. A queen's household was thought, felt and understood to be her own, and its servants were seen to be under her charge. It was the responsibility of the queen, as mistress of the household, to govern her servants, and govern them well. This is reflected in Latymer's *Cronickille*, as Anne Boleyn repeatedly describes her household as 'my courte', observing that 'the prince is bounde to kepe his awne persone pure and undefyled, his house and courte so well ruled that all that see it may have desyre to follow and do therafter', and 'as I have attayned unto this highe place nexte unto my sovereigne, so I might in all godlynes goodnes duely administre the same'.[17] To command service was in itself powerful and prestigious. Queens consort presided over their own servants, commanding their obedience and conformity. By attending upon her person and performing menial or routine tasks on her behalf, they were a visible and tangible expression of her status and authority. Latymer recalled how the queen gave 'carefull charge' to her lord chamberlain and vice-chamberlain, who 'reprehended dyvers and sondrye persons... for their horrible swearing as for their inordinate and dissolute talke, together with their abhomynable incontynencye'. Upon 'fynding certayne persons incorrigible', they were to report them to the queen herself, 'whoo either pryncely rebuked them or sharpely punisshed, or els utterly exilide them her majesties courte for ever'.[18]

As mistress of the household, the queen's authority had to be continually practised and constantly legitimated, sometimes through ritual and ceremony, though more often, through discourse. It had to be constructed socially, by her interaction with her servants. The 'good' mistress, in the view of Latymer, gave her servants moral guidance, 'to instruct them the waye to vertue and grace, to charge them to abandone and eschue all maner of vice', 'vigilantly to wache their doinges', and to 'suffer noo contencion emonges them, admitt noo brawling altercacions nor sedicious quarrels'.[19] Anne herself would, apparently, on occasion, 'call before her in the prevy chambre' her ladies and gentlewomen and 'wolde many tymes move them to modestye and chastertie'. She 'wold geove them a longe charge of their behaviours', warning them that they 'shoulde not consume time in vayne toyes and poeticall fanses'.[20] Anne gave her maids-of-honour 'a booke of prayers' to hang from their girdles for each of them to use as 'a myrroure or glasse wherin she might learne to address her wandering thoughtes'.[21] When Anne learned that Mary Shelton had 'written certeyne ydill poeses' in her book of prayers, she called her maid before her and 'rebuked her that wold permitte suche wantone toyes'.[22] This view, or memory, of Anne, as the strict, matronly, or 'good' mistress, is corroborated by at least two more of accounts: Joan Wilkinson, Anne's silkwoman, would tell John Foxe that 'in all her time she neuer saw better order amongst the ladies and gentlewomen of the Courte, then was in this good Queenes dayes',[23] whereas another of the queen's attendants, probably Anne Gainsford, informed Wyatt in observing that she 'had in court drawn about her, to be attending on her, ladies of great honour, and yet of greater choice for reputation of virtue' whom the queen had 'trained upon with all commendations of well ordered government'.[24]

Publicly, interactions between queens and their servants were necessarily governed by set expectations and conventions. Privately, queens could engage their servants in ways that were more relaxed, personal and intimate. This intimacy did not necessarily defy or break conventions laid out in didactic literature on service. Queens were warned not to be autocratic in governing their servants, but benevolent, so that they might obey with reverence, and without contempt or resentment from oppression. Anne, according to Latymer, would show her servants 'tendre affeccion... then ever they dusrte have hoped or wysshed for'.[25] 'You must love your mistress... as you love yourself', Pizan urged, before tying affection between mistress and servant to the conduct of the household: a lady or gentlewoman in service was 'expected to love her lady and mistress with all her heart (whether the mistress is good or bad or kind), or otherwise she damns herself and behaves very badly'.[26]

The very nature of these interactions means that they are difficult to uncover. Only rarely does the evidence provide an extraordinary, if tantalising, view, of how queens and their servants might have interacted more intimately. Like the king and his 'boon companions', queens treated their servants with familiarity. When Anne Boleyn was served Ipocras 'and other wynes' at her coronation, she had them 'sent doune to her ladyes, and when the ladyes had dronke', Anne 'withdrew her selfe with a fewe ladyes' to relax in her chamber.[27] Albeit anecdotal, and fragmentary, the evidence would indicate that queens often spoke candidly with their servants. Anne Gainsford, Anne's maid, would later recall that, before her marriage to the king, when her mistress came upon a book of 'old prophecies' in her chambers, she 'called to her maid': 'Come hither, Nan', the queen beckoned, 'see here a book of prophecy; this he saith is the king, this the queen, mourning, weeping and wringing her hands, and this is myself with my head off.' 'I would not myself marry him', Gainsford remarked, before her mistress assured her, 'I am resolved to have him whatsoever might become of me.'[28] With a word or gesture, queens could break down the formal and rigidly-hierarchical relationship between mistress and servant. Mary Woodhull, Katherine Parr's chamberer, shared the queen's bed during her pregnancy, and Mary, Katherine would later recall, 'beyng abed with me had layd her hand vpon my bely to fele yt styre'.[29]

Queens and their servants provided each other with comfort in difficult times. In 1515, Catherine of Aragon remarked that her maid-of-honour, Maria de Salinas, whom she loved 'more than any other mortal',[30] had 'always comforted her in her hours of trial'.[31] At Blackfriars in 1529, in the midst of the king's Great Matter, after making an impassioned speech knelt before Henry, Catherine 'rose up' and, strikingly, 'took her way straight out of the house, leaning (as she was wont always to do) upon the arm of' Griffith Richards, her receiver-general.[32] In 1540, when Anne of Cleves heard that her marriage to the king was to be annulled, Thomas Manners, Earl of Rutland, the queen's lord chamberlain, commiserated with her: 'And for that I dyd see her to take the matter hevely, I desired her to be of good comfort'.[33]

Some time between 1529 and 1532, when Anne Boleyn was queen-in-waiting, one of her attendants, Bridget, Lady Wingfield, abruptly left court, and Anne, seemingly in haste, wrote her a letter.[34] It is clear that these women were close, with Anne declaring herself to be an 'assured friend' of Bridget, remarking that, 'next mine own mother, I know no woman alive that I love better'. Yet it would also appear that they parted on uncertain terms, as Anne was anxious to reconcile with her, stating that, 'though at all times I have not showed the love that I bear you as much as it was indeed, yet now I trust that you shall well prove that I loved you a great deal more than I made feign for…', or, in other words, that Lady Wingfield will, in time, see that Anne's love is genuine. At the end of the letter, Anne writes, 'I pray you leave your indiscreet trouble, both for displeasing of God and also for displeasing of me, that doth love you so entirely.' Precisely what 'trouble' Lady Wingfield found herself in is not known, but it must have been serious enough to force her withdrawal from court, and for Anne to write so urgently.

Christine de Pizan characterised the queen's women in particular as caretakers of her welfare, who in their own state and demeanour should represent her body, mind and soul:

> If she is ill or unhappy, you must be as sad as if it were your own misfortune, and likewise joyous at her well-being and prosperity. When you see her displeased, be sad with a sorrowful expression, and when good comes to her be joyful, and not just in front of her, but even more when you are out of her presence.[35]

Anne suffered a miscarriage in 1536, and it was, surprisingly, the queen, who 'consoled her maids who wept, telling them it was for the best, because she would be the sooner with child again'.[36] Katherine Parr wrote a letter of condolence to Jane, Lady Wriothesley, in 1544, upon learning of the death of her son: 'my lady wreseley', the queen urged, 'put awaye all immoderate and vniuste hevynes... yt hathe pleased hys mayeste to accepte and able hym to hys kyngdome then that yt fyrst pleased hym to comforte you wythe suche agyfte'.[37] When Katherine lay on her deathbed in 1548, she confided in her gentlewoman Elizabeth Tyrwhitt that 'she did fear such things in herself, that she was sure she could not live'. 'My Lady Tyrwhit,' Katherine confided, 'I am not well handled, for those that be about me careth not for me, but standeth laughing at my grief. And the more good I will to them, the less good they will to me.'[38]

The outpouring of emotion from servants of a queen is most striking in their grieving for their mistress. After being found guilty of treason in 1536, Anne Boleyn, incarcerated in the Tower, was 'prepared to die well'. Lancelot de Carle remarked that, upon learning that the hour of her execution was postponed, her attendants, distraught, were already grieving for their mistress:

> ...upon seeing her ladies plagued
> By great anguish, she consoled them,
> Continually, telling them that death,
> To true Christians, requires no comforting,
> Since eternal life exists in heaven,
> Beyond the danger of this wicked world,
> And, for this reason, they must not lament her death at all,
> For she assuredly hopes to reach
> The place of happiness and prosperity,
> Leaving all sadness here behind.[39]

Many years after Anne's death, Latymer recalled that 'wee that did attende her majestie muste nedes justly lamente the soudaine departinge of so god a princes', so much so that their 'hertes might seeme for sorrow to pynne and melte awaye'.[40] Relationships, between 'mistress' and 'servant', could thus have emotional significance, with such evidence revealing ties of companionship and friendship which amounted to more than the strictest obligations of service.

10

'Sythens I injoye their service they may have some porcion of my lyving'
ADVANCEMENT

In 1534, a young man named James Billingford visited abbeys and priories in Warwickshire, Oxfordshire and Northamptonshire to 'extort money' from them, calling himself the 'quenys chapelayn'. He was not Anne Boleyn's chaplain, but acting in the queen's name, and 'yn many places' invoking her authority, Billingford was able to take various sums of money, and their horses. He even made threats to punish and depose those who did not comply with his demands, 'to the great dishonor and slaunder of the quenys grace'.[1] A witness to his extortion later recalled how Billingford, a 'crafty witted fellow', appropriating the office of chaplain to her household, inferred that he knew the queen personally, and as such, warned him 'to take care how I meddled with him'. Billingford's extortion reflects the status held by servants of the queen, and suggests that their interests were protected by the crown.

What made serving the queen a viable, if not attractive and lucrative, career for Jane, was the potential for advancement. The 'good' servant performed their duties, tasks and functions competently and faithfully, whereas the 'good' mistress maintained, rewarded and advanced her servants. Relationships between mistress and servant were thus reciprocal. William Latymer, who actually was Anne's chaplain, acknowledged this connexion between the 'good' mistress, and the 'good' service which she, as queen, could expect to receive in return:

> I may not here forgett the loving kyndenes of this gracious prince towardes her trustye servauntes, whose necessities, siknesses and other adversityes she releved so abundantly that they all protested them selves

more bownde to her highnes for her gracious benevolence then they might be hable in any kynde of service to acquitt.[2]

Conceptually known as 'good lordship', this mandated the involvement and continual interference of queens as mistresses of the household into the lives and careers of their servants.[3] Unlike wages and other perquisites, this was undefined, non-institutional, and depended on the whims and will of the queen. When the master or mistress of a household was the sovereign, or the wife of the sovereign, favour became *royal* favour, giving maximum scope to the advancement of even the most lowly and humble of servants.

The 'good' mistress maintained the physical wellbeing of their servants, ensuring that they were kept in good health and properly cared for when they fell ill. Latymer recalls how, in 1533, when one of Anne's servants fell 'greviouslye sick', he, 'feling his maladye to increase, sente for his wyefe to come unto him'. His wife, Anne Joscelyn, 'attended the quenes highnes in her prevy chambre'. Joscelyn, Anne's chamberer, had been 'denyed licence to visitt her weake husbande', and thus 'moved one of her chapellayns to solicite her cause to the quenes majestie'. Upon hearing the request, the queen 'not only graunted her licence to departe, to the comforte of her weake and sicke housbownde, but also most bountyfullye commaunded to be prepared for her sufficiente furniture of horse and other necessarys for her jorney, and tenne poundes in monye towarde the charge of her travaill'.[4] Similarly, in 1502, Elizabeth of York covered the cost of boarding for eight weeks for her gentlewoman, Anne Say, 'being sikke' at Woodstock, and later, at Abingdon. On another occasion Elizabeth laid out 26*s*. 8*d*. for Nicholas Matthew, yeoman of her Chamber, 'towardes his charges whan he was hurte by the seruauntes of sir William Sandes'.[5] Much of the evidence examined alludes to informal exchanges or conversations between mistress and servant – how else did Elizabeth know to reward William Paston, her page, with 40*s*. 'towardes the byeng of his Wedding clothing', Nicholas Grey, her clerk, 60*s*. 'towardes suche losses as he susteigned at the birnyng of his howse', or Bridget Crowmer, her gentlewoman, with 40*s*. 'at hir departing from the courte'?[6]

Latymer understood that, for Anne, as for all queens, 'to be ladye over manye' meant 'that principally she was bounde to provide for suche as were in her awne housholde'.[7] Alleviating their financial hardship, Anne lent her servants various sums of money. 'Out of her privy purse', one of Anne's maids later remarked, 'went not a little'.[8] A book of debts which were 'due to the Late Quene Anne', and which, after her death, were owed to the king, show that Sir Edward Baynton, her vice-chamberlain, owed her £200, John Ashley, her sewer, owed her £100, Sir James Boleyn, her uncle and chancellor, owed her £50, George Taylor, her receiver-general, owed her £30, and Elizabeth Browne, Countess of Worcester, a lady of her Privy Chamber, owed her the sum of £100.[9] 'As tochyng the some off one hundryth pownds whych I dyd borrow off quene Ane', the Countess of Worcester wrote to Thomas Cromwell, the king's secretary, some time after, 'I dowte yt not but she wold have bene good to me'.[10] The late queen Anne, Worcester felt, was unlikely to have called in the debt of £100, and that this was an informal loan between friends is indicated by the fact that she had borrowed it in confidence: even her husband, Henry Somerset, Earl of Worcester, was 'otterly ignorant both off the borowyng and usyng off the sayd hundryth pownds'. 'And yff he should now have knawlege tharoff', the Countess feared, 'I am in dowt how he wold take yt'.[11] In contrast, Elizabeth of York often had to borrow money, pledging her own plate to secure repayment, as her own income was insufficient to cover her expenditure. Often the queen borrowed small sums from her attendants: in 1502, 20s. was 'lent to the quene' by Lady Verney, 26s. 8d. by Lady Bray, and £13. 6s. 8d. by Mary Ratclif.[12]

Queens took care to provide generously for their households. George Taylor, Anne's receiver-general, accounted for £186. 8s. 7d. laid out by the queen on gifts and rewards between 1534 and 1535.[13] At New Year in 1534, for instance, Anne gave her ladies palfreys and saddles for their horses.[14] Unfortunately, an itemised list of all that which was laid out by Anne does not survive; the account books for other Tudor queens reveal genuine affection and concern for the livelihood of their servants.[15] Gifts and rewards from queens to their servants could vary from money, food, drink, clothes, jewels, plate or tokens. Such royal generosity, or 'largesse', strengthened emotional ties and reaffirmed bonds of obligation between mistress and servant.[16] Inventories of Jane's possessions from

1536 and 1541 illustrate that she held many valuable items, most of which she likely accrued throughout her career in royal service:

1536
Thez parcelles of Stuff here being wrytten ben the Lady Rochefords And they doue remayne a chest beyng in the chambr over the kechen[17]

a pear Slyvez of crymsen velvett set wt goldsmythez
a pear Slyvez of cheker damaske whitt
a pear slyves of blak velvet wt eight pear aglettes . . . enamyled wt blak . . gold
pear Slyvez of crymsen satten
a pear Slyvez of yoloes satten
Item a pear Slyvez of a Satten whitt
Item a pear Slyvez of cloth of silver
Item a pear Slyvez of Tynxell Crymsen
Item a pear Slyvez of Tynxell blak
Item a plackard of tynxell
Item a plackard of blak velvet
Item a plackard of velvet of. . . carnassion coloure
Item a plackard of tawney velvet
. . . a plackard of crymsen satten
. a plackard of whitt satten
Item ij plackardes of russett satten
Item a plackard of blak damask
Item a Prymer borded wt silver & gilt wt one clasp
Item ij pear knyvez wt shethez of blak velvet
Item a fote of silver and gilt of a Ivory coffer
Item a pear of broken bedes of gold and perle
Item a pear broken bedes of gold and whitt bone
Item a pear of lawnez
Item a boke covered wt blak velvet and a clasp of silver
Item a boke covered wt crymsen velvet
Item a pear of knyt hosez of whit silke wrought wt gold for maslcyng
. . . ij squarez of black velvett
. . • one square of satten whitt
. . . ij squares of satten crymsen

1541
Plate, apparel and Juells that were the Lady of Rochford's[18]

Plate
A payre of flagones of sylver wherof one lacketh a stople
A salt of sylver and gilt wt owt a cover
A newer of stone wowt a cover wt a hope of sylver and gilt

An nother newer of stone wt cover hope and fote of sylver
a bason and an Ewer of sylver parcel gilt
A litle tase of sylver
A Casting botle of sylver and gilte
A litle crewes of sylver

Apparel
A kirtel of black velvet
A kirtle of black saten
A nyght gowne of black taffeta
A gown of black damaske
A gown of black saten
iij fayre bordures of my ladyes of goldsmithes work black enameled
xviij fayre perles
A fayre broche black enamelled wt six small diamondes
A litle stele casket wt a purse and forty pounds in it
v perles and certyn peces of broken gold in a box
xi small perles

Juells
A broach wt an agate
A cross of dyamonds with three perles pendant
A flower of Rubies
A flower wt a ruby and a great emerald wt a perle pen[dant]
A tablet of gold wt black, grene and whit enamelled
A pair of brasselletts of red cornelyns
A pair of bedes of gold and stones
A broch of gold wt an antique hed and a whit face

Perhaps the 'Prymer', or Book of Hours, from 1536 was a gift from her sister-in-law. One wonders if, after Anne's fall, Jane left the book, normally a rich and perhaps sacred object, to rot in the chamber above the kitchen where it was found. 'A tablet of gold wt black, grene and whit enamelled' was surely the 'tablet of gold' that Jane received from Anne's successor, Jane Seymour.[19] Were the 'fayre broche' and 'flower of Rubies' found alongside the gold tablet gifts of royal favour too?

Queens consort shared in the custody of patronage. When Sir William Compton, the king's groom of the stool, died in 1528, the various offices which had been granted to him by the queen, Catherine of Aragon, were to be redistributed at her discretion. For 'such offices as Compton had of her', the king was explicit in that he desired to leave Catherine to 'bestow them at hir pleasur, to hir owyn servauntes'.[20] Queens often acted as patrons for their servants, showing them favour in all manner of suits for the advancement of their careers. 'Sythens I injoye their service', Anne Boleyn remarked, 'they may have some porcion of my lyving'.[21] Queens consort were granted a large jointure in marriage to the king which made them one of the principal and wealthiest landowners in England.[22] A document entitled 'Fees and annuities going out of divers honours, castles, lordships, manors, lands and tenements', dated to 21 March 1534, was drawn up in preparation for when Catherine of Aragon's estate was to be handed over to Anne as her successor.[23] Upon inheriting these lands, the new queen would have rewarded her own servants with 'greate sommes of monye, some with offices, baylywickes and other places of charge wherento was annexed commodittis'.[24] Jane herself was unlikely to have been in receipt of offices in the queen's lands. Of the 84 entries for payments, totalling £778. 19s. 6d., laid out by Catherine of Aragon to individuals administering her estate, at least thirty can be identified as her servants, but only one of them was a woman. Margaret, Lady Grey, received £9. 2d. 4d. as keeper of Lytley and Donmore parks, and as bailiff of Donmore.[25] As a woman, and a wife, much of the favour that Jane enjoyed with the queen, or the king, is difficult to trace. Grants, like the wardship of Edmund Sheffield, the young son and heir of the late Sir Robert Sheffield and Jane Stanley, were awarded specifically to her husband George, but we can presume that both he and Jane benefited from patronage of this kind.[26] The insufficiency of surviving grants, particularly where it concerns women, is apparent. For instance, a warrant granting both John Stonor, the king's Sergeant-at-arms, and his wife, Isabel, the queen's Mother of the Maids, the farm of the priory of Goring, Oxford, acknowledged Isabel's service to the crown, but as a married woman she was unlikely to have been considered first-hand, and thus, her role is obscured.[27]

Often it is unclear if the initiative to reward and advance servants came from the queen or the king. Sometimes these records are more precise, and the queen's intervention on behalf of her servants is clear, as in the case of Elizabeth Lysle, Catherine of Aragon's gentlewoman, who in 1514 was granted the field or enclosure of Northburghilles, among other lands, specifically 'at the Queen's request'.[28] In 1544, Katherine Parr petitioned directly to Henry on behalf of one of her gentleman ushers, Henry Webbe, for the house and demesnes of the nunnery of Hallywell.[29] 'We shall hartely desire, and pray you, to be so favourable to hym,' the queen wrote, 'at this oure earnest request, as that he may for his monye have ye purchase at your hands, of the saide vj li. whereof he hath thindenture'.[30] In a poem on the life of Sir Nicholas Throckmorton, Katherine's sewer, composed in c. 1571, her servant would recall that:

> She, willing of herself to do us good,
> Sought out the means her uncle's life to save;
> And, when the King was in the pleasing mood,
> She humbly then her suit began to crave.
> With wooing times denials disagree,
> She spake, and sped: my father was set free.[31]

The relationship between the 'good' mistress and the 'good' servant is clear. By maintaining, rewarding and advancing their servants, queens encouraged, and gave recognition to, their service. The matter of advancing their own servants was thus treated urgently. Catherine of Aragon was particularly anxious to provide for those who, as she felt, in her own words, were 'good, and taketh labour doing me service'.[32] Anne Boleyn 'wolde assuredly preferre her awne servauntes furste', and was, according to Latymer, 'resolved that of duetye her paynfull and auncient servantes shoulde furste injoye such benifittes as were in her majestie to employ, for they are true servauntes to yeld me their service, take payne to death'.[33]

Clearly the fortune, or misfortune, of the queen's servants, was closely aligned with her own. When Catherine of Aragon was exiled from court in 1531, she struggled to maintain the men and women in her service. 'The Queen dreads most,' Chapuys reported, that 'her marriage portion', or estate, 'be taken from her'. Catherine feared that if she were 'dispossessed of her rank and dignity' as queen, her servants would suffer for it. 'She is the more afraid', as a result, 'that her servants and domestics, besides other people whose fidelity she has rewarded with sundry offices in her household, will henceforward be deprived of their pensions and salaries'.[34] The power to maintain, reward and advance, and thus to bind, or oblige, the queen's servants, and their loyalty, was constricted by the king, who, as sovereign, remained in control of the royal bounty. Catherine died at Kimbolton on 7 January 1536.[35] English law forbade a wife from drafting a will while her husband was still alive, so Catherine wrote a list of requests for Henry, chief among them that she may be granted various goods, gold, silver, and money due to her, so that she might reward her servants for 'the good seruices they have don vnto me'. Francis Phillip, her sewer, was to be granted £40 and 'all that I owe him', Isabel de Vargas, £20, and Mary Victoria, the wife of her physician, £40. Elizabeth Darrell was to receive £200, Blanche Twyford, £100, Margery Otwell and Dorothy Wheler, £40, Dr Miguel de la Sá and John Sotha, a year's wages each, and Philip Greenacre, Anthony Rocke and Bastian Hennyocke, £20. Most of these attendants were discharged from her service for the loyalty they had shown to their mistress when they refused to swear an oath to her as 'Princess Dowager'.[36] It is unclear if they ever received what was bequeathed to them. Nearly six months after Catherine's death, Elizabeth Darrell had not received what was owed to her, and wrote to Sir Francis Bryan, a gentleman of the king's Privy Chamber, requesting the '300 marks which the Dowager gave her by her will'.[37] When Richard Rich travelled to Kimbolton shortly after Catherine's death to take inventory of her jewels, plate and wardrobe, he found that her servants had claimed 'divers apparel' and other materials for their fees. Rich advised that Henry 'cannot seize her goods' as she was a 'sole' woman and 'it would not be honorable to take the things given in her lifetime'.[38] In contrast, these servants, remaining at Kimbolton having sworn to serve Catherine as 'Princess Dowager', were to be assured of the king's favour, by which they were 'greatly comforted'.[39] It was ultimately Henry who had custody of the queen's 'goods', suggesting that the fortunes and the fates of mistress and servant, albeit closely aligned, were not inextricable. As we shall see, this fact would prove critical for Jane, who forged her career through the 1530s and 1540s in spite of Henry's marital instability.

11

'Preserve my courte inviolate'
PIETY AND PASTIME

The 'good', or 'godly', mistress, kept her servants constant and conspicuous in their piety. Much of Jane's time each day at court would have been spent in religious ceremonial. Publicly, queens, at least once, often twice or even three times a day, emerged from their private apartments with their ladies and walked in procession from their Privy chamber to their Presence chamber, through their Guard chamber and then by a gallery to the Chapel Royal, where they heard mass 'before the highe aulter', and on occasion, gave confession and received penance.[1] Eustace Chapuys reported on 15 April 1533, the day before Easter Sunday, that Anne Boleyn 'went to mass in Royal state, loaded with jewels, clothed in a robe of cloth of gold friese'. Mary, Duchess of Richmond, carried her train, and in attendance were as many as sixty women who conducted her 'to and from the church with the same or perhaps greater ceremonies and solemnities than those used with former queens on such occasions'.[2] Privately, in her Privy chamber, the queen and her servants heard mass, prayed, and would take confession in the queen's closet. Queens and their ladies and gentlewomen servants often attended divine services in her privy closet, where sermons and devotions were ministered by her own chaplains: a chaplain was to be ready at eight o'clock in the morning every day 'in suche place as shalbe appoynted' to say 'suche divine service'; and again between nine and ten o'clock 'in her chapell closet to say like service before her grace's gentylwomen and other of her famylye'; and finally, before five o'clock in the afternoon 'to say like service', and otherwise 'at all tymes' to be 'declared within her sayd house'. If any of the queen's attendants were found to be absent, they were 'to be charitably monishyd and reconsylid', or, for a second offence, discharged.[3]

Household piety, the daily routine of religious observances and ceremonial, engaging in theological debates, prayer sessions and the study of scripture, attending sermons from visiting preachers, and possessing or exchanging of religious texts, was led and dictated by queens as mistress of the household. Anne apparently 'kepte her maides and suche as were about her so occupied in sowing and woorking of shirts & smockes for the poore';[4] she kept an English bible in her chambers for her servants 'to rede upon when they wold', and even urged her chaplains to 'exhorte them to feare God,' and 'cause them dayly to heare the devine service.'[5] The 'good' mistress, in the words of Latymer, ruled her servants 'in moste godly wyse and princely maner', and 'beganne ymediatly after her royall coronacion to converte her whole thought, ymaginacion and indevour to the godly order, rule and goverment of suche as was committed to attende her highnes in all her affayers'.[6] Anne preferred many known reformers, Hugh Latimer, William Betts and William Latymer, to her household as her chaplains, and this characterised the nature of religious life in her chambers. She was likely responsible for securing bishoprics for Hugh Latimer, who was made Bishop of Worcester, and her almoner, Nicholas Shaxton, who was made Bishop of Salisbury. 'By her meanes and continuall mediacione', these men, according to Latymer and Foxe, 'were brought in fauour wt the king'.[7] Neither Latimer nor Shaxton could meet the charges, or 'first-fruits', for their elevation to the episcopate, and thus Anne lent them each the sum of £200.[8] John Smyth, one of the canons of St. Paul's, wrote to Sir Edward Baynton, Anne's vice-chamberlain, for her intervention with infighting over offices:

> ...in the matere with the Queenes Grace for me, consyderinge my tender and moste faithefull and diligente love and servis alwaies shewed unto hir Grace... and at all other tymes in expedissyon of hire honorable letteres for the promossyones of hir chaplenes and servants.[9]

When William Betts died in March 1535, Anne actively recruited Matthew Parker to replace him. Through John Skip, her almoner, she exhorted Parker to be one of her chaplains ('I pray you resist not your calling, but come in any wise to know further of her pleasure').[10] She was particularly fond of Parker, and entrusted her own daughter to him shortly before her death. Later, in 1559, with Elizabeth now queen, Anne's former chaplain related, 'my heart would right fain serve my sovereign lady the Queen's majesty, in more respects than of mine allegiance, not forgetting what words her grace's mother said to me of her, not six days before her apprehension'.[11]

William Latymer and Nicholas Shaxton, with Thomas, Lord Burgh, the queen's lord chamberlain, Sir Edward Baynton, her vice-chamberlain, Sir James Boleyn, her chancellor, and others 'of her sidd', in the queen's Presence chamber 'in all their denars and suppers' apparently 'gave them selfes wholie' to 'the discussing of some one dought or other in scripture'. This was, occasionally, done in the company of the king: 'Wherin the kinge his majestie to some tyme such pleasure', Latymer recalled, 'that dyverse and sondry tymes he wolde not only here them but somtyme wolde argue and reason hym selfe.'[12] Queens and their servants might recite and debate scripture, or read, study and exchange books for learning and devotion. If queens went on pilgrimage, they were accompanied by their servants, and in travelling from palace to palace, both mistress and servant could be engaged in almsgiving and poor relief.[13] Foxe wrote that Anne 'caried euer about her a certaine little purse, out of the which she was wont daily to scatter abroad some almes', engaging her servants in poor relief, with the queen urging them to 'commaunde mynne almes liberally' and to 'take esspeciall regarde in the choise of suche poore peopell as shalbe fownde moste nedye'.[14]

Anne was held personally responsible by hostile observers for promoting heresy, or Lutheranism. Strict laws forbade, for instance, the purchase and possession of prohibited books of a heretical nature. Anne had in her chambers a copy of William Tyndale's *Obedience of a Christian Man*, which she had lent to one of her maids, Anne Gainsford, some time in 1529. George Zouche, another of the queen's servants, 'plucked' the book from the maid, which was then snatched from Zouche by Dr. Richard Sampson, dean of the king's Chapel, who confiscated and delivered it to Wolsey. A fearful Gainsford 'wept', because 'she could not get the book back from her wooer'. She knew that possession of the book in question 'was enough to make a man a heretic, and reading of it a dangerous article against any in these days'.[15] Wolsey sent for and examined Zouche, who informed him that 'it pertained to one of the queen's chamber'.[16] But before the cardinal could report it to Henry, the queen herself went to him. 'Upon her knees she desireth the King's help for her book', and even 'besought his Grace most tenderly to read it'.[17] Some years later, in 1536, the queen entrusted her chaplain, Latymer, and her silkwoman, Wilkinson, to purchase and import what were, potentially, forbidden books to her chambers.[18] Latymer was apprehended upon his return from Flanders. The titles of these books and the nature of the material cannot now be known, though it may reasonably be speculated that 'the irregularity of the shipment', in that 'silkwomen were not normally purveyors of books to the royal household', indicates that such works were of a 'radical religious character'.[19]

Anne was not the only queen who was vulnerable to accusations of heresy. In 1546, Katherine Parr and her attendants aroused the suspicion of Stephen Gardiner, Bishop of Winchester, Thomas Wriothesley, Lord Chancellor, 'and others more aswell of the kings priuie chamber, as of his priuie councell'.[20] Thomas Howard, Duke of Norfolk, was brought before the Privy Council and examined 'for disputing indiscreetly of Scripture with other young gentlemen of the Court' in 'the Quenes chambre'.[21] The queen's chambers were to be searched to uncover 'what bokes, by law forbidden, shee had in her closet',[22] some of which were thought to have been sent to Katherine by Anne Askew, a Lincolnshire gentlewoman and known heretic who was acquainted with her servants.[23] When Askew was arrested and tortured in 1546, she was examined as to their involvement as agents of religious dissent.[24] The king's councillors specifically named and questioned Askew on the queen's ladies and gentlewomen, Katherine Willoughby, Lady Suffolk, Mary Arundell, Countess of Sussex, Anne Stanhope, Countess of Hertford, Joan Champernowne, Lady Denny, and Lady Fitzwilliam, of whom she stated, 'if I should pronounce any thing against them, that I were not able to proue it.' All that Askew admitted to under torture was having received money, ten shillings from 'a man in a blew coate', apparently from the Countess of Hertford, and eight shillings delivered by a man 'in a violet coat', sent from Lady Denny.[25] Askew could not have been mistaken in that the king's councillors were targeting the queen's servants: 'they did put me on the racke,' she felt, 'because I confessed no Ladies or Gentlewomen to be of my opinion'.[26] Katherine Parr and her servants were drawn together by their commitment to defining, developing and advocating for reform. The queen 'at al times conuenient', would 'haue priuate conference touching spiritual matters' in her chambers. 'Euery day in the after noone for the space of an houre, one of her sayd Chaplains in her priuie Chamber made some collation to her and to her Ladies and Gentlewomen of her priuie Chamber, or other that were disposed to heare', Foxe recorded, 'in which sermons, they oft times touched suche abuses as in the churche then were rife'.[27] The queen, accompanied by the ladies and gentlewomen of her Privy Chamber, 'oftetimes' would exhort the king, as

> shee did with all painfull endeuor apply her selfe by all vertuous meanes, in all thynges to please hys humour... sometymes of her selfe would come to visite him, either at after dinner or after supper, as was most fit for her purpose. At whiche tymes shee woulde not fayle to vse all occasions to moue him, according to her maner, zelously to proceede in the reformation of the Church.[28]

It is significant that Foxe situated this activity between Katherine and her servants as specifically 'in her priuie Chamber',[29] which was a defined, restricted space, and functioned to facilitate and potentially conceal forbidden religious practices. Yet, clearly Katherine and her servants had endangered themselves by their activity in the queen's chambers. Anne Parr, Lady Herbert, Countess of Pembroke, the queen's sister, Maud Parr, Lady Lane, her cousin, and Elizabeth, Lady Tyrwhitt, were due to be apprehended, questioned, and their coffers searched, 'wherby the Queene myght be charged' and 'caried by barge by night vnto the Tower'.[30] A warrant for the queen's arrest was produced,[31] but a draft of articles drawn up against her was mislaid, and Thomas Wendy, her physician, brought it to the queen. When the queen learned of it, 'for the sodayne feare therof', she 'fell incontinent into a great melancholy and agony, bewailing and taking on in such sorte, as was lamentable to see'.[32] Her physician, 'for the comforting of her heauy minde, began to breake with her in secrete maner, touching the said articles deuised against her' and 'exhorted her somewhat to frame and conforme her selfe vnto the kings minde'. The queen panicked, 'commandyng her ladies to convey away their bookes which were against the law'. 'The next night followyng after supper', two ladies of the queen's Privy Chamber, Lady Herbert and Lady Lane, 'who carried the candle before her', accompanied Katherine 'unto the kynges bead chamber', where, by pleading ignorance and acting with the utmost deference, the queen was able to convince Henry of her innocence. When Wriothesley later confronted the queen to arrest her, Henry intervened: 'Knave! Arrant knave, beast and fool!' the king berated him.[33]

Clearly there were limits to what, and how, queens and their servants could advocate for reform. Whereas many would have outwardly conformed, as an overzealous, or even unorthodox faith, could risk attracting hostility and incurring the king's wrath, behind this conformity, a religious, reformist zeal, which may otherwise be seen and judged as heretical, could be practised, and potentially hidden, in the cloistered chambers of the queen. So hidden were these practices that we can only speculate as to Jane's involvement in Anne Boleyn's religious circle. This may even have been a point of contention, if Jane, like her father, was strictly orthodox, while Anne, and George, Jane's husband, were leaning 'evangelical'.[34] We cannot know, as Jane left so few traces behind. If she did not share in the religious convictions or personal faith of her mistress, as a member of the queen's household, she would still have been drawn into its distinct pattern of piety.[35]

It remains difficult to determine if, and how far, queens *actually* kept their servants constant and conspicuous in their piety, as much of the evidence which survives is determinedly one-sided, even hagiographic, in nature. The most useful and descriptive accounts for Anne and her servants' religious activity were written during in the reign of Elizabeth I, Anne's daughter, and as such may have been written in an attempt, firstly, to rehabilitate or retrieve her reputation, and secondly, if indirectly, influence the Elizabethan religious settlement.[36] It is significant that these accounts are strikingly similar to – and perhaps, even echo – those on Catherine of Aragon by Catholic authors, who invoked the same imagery and rhetoric. In *The history of Grisild* (1558),

William Forrest, who served Mary I as her chaplain, remembered her mother, Catherine of Aragon, as a 'godly' mistress who kept order amongst her servants, and described her court as 'religious', avoiding all manner of 'vayne' and 'idle' pastimes.[37] In *A Treatise on the Pretended Divorce Between Henry VIII and Catharine of Aragon*, Nicholas Harpsfield, a Catholic priest writing in Mary's reign, (c. 1553-1558), described Catherine 'in much prayer, great alms, and abstinence', and 'when she was not this way occupied, then was she and her gentlewomen working with their own hands something wrought in needlework costly and artificially, which she intended to honour of God to bestow upon some churches'.[38] Nicholas Sanders' *The Rise and Growth of the Anglican Schism* (1585) had Catherine 'present every morning in church for six hours together during the sacred offices', and 'in the midst of her maids of honour, she read the lives of saints'.[39] Certainly these authors intended to preserve strictly the most idyllic image and 'pious' representations of these queens in the reigns of their respective daughters, Elizabeth and Mary. Although the accuracy of these accounts has been questioned, and closely scrutinised,[40] the parallels which can be drawn between them establishes the 'good', or 'godly' mistress as a strict, pious, devout and sombre figure who kept herself and her servants, in the words of Latymer, in 'vertuous demeanour, godly conversacion, sobre communicacion and integritie of lyf'.[41]

The character and demeanour of the queen's servants, like that of the queen herself, had to be irreproachable. As Pizan observed, they 'must preserve their honour more than other women because their honour or dishonour reflects and rebounds upon their mistress'.[42] Latymer's Anne understood that she was 'bounde to kepe her owne person pure and undefyled her house and Courte so well ruled that all that see it may have desire to follow and do thereafter, and all that heare therof may desire to see it'.[43] She urged her chaplains 'to omitt nothing that may seeme to apperteinge to my honour': 'in this wyse you may preserve my courte inviolate, and garde it from the obloquie of the envyous'.[44] How servants led their own lives, in what they said, what they did, where they went and with whom, reflected upon queens as their mistress. Even Catherine of Aragon, whose piety is reasonably well-documented,[45] could be accused by the king, in the midst of his Great Matter, of exhorting her ladies and gentlemen far too often 'to dance and pass time'.[46] Queens were held accountable for their servants, and a queen who failed to censure her servants' behaviour and instruct them in moral discipline might be judged incapable of governing her own.[47] In the words of Pizan, 'the lady who is chaste will want all her women to be so too, on pain of being banished from her company'.[48] It is not unreasonable to suggest that queens kept up a pious appearance to protect their own reputations and that of their households. The evidence remains ambiguous. If the queen's household in this period was 'godly', pious and virtuous, if it was judged as such by its contemporaries, or if this was merely constructed later, is unclear. Certainly this is what queens would have aspired to, the expectation against which all queens would be measured, but in reality, how strictly servants were kept in this manner would have varied considerably from household to household.

Life in the queen's chambers was not all prayer books and private devotions. It is not plausible that queens always ruled their households so firmly, and piously, with their servants 'so occupied' in moral discipline as to avoid 'vayne' and 'idle' pastimes. There was time for dancing, singing, writing and reciting poetry, idle conversation, and playing music, cards and wordgames.[49] Like Henry and his gentlemen servants, who would engage in hunting, hawking and archery, his queens and their ladies had their own 'recreacion', during which they would 'passe tyme' and 'playe'.[50] Anne kept her ladies, gentlewomen and maids occupied with needlework. George Wyatt wrote that many of the 'rich and exquisite works' which adorned Hampton Court were 'for the greater part wrought by her own hand and needle, and also of her ladies'.[51] Similarly, in 1527, when Catherine of Aragon was visited by Wolsey, who sought her consent for the annulment of her marriage to the king, 'she came out of her Privy chamber with a skein of white thread about her neck', and excused herself: 'but to make answer to your request I cannot so suddenly, for I was set among my maidens at work, thinking full little of any such matter'.[52] The material culture of the queen's household espoused the feminine virtues of the crown, yet it is difficult to discern the nature of, or motive behind, their activity. Did Catherine emerge from her Privy chamber with a thread about her neck merely to excuse herself, or were she and her women actually engaged in needlework?

These women would have sewn not only shirts and smocks for the poor, but costumes for court revelry, theatrical spectacles which incorporated verse, music and dance, in which they often took part. Likewise the 'booke of prayers' hanging from the girdles of Anne's maids-of-honour may have functioned too as an item for self-fashioning.

Queens regularly played cards and dice with their gentlewomen. The accounts of Anne of Cleves, for instance, reveal that she laid out, in 1540, 33*s.* 4*d.* for 'playng at cards', and the next day, 60*s.*, for 'playng at blanke dycce', 40*s.* 'for Cards', and 20*s.* for 'grots to play', which were delivered to and kept in the hands of one of her chamberers.[53] A near-contemporary account suggests that it was during a game of cards that 'wherein dealing', Catherine of Aragon, seeing that her maid and rival, Anne Boleyn, had in her hand a king, playfully and quite memorably remarked 'you have good hap to stop at a king, but you are not like others, you will have all or none'.[54] On one occasion in 1519, several gentlemen at court even played 'shouffulborde', with various sums owed 'for playing money in the queen's chamber'.[55] Minstrels, musicians and fools performed for the entertainment and merriment of queens and her servants. Anne Boleyn's accounts reveal that, in 1536, she paid for twenty-five yards of 'cadace fringe' for her tailor, John Scut, to make a gown and a green satin cap 'for her Grace's woman fool'.[56] Perhaps this was 'Jane Foole', later in the households of Jane Seymour, who also covered the cost of her gown and kirtle, and Katherine Parr, who provided her with three geese and a hen.[57] She was closely acquainted with Princess Mary too, who, on one occasion, sent her 22*s.* 6*d.* 'for the tyme of hir seeknes', and paid for her 'housen', 'a payr of Shoes', 'Smocks', a 'Coffre', 'nedles', and 'for Shaving hir hede'.[58]

Paradoxically, the queen's household had to be the epitome of morality, and virtue, yet this was a difficult, if not impracticable, ideal to reconcile with the king and his court, in all its worldliness and splendour. Sir Edward Baynton, Anne Boleyn's vice-chamberlain, reported to her brother, George, on 9 June 1533, that, 'as for passe tyme in the queens chambers', there 'was never more'.[59] 'Yf any of you that bee now departed have any ladies that ye thought favoured you, and somewhat wold moorne att parting of their servauntes,' Baynton continued, 'I can no whit perceyve the same by their daunsing and passetyme they do use here, but that other take place, as ever hath been the custume'.[60] These interactions, or 'fantasyes' as Baynton described them, between the queen's women and gentlemen at court ('their servauntes'), represent *amour courtois*, or the 'courtly love' tradition, an integral element of chivalric culture in which gallant knights would, feigning their love, court and flatter their ladies with dances, poems, songs and gifts and other 'favours' in an unending pursuit for her affection.[61]

This tradition ran through the Devonshire manuscript, an anthology of nearly two-hundred poems of courtly verse, many of which were composed and circulated by women in Anne's innermost circle.[62] The manuscript illustrates a courtly circle-in-action – led by Lady Margaret Douglas, Mary Shelton and Mary Howard, the Duchess of Richmond, three of Anne's servants – and is a material witness to how they interacted with one another in the queen's chambers. By their literary expression, annotation and circulation of the manuscript, the queen's women provide a view not only of the pastime enjoyed and pleasure taken in 'poeticall fanses' and amorous repartee,[63] but also of the impassioned and unrestrained environment in which even Anne herself incautiously flirted with gentlemen at court. Thematically, forbidden, or improper love, loyalty, and fidelity, are contextualised by the scandals which arose in the queen's chambers. Lady Margaret Douglas conducted her liaisons with Thomas Howard, the younger son of the Duke of Norfolk, in secret. But when their affair was discovered, it was the queen's servants who were examined: John Ashley, Anne's sewer, apparently 'perceyved love between them' for at least 'a quartr of a yere', while Thomas Smyth, clerk of the council, remarked that often the Duke 'wold watche tyl my lady bulleyn was goon and thenne stele in to her chambre'.[64] Reflecting the conventions within which they interacted, the poems often evoke paranoia, and vulnerability, and the difficulty, even danger, for women to, in the words of Castiglione, keep 'a certaine meane verie hard', and in their interactions with men to 'come just to certaine limittes, but not to passe them'.[65]

If the 'courtly love' tradition was meant to regulate and constrain gender relationships 'within an accepted convention',[66] there was still potential for it to inflame such interactions. Clearly there was tension between the queen's household and the wider court to which it belonged. Anne Boleyn herself acknowledged the potential for 'wantones', 'pleasurs' and 'licencious libertie' in her chambers, and was acutely aware of such dangers in her own 'courte', and as such urged her chaplains to admonish her servants if they were to 'yelde to any maner of sensualitie'.[67] Pizan advised queens to 'so enforce her regulations that there will be no visitor to her court so foolhardy as to dare to whisper privately with any of her women', nor would they 'disobey her commands in any respect or to question her will'.[68]

A woman's capacity to rule and govern, in view of her contemporaries, could be judged from her ability to keep the ladies and gentlewomen of her household chaste and virtuous. Unfortunately for Anne, her household was afflicted by scandal. In addition to Margaret Douglas' affair with Thomas Howard, and her sister Mary Boleyn's secret marriage and pregnancy in 1534, there was Elizabeth Holland, for instance, who was Anne's maid-of-honour, but also the mistress of the Duke of Norfolk, and the aforementioned Bridget, Lady Wingfield, who abruptly left Anne's household. Why Wingfield withdrew from court, and why Anne was so anxious to reconcile with her, would have remained their secret, if it had not been for the report by Spelman in May 1536, some three or four years later, when Anne was arrested on suspicion of committing adultery. An intriguing detail of Spelman's report which is often overlooked is that the Lady Wingfield apparently 'shared the same tendencies' as Anne. He could only have meant sexual misconduct. Surely this is why the Lady Wingfield was forced to withdraw from court: what could have been more 'displeasing to God' and 'displeasing to Anne' as a lady of her household who lacked virtue? For this, Anne, as her mistress, may have felt in some way responsible, declaring that although she would not, or perhaps could not, write to the Lady Wingfield in her trouble, she claimed that she would abide by, and herself bear it, for as long as she lives.

Anne's governance, or lack thereof, would have severe consequences in 1536, when Elizabeth, Countess of Worcester and lady of the queen's Privy Chamber, was accused by her brother of 'showing many signs of loving others by dishonest love'. It has been suggested that the Countess may have been pregnant ('showing many signs') potentially by a man who was not her husband ('of loving others by dishonest love').[69] As we shall see, this more than likely led to the queen's own indiscretions coming to light. The conventions of 'courtly love' may have excused married courtiers when flirting with others. Perhaps it was for his philandering that George, Anne's brother and Jane's husband, earned his reputation as a womaniser. Was Jane herself free from scandal? Had she committed her own indiscretions at Anne's court? Sleidan regarded her as an 'errant strompet';[70] Cavendish would remember that she, 'withouten bridle of honest measure', followed her 'lust and filthy pleasure'.[71] It is impossible to say now what either of them meant by their remarks, though it is rather more likely that it was simply Jane's involvement in contriving Katherine Howard's affair with Thomas Culpeper in 1541 which tarnished her reputation.

If Anne Boleyn's household was flirtatious and given to vanity, the household of her successor, Jane Seymour, would, by her rigid enforcement of discipline and decorum, maintain an outwardly virtuous and incontestably high moral standard. Jane may have been eager to set herself apart from her predecessor and rid the queen's household of its previously wayward influence, by consciously and carefully constructing her own image – and that of her servants – as gentle and virtuous. Thomas Cromwell remarked that 'his grace I think chose the vertuost lady and the veriest gentlewoman that lyveth and oon that variethe asmoche from the conditions of thother as the daye varietie from the night'.[72] Besse Harvey, who had served as Anne's maid and had hoped to retain her place with Jane, wrote to Sir Francis Bryan, gentleman of the king's Privy Chamber, asking 'why she was discharged of the Queen's service', soliciting him to find her preferment. Bryan 'sent her word that he had moved it', but 'the King bade him meddle with other matters'.[73] Perhaps Besse, whose reputation, it seems, was far from beyond reproach, was discharged, and kept out of the queen's household, on account of Jane's rigidly-enforced morality.[74] Certainly a woman whose reputation had been brought into disrepute was unfit to serve a queen. 'To serve God and to be virtuous' was reportedly 'much regarded' in Jane's household.[75] 'Here is a very great and triumphant court' with 'many ancient ladies and gentlewomen in it', another remarked, shortly after Jane's household was established, suggesting that she had recruited more matronly, 'sober' ladies to serve her.[76] Jane even banned the French fashions popularised by her predecessor, enforcing a more traditional English apparel for her women. She gave strict orders to her maids-of-honour regarding their formal attire. Shortly after her arrival at court in the autumn of 1537, Anne Basset was instructed by the queen that she must 'wear no more her French apparel', and instead 'must have a bonnet or two with frontlets, an edge of pearl, a gown of black satin, and another of velvet'.[77] 'Your ladyship must provide a gown of tawny velvet for Mrs. Anne', Husee reiterated to Anne's mother weeks later.[78] In the meantime, Mary, Countess of Sussex, one of the queen's ladies, let Anne 'lieth in her chamber', and gave her a 'velvet bonnet' and 'a kirtle of crimson damask and sleeves' until her proper attire could be made.[79] Husee 'thought it became her nothing so well as the French hood... but the Queen's pleasure must be done'.[80] This marked change between these two households reflects how far the environment and culture therein was influenced by the personality and character of the mistress who presided over it.

Serving Anne Boleyn, like serving any queen, would surely at times have been onerous or difficult; at others it must have been amusing, exciting and entertaining. Jane, Lady Rochford, as a lady of the queen's Privy Chamber, was at the peak of her career in the royal household. Her relationship with the new queen, not only as her sister-in-law, but as her servant, could be close, intimate and meaningful. We can imagine that she enjoyed all the perks and privileges of court life, not least the sumptuous feasts, merriment and everyday revelry. And yet, unfortunately for Jane, it was not to last.

12

'Poor banished creature'
EXILE

In the autumn of 1534, the Imperial ambassador Eustace Chapuys reported that Jane, 'the wife of Mr. de Rochefort', had 'lately been exiled from Court' for having 'conspired' against a 'young lady whom the king has been accustomed to serve'.[1] Who was this unnamed 'young lady' with whom Henry was infatuated in 1534? The earliest mention of her is probably in a dispatch from Chapuys to Charles V, dated 3 September 1533. A mere three months after Anne's coronation, and a year prior to the incident that led to Jane's banishment from court, the king had taken a mistress. Anne reportedly grew 'jealous' of Henry and upbraided him for his philandering, to which he remarked 'that she must shut her eyes and endure as those who were better than herself had done'.[2] That Henry had taken a mistress did not necessarily mean that Anne was insecure in her position; in November of that same year, one of Anne's ladies told Chapuys that the king 'said several times he would sooner go begging from door to door than ever abandon' the queen.[3] A year later, on 27 September 1534, the ambassador observed that the king had 'renewed and increased the love he formerly had for a very beautiful damsel', suggesting that she had been at court for some time.[4] We know that she was one of Anne's ladies, as Chapuys wrote that the queen 'attempted to have the damsel dismissed from her service'.[5] It is not clear whether the unnamed 'damsel' was already in the queen's household when the affair began, or if the infatuated king appointed her as such to be close to his new mistress. She was apparently a friend of Princess Mary, having, rather boldly, sent a letter encouraging her 'to take good heart' because 'her tribulations will come to an end much sooner than she expected'. 'Be assured that,' the unnamed 'damsel' continued, 'should the opportunity occur, she will show herself her true friend and devoted servant'.[6]

Did the anonymous 'young lady' with whom the king was infatuated in 1534 pose a threat to Anne? It was not unusual for a king to take a mistress, and nor did the presence of a mistress in the royal bed necessarily mean that the queen was any less secure in her position. Queens were expected to tolerate their husband's infidelities. When the king told Anne that 'she must shut her eyes and endure as those who were better than herself had done', he was speaking of his first wife, Catherine, who had been praised for 'the great modesty and patience she had shown' when her husband had shown himself 'continually inclined to amours'.[7] The unnamed 'damsel' may have had the king's affection, but could she be considered a rival to the queen for the crown? One ambassador remarked that the king was 'entertaining another lady', apparently encouraged by courtiers hostile to the queen 'with the object of separating him from Anne'.[8] Anne will surely have remembered the circumstances in which she herself had become his wife. In dethroning a queen, Anne had set a dangerous precedent. In the urgency to secure the succession, it is understandable that she would have felt vulnerable. Chapuys too tied the king's philandering to his 'doubts' as to whether Anne 'was *enceinte* [pregnant] or not'. It was apparently only then that he had 'renewed and increased the love which he formerly bore to another very handsome young lady of this court'.[9]

What was the significance of the relationship between the unnamed 'damsel' and the Princess? Mary was a rival to Anne and her daughter, Elizabeth. It was in Anne's interests that Mary remained 'bastardised' and excluded from the line of succession so that Elizabeth would inherit the throne before her. This may explain why the queen adopted a 'strategy of humiliation' and, at least, according to Chapuys, took every opportunity to ridicule and degrade Mary. She apparently 'boasted that she will have the said Princess for her lady's maid', and moreover, threatened 'to marry her to some varlet' beneath her station.[10] She ordered that Mary should be served her breakfast, not, in her chamber, as a Princess would be accustomed, but in public.[11] If all this was not humiliating enough for Mary, Anne wanted the Princess to carry her train![12] The ambassador also attributed the severe reduction made to Mary's household and allowance in October 1533 to the 'importunity and malignity' of the queen.[13] Fearing that the king's 'easiness or lightness' might lead the king to treat the Princess better, Anne would apparently solicit Cromwell 'and other messengers' to deter the king from 'seeing or speaking with' his daughter.[14] Anne, Chapuys maintained, 'did not cease day and night to plot the most she could against the Princess'.[15] This he would reiterate through 1534 alongside reports of the king's infatuation with the unnamed 'damsel'. Chapuys observed on 13 October that 'her influence increases daily, while that of the concubine', or Anne, 'diminishes';[16] the ambassador would report later that month that 'the young lady… who is quite devoted to the Princess, has already busied herself in her behalf'.[17] She was apparently sharing more than his bed; she had his ear. More than that, she had an agenda, and that was quite enough to make her a threat. The 'young lady' whom the king had taken for a mistress had already postulated on an 'opportunity' whereby she could prove her loyalty to Mary. Such an opportunity would only materialise if the Princess was first restored to the succession. Is this the matter in which the 'young lady' had 'busied herself in on her behalf'? The implication is there, and Cromwell, who must have been aware of his sovereign's newest infatuation, only provoked the ambassador's already wild speculation by suggesting that if the king 'would change his fancy', then he could be reconciled to his daughter, Mary.[18]

In hindsight it appears that Chapuys may have been overestimating the influence of the unnamed 'damsel'. A few months later, the ambassador was reporting that she was no longer in the king's favour.[19] In her place, in around February 1535, came Madge Shelton, Anne's cousin (who, because of her kinship ties, did not pose a threat, and was apparently 'deliberately selected' by the queen herself to encourage Henry's advances and oust the anonymous rival).[20] What is more, it is unlikely that the unnamed 'damsel' could ever have successfully moved the king to reconsider his treatment of the Princess. When Jane Seymour, Henry's third wife, endeavoured to reconcile her husband to Mary, he apparently called her a 'fool', muttering that she 'ought to solicit the advancement of the children they would have between them, and not any others'.[21] If his own wife and queen could not move Henry to reconcile with Mary in 1536, it is unlikely that his mistress would have broken his will in 1534.

Yet Anne felt humiliated, angry and desperate. In the words of the Imperial ambassador, the queen was 'visibly losing part of her pride and vainglory'.[22] That both Anne and Jane would dare to contrive a way of ousting Henry's mistress from court suggests that the presence of the unnamed 'damsel' had greatly unnerved the queen. It is significant that the queen could not discharge her from her own household, against the will of the king. Anne could see no other way to extricate herself from what must have been an uncomfortable situation. If Henry was to cast her aside as queen, Jane too would lose her place at court as the queen's confidante. The motive is clear, but how did Jane become involved, and who led the plot? We do not know for certain, but it is plausible that Anne, 'visibly' upset and unnerved by the unnamed 'damsel', first confided in, or was approached, by Jane herself. It was Jane who, to relieve the emotional strain felt by her sister-in-law and secure her own position, then took action and 'conspired' to physically separate the king from his new amour. This would be done by 'quarrelling', or in other words, by provoking the 'young lady' to insult or attack the queen, or stirring up some trouble so intolerable that would force her to withdraw.[23]

But the plot backfired. Jane must have provoked the king's mistress, leading to some altercation, because Anne reportedly confronted the king with 'certain remonstrances' or 'proofs' that 'the young lady in question did not treat her with due respect in words or deeds'.[24] Henry was enraged, not with the 'young lady', but with Anne, and 'went away in a great passion' while 'complaining loudly of her importunity and vexatiousness'.[25] Henry warned that 'she ought to be satisfied with what he had done for her; for, were he to commence again, he would certainly not do as much'.[26] The king could not well punish Anne as his queen, so in 1534 it was Jane who took the fall. 'The wife of Mr. de Rochefort' was promptly 'exiled from Court' as punishment.[27] There was precedent for this, as the king could, and often did, exercise his prerogative as sovereign, and where he saw fit, punished and discharged his queens' servants at will. In 1510, when Elizabeth Stafford was caught 'about the palace, insidiously spying out every unwatched moment, in order to tell the Queen', Henry intervened and, for her 'suspected tale-bearing', Elizabeth was discharged from the queen's household, which, reportedly, left Catherine 'vexed'.[28] In 1525, Henry discharged three of her Spanish ladies, known to be her 'chief counsellors', suspecting them of encouraging the queen to protest the elevation of Henry Fitzroy, the king's bastard child, as Duke of Richmond and Somerset. 'A strong measure', remarked Lorenzo Orio, the Venetian ambassador, 'but the Queen was obliged to submit and to have patience'.[29] By 1530, Anne was so far in Henry's favour that, 'at her request', three more of Catherine's ladies, 'most devoted to the Queen, and in whom she found more comfort and consolation than in any others', were, by the king, to be 'dismissed from Court and sent home'.[30] And thus, upon learning of Jane's involvement in the latest plot, Henry ensured that she suffered the same fate for meddling in his affairs.

What were the consequences of Jane's exile? When Cardinal Wolsey was placed 'under a sentence of exile from Court' in 1529, he was 'ordered to reside three miles away from it, and not to appear unless summoned'.[31] The physical distance at which Jane was kept away could be seen as representative of how far she had fallen from favour. Although there is no indication as to Jane's whereabouts immediately following her exile, she was no longer serving in the queen's chambers. It is not 'impossible' to determine 'whether in fact she had left court'.[32] A few months after the incident Chapuys confirms his earlier report: 'it is true that Rochford's wife was sent from Court for the reason that I have heretofore written'.[33] He was not mistaken. Jane had been exiled. It is likely that, for a place of residence, she was forced to return to either Grimson Manor in Norfolk or the Palace of Beaulieu, which had been granted to her husband George in 1533.

Three months prior to the incident which led to Jane's exile, Mary Boleyn, Anne's sister and Jane's sister-in-law, fell pregnant, at which time it was disclosed that she had secretly married William Stafford. Her family were furious, and they abandoned her. Mary too was banished from court 'in consequence of gross misconduct'. 'Her exile', Chapuys remarked, was felt necessary as 'it would not have been becoming to see her at Court *enceinte* [pregnant]'.[34] The consequences of Mary's exile were quite serious. Ostracised, she was left in a perilous financial state and, in her own words, the 'poor banished creature' was forced in 1535 to petition Cromwell to intervene on her behalf with the king and queen for forgiveness, 'pity' and relief from her 'vile conditions'.[35] Whereas Mary had outraged all decency, embarrassing her kith and kin by her 'gross misconduct', Jane acted to preserve Anne's position as queen and the Boleyn ascendancy. Yet there is no indication that Anne, George, or Sir Thomas Boleyn, Jane's father-in-law, did anything to intervene with the king on her behalf. Henry's volatile moods may have precluded this; perhaps they knew better than to question his judgment. Jane left the court in disgrace, and the Boleyns shrewdly kept their distance, consciously disassociating themselves from the scandal and their meddlesome kinswoman. Far from 'comfortable',[36] Jane would be isolated, alone, anxiously waiting in vain for news from court of her reinstatement. She became the scapegoat in the 'plot' to oust the king's mistress, while the rest of the Boleyns appear to have survived the incident virtually unscathed: 'neither is there any further sign of the King's ill-humour towards the Lady's relatives,' it was observed, 'except that which is naturally connected with their occasional quarrels'. Chapuys reported in December 1534 that Jane remained in exile,[37] and there was no sign that she would be recalled. They failed to protect Jane from banishment, and appear to have made little or no effort to see her reinstated, which she must have bitterly resented. Some accounts imagine that 'it was not long before Jane was back in the royal bedchamber again', perhaps 'in the early months of 1535',[38] but there is no evidence that Jane *ever* returned to court while Anne was queen. Chapuys, who closely documented the incident, makes no further mention of Jane until her husband George's trial in 1536.

13

'...apon a certeyn tyme waytynge on your Grace at Honesdon'
JANE AND PRINCESS MARY

In October 1535, while the king and his court were on progress in Hampshire, a group of women gathered at Greenwich in London for a public demonstration in support of Princess Mary. It was recorded in a dispatch from the French ambassador Anthoine de Castelnau, the Bishop of Tarbes, to Jean de Dinteville, the Bailly of Troyes.[1] As Mary was moving to Eltham from her lodgings in Greenwich, 'a great troop of citizens' wives and others, unknown to their husbands,' it was reported, 'presented themselves before her, weeping and crying that she was Princess, notwithstanding all that had been done'. 'Some of them, the chiefest,' the report continues, 'were placed in the Tower', with an additional handwritten note in the margin which reads 'Nota. Millor de Rochefort et Millor de Guillaume', or 'Note. my Lord Rochford and my Lord William'.[2] Did this mean to indicate, as has been supposed, that their wives, Jane, Lady Rochford, and Margaret, Lady Howard, were chief among the women who were arrested?[3]

The evidence for placing Jane at the demonstration in Greenwich has been described as 'thin', 'ambiguous' and 'not convincing'.[4] She is not identified in the main body of the document. Neither Castelnau nor Dinteville would have speculated as to the identity of those ladies who participated in the demonstration at Greenwich if their reports were intended to be accurate. It would appear that the marginal note could only have meant to identify George, Lord Rochford, and William, Lord Howard, and not their wives. Howard's first wife, Katherine, died in April 1535, several months prior to the demonstration, and he did not remarry until June 1536.[5] His second wife, Margaret Gamage, was still serving as a maid to the queen in October 1535. And thus Castelnau's dispatch probably meant that Rochford and Howard were sent to deal with the protestors at Greenwich, not that their wives were among them.

In any case, Jane, we are told, 'knew her destiny lay with the Boleyns; to jump ship at this stage would have been folly'. Is this really an accurate assessment of her position in October 1535?[6] As inexplicable as it might first seem that Jane would attend a demonstration in favour of the Princess, the two women were far from mortal enemies. Jane held Mary's train at the funeral of Jane Seymour, Henry's third wife, in 1537, as one account observed that 'the Ladye Marie, the Kinges daughter, beinge cheife mourner, with a great companye of ladies and gentleweomen waytinge on her, and ridinge all in blacke allso' had 'her train borne by the viscountess Rochforde'.[7] Although the records of Mary's privy purse are somewhat fragmentary, they too indicate that Jane was on friendly terms with the Princess. Jane would exchange New Year's gifts with Mary in 1537, 1538 and 1540. We know that, on an earlier occasion, some time in 1536 or perhaps even earlier, Jane had presented Mary with a clock, as records show that a payment of five shillings was made in 1537 'for mending of the Clocke which my lades grace had of my Lady Rochford'. Mary closed the exchange, presenting Jane with 12 yards of black satin, costing £4 10s.[8] Rewards were often granted by Mary to Jane's servants as gratuity for delivering various letters, gifts and tokens. In 1538, the Princess made payments, of eleven shillings and twelve pence, and on another occasion, twelve pence, to 'my Lady of Rochford's woman'.[9] It may be that Jane first struck up a friendship with a young Mary in the 1520s while serving in the household of her mother, Catherine of Aragon.

There is evidence that Jane's family too were associated with the Princess. Our earliest indication of a 'Morley-Mary' connexion is in the preface to one of the works which Jane's father, Henry, Lord Morley, presented to Mary upon her accession in 1553, in which he wrote of 'the love and truth that I have borne to your Highness from your childhood'.[10] Morley recalled that he was so impressed with Mary's proficiency in Latin when she was around twelve years old (c. 1528), he had made an 'exemplar', or copy, of one prayer by Thomas Aquinas that she had translated and 'set yt as well in my boke or bokes, as also in my pore wyfes, youer humble beadwoman, and my chyldren, to gyue them ocasion to remember to praye for youer grace'. In other words, Morley claimed to have brought Jane and his other children up to revere and respect the Princess.[11] In early 1537, Mary made payments to a nurse and a midwife on their safe delivery of Morley's grandson and Jane's nephew, for whom she was made godmother. At the end of that same year, Mary's accounts reveal that she laid out 3s. 4d. in reward to Morley's servant, who was presumably sent to the Princess on more than one occasion on errand to deliver letters or gifts from his master. Lord Morley remained devoted to Mary, and their acquaintance was kept up through his lifetime. They too exchanged gifts at New Year. In 1543, for instance, Morley had gifted her 'a Boke'.[12] Morley dedicated a number of his literary works and translations to the Princess. Six of them can be dated between 1537 and 1547, and in all of them he addressed Mary with the utmost admiration and respect. He attended her coronation in 1553, and in 1556, three years into her short reign and the restoration of religious orthodoxy, Morley would thank her for granting him the 'libertye to ende myne olde dayes in quyet'.[13]

It has been suggested that Jane became effectively estranged from the Boleyns and, somewhat disaffected, realigned herself with Mary. The drawback of the evidence for this is that almost none of it predates the fall of Anne Boleyn.[14] Of course, any association in the 1530s predating Mary's reconciliation with the king would have been kept secret. On 4 June 1536, just over a fortnight after Anne's execution, Henry, Lord Morley, his wife, Alice, Lady Morley, and one of their two daughters, possibly Jane, visited Mary at Hunsdon. Great Hallingbury, the principal Morley residence, was in close proximity to Hunsdon.[15] Details of their visit emerged when Anne, Lady Hussey, formerly one of Mary's attendants, was apprehended and thrown in the Tower for allegedly calling Mary by the title 'Princess' (which had been made treason under the Act of Succession in 1534). She was interrogated, and asked specifically who accompanied her when she visited Mary. Anne maintained that 'she was not sent for' by the Princess, but in fact, rather took the opportunity to visit and pay her respects to her at Hunsdon as she was travelling through to London with her husband. Unfortunately, the manuscript containing her deposition is mutilated. When questioned on who else was at Hunsdon on the day of her visit, Anne answered, among others, that 'lord Morley . . . . his wife and daughter, m . . . . . .' were in attendance. We do not know if the daughter present at Hunsdon was Jane, or her sister, Margaret (where it breaks off, we can presume that it read as either 'my Lady Rochford', or 'my Lady Shelton').[16]

What makes the Morley's family visit to Hunsdon so compelling as evidence of a 'Morley-Mary' connexion is that, although it occurred after the fall of Anne Boleyn, at which time, it appears that Mary's friends, supporters and sympathisers began rallying around the Princess with renewed hope of restoring her to the line of succession,[17] it was *before* Mary's reconciliation with her father, the king, and thus took place at a time when their association with the Princess could still arouse suspicion. Within a week of the Morley's visit to Hunsdon on 4 June, not only the Princess but 'all her friends' reportedly found themselves in 'the most extreme perplexity and danger'. Mary hoped to reconcile with her father without being forced to swear to the 1534 statutes decreeing her own bastardy and the abolition of the papal jurisdiction as, in her own words: 'my conscience will in no ways suffer me to consent thereunto'.[18] Henry was determined that she acquiesce unconditionally. When Mary was visited by the king's commissioners in June and ordered to 'obey his commands and accede to his wishes', she outright refused.[19] Upon learning of Mary's resistance, her father was reportedly agitated, 'displeased' and 'grew desperate from anger'.[20] Her stubbornness and 'ingratitude' infuriated Cromwell too, who mere days after approaching the king on her behalf now declared her to be 'the most ungrate, unnatural, and most obstinate person living, both to God and your most dear and benign father'.[21] One of the king's commissioners even apparently threatened that, if she were not the Henry's daughter, 'he would beat her to death, or strike her head against the wall until he made it as soft as a boiled apple', while another remarked that 'she was a traitress, and would be punished as such'.[22] Clearly the situation was tense. None of Mary's supporters would have been unaware of the danger they would soon find themselves in if they were seen sympathising with her.

Henry suspected that Mary had been 'encouraged' in her 'obstinate refusal'. 'Several of her attendants', chief among them Anne, Lady Hussey, with 'certain ladies of the Court' and 'several of his courtiers', namely Sir Francis Bryan, Sir Anthony Browne and Sir Nicholas Carew, essentially, anyone at all with whom Mary was known or even likely to have had communication, were arrested, summoned before the Privy council, and interrogated.[23] Some of them were questioned about the nature of their communications with Mary; Bryan, who, in the days prior to Anne's fall, had visited Lord Morley at his home in Essex, admitted that he had discussed the possibility of the Princess being restored to the succession, though only 'if it stood with the King's pleasure'.[24] Carew later confessed that he and others of Mary's friends urged her to reconcile with the king, and again, the possibility of Mary being reinstated in the line of succession was raised.[25] The king may have felt that Mary could become the focus for opposition to his rule, and the line of questioning adopted by his commissioners shows that, what was already quite a sensitive situation, was escalating into a crisis. Mary eventually succumbed to the king's demands unconditionally, if only to protect these men and women who, by their 'great and almost excessive love and affection', Cromwell observed, were 'determined to risk every thing for her sake'.[26] We will never know how close Jane, or her family, came to committing treason. What, exactly, was the nature of the Morley family's visit on 4 June 1536? Lord Morley would recall in the preface to one his translated works, later presented to Mary, that 'apon a certeyn tyme waytynge on your Grace at Honesdon' the two of them spoke 'of thynges touchynge to vertue'.[27] But had it gone further? Did they address hopes of Mary being restored to the succession?[28] Had they, even if indirectly, encouraged Mary in her obstinacy?

Jane may not have been foolhardy enough to make a public display of support and affection for the beleaguered Princess. Mary was not viable as a political ally in 1535. Certainly she could have been a real friend of the Morleys.[29] Although a 'Marian' faction cannot be substantiated in the evidence,[30] and Jane's attendance at the demonstration at Greenwich in 1535 cannot be proven, it must be remembered that she was not inextricably tied to the Boleyns. Jane's allegiances were many, complex, and inherently conflicted. She was not only a Boleyn, but a Parker too, and it is reasonably well-established that her father was staunchly loyal to Mary. Jane may even have been moved by Lord Morley's sympathy for the Princess.[31] Some find it inexplicable that Jane would turn against the Boleyns, but it is far from implausible that she, who, in 1534, had put her neck on the line to comfort her royal mistress, and was severely punished as a result, became frustrated, even angry and embittered. Jane's husband and sister-in-law continued to revel in court life, and had seemingly abandoned her, providing her with little comfort in the isolation of her exile.

14

'Certain other little follies'
ARREST, INVESTIGATION, TRIAL

On 30 April 1536, Mark Smeaton, a court musician, was apprehended and interrogated. He confessed that he had slept with the queen, Anne Boleyn, on three occasions, though he may have been tortured.[1] The next day, Smeaton was taken to the Tower of London, while the king and his court attended the May Day jousts at Greenwich. At the end of the tournament, Henry abruptly left, without Anne, of which 'many men mused, but moste chiefely the quene'.[2] Perhaps the king had been informed of Smeaton's confession, or took offense when Anne dropped her handkerchief to 'one of her lovers' so that he might 'wipe his face running with sweat'.[3] On his journey to Westminster, Henry accused Norris too of having slept with the queen, which he denied. Norris 'wold confess no thing to the Kynge, where upon he was committed to the towre in the mornynge'.[4] The arrests did not end there. On 2 May, Anne's brother, George, and the queen herself were apprehended at 'about five of the clocke at night' and thrown in the Tower, as were Sir Francis Weston and Sir William Brereton two days later.[5]

Anne was accused of 'following daily her frail and carnal lust', having 'falsely and traitorously' procured five gentlemen at court, Mark Smeaton, Henry Norris, William Brereton, Francis Weston, and her own brother George, to 'be her adulterers and concubines'.[6] Within two weeks of her arrest, Anne stood trial. She was found guilty of treason and was condemned to death. A few days later, on 19 May, Anne was taken from her lodgings within the Tower to a nearby scaffold, where her head was stricken off with a sword. Why was Anne executed? Was she innocent, or guilty, of the crimes of which she was accused in 1536? And what was Jane's role? Was Jane arrested, or interrogated? Did she provide any evidence at all? If so, against whom? How useful, and how truthful, was her statement? What was her motive? Did Jane betray her own husband and sister-in-law? Did she have a choice?[7]

John Husee, Lady Lisle's agent in London, wrote to her on 24 May identifying the first accusers as 'the lady Worserter', or Elizabeth Browne, countess of Worcester, 'and Nan Cobham', or Anne Cobham, 'with one mayde mo', often thought to be Margery Horsman, 'but the lady Worseter was the fyrst grounde'.[8] He was not mistaken, as a day later he wrote again: 'Tuching the Quenys accusers my lady Worsetter barythe name to be the pryncypall'.[9] Elizabeth, Countess of Worcester, was serving in Anne's household in 1536 as a lady of the Privy Chamber.

Her allegations are found in a printed poem entitled *A letter containing the criminal charges laid against Queen Anne Boleyn of England*, written by Lancelot de Carles, secretary to the serving French ambassador in England in 1536, Antoine de Castelnau. The poem describes how 'a lord of the Privy Council', Sir Anthony Browne, Elizabeth's brother, 'admonished' or berated his sister after seeing that she 'loved certain persons with a dishonourable love'. Elizabeth then accuses Anne of 'a much higher fault', one which her brother 'might ascertain from Mark [Smeaton]'.[10] 'The one thing that seems the worst of all to me', she would admit, 'is that her brother often had carnal knowledge of her in her bed'. Upon hearing his sister's allegations, Sir Anthony and two other unnamed gentlemen would, we can expect, rather gently, inform the king.[11]

Some remain sceptical of this account. A copy of the poem presented to the king was described as a 'French book written in form of a tragedy by one Carle being attendant and near about the ambassador', suggesting that de Carles was much less an eyewitness than he was merely relating a version of events which correlated with that communicated by Cromwell to the French embassy on 14 May: 'the quenes abhomynacion both in incontinent lyving, and other offences towardes the kinges highness was so rank and commen, that her ladyes of her privy chambre, and her chamberers', Cromwell reported, 'could not conteyne it within their brestes'. 'It cam soo plainly to the eares of some of his graces counsail', he continues, 'that with their dieutye to his Majestie they could not concele it from him, but with greate feare, as the cace enforced declared what they harde unto his highnes'.[12] One author concludes that de Carles' account is 'in effect, the government line in translation'.[13] On the other hand, that the accusations emerged out of 'the accident of a quarrel between one of the queen's ladies and her brother' is not only plausible, but corroborated by the few facts that we do have.[14]

Alternatively, the confession of Bridget, Lady Wingfield, may have sparked the initial investigation into Anne's conduct. John Spelman, the judge at Anne's trial, identified Bridget as the queen's confidante, who conveyed information about Anne's sexual habits. Spelman remarked that

> All the evidence was on bawdy and lechery, so that there was never such a whore in the realm. And note that this matter was disclosed by a woman called Lady Wingfeilde who was a servant of the said queen and shared the same tendencies. And suddenly the said Wingfeilde became ill and a little time before her death she showed the matter…[15]

Wingfield's confession, later presented at Anne's trial, has been hastily dismissed by historians who maintain the queen's innocence. One historian remarked that its 'opportune appearance invites suspicion'. Whoever disclosed her confession had apparently kept the evidence to themselves for at least two years. 'It is hard to believe that anything of substance would have been left to gather dust until Cromwell started to ask questions', reasoning that 'hostility to Anne' would have seen Lady Wingfield's confession produced much earlier than 1536.[16] When did Lady Wingfield die? It is presumed that she died in 1534, as this was her last appearance in court records, and thus the last time she was known to be alive.[17] The actual date of her death is unknown. Some may be sceptical, but Lady Wingfield was felt by Spelman to be a compelling witness. Few documents survive on Anne's fall, yet Spelman's report is that of an eyewitness to her trial. And in that report, albeit brief, Spelman observed that 'this matter was disclosed by a woman called Lady Wingfeilde'. Alternatively, it has been suggested that when Spelman wrote that 'this matter was disclosed by a woman called the lady Wingfield', he intended to write 'the Lady Worcester': yet Spelman names Wingfield twice in his report, clearly stating that she made this confession on her deathbed, and Elizabeth, Countess of Worcester, did not die until 1565.[18] Is the most plausible explanation to all this that Lady Wingfield died and made her statement not in 1534, but in 1536, preceding Anne's arrest not by years, but by mere days?[19] Perhaps she felt it necessary to 'die well', to unburden her soul and in her last words confess her own indiscretions, even if it meant disclosing those of the queen too. Exactly what Lady Wingfield revealed in her deathbed confession is unknown. What is clear, however, is that it cast doubt on Anne's morality, that it was presented at her trial, and that it must have been sufficiently damning to the queen in 1536.

The evidence which was turned out from the initial investigation, however, was felt to be inconclusive, and the case against Anne manifestly weak. No overt act of adultery could be proven. Sir Edward Baynton, Anne's vice-chamberlain, expressed this concern in a letter to Sir William Fitzwilliam, the king's treasurer: 'There is much communication that no man will confess anything against her', reported Baynton, 'but only Marke of any actual thing'. 'It would', Baynton suggested, 'much touch the King's honor if it should no further appear'.[20] Baynton's remarks here are unsettling, as they suggest that the prosecution were quite determined to find Anne guilty. Henry was convinced of her guilt, and the suspicion alone as to her conduct was an affront to his honour. In order to substantiate the charges and secure a conviction, the investigation turned to Anne's household. The ladies of her Privy chamber and 'others of her side were examined'.[21] Lacking anything like proof, such as an eyewitness account of illicit lovers caught *in flagrante* or a valid confession from the accused, the case against Anne rested on their compliance. Transcripts of their depositions no longer survive, but their words would have been extracted to reconstruct the alleged incidents, later drafted in the form of an indictment. Indictments were written statements of the crimes of which the subject or subjects were accused, in explicit detail, for presenting at a trial to a grand jury, who would then deliver a verdict. It is clear from Anne's indictment that her ladies, willingly or reluctantly, provided full and frank statements. Their testimony 'carried weight'.[22]

What is not clear, even upon deconstructing the indictments and analysing the specific allegations contained therein, is exactly who provided them. We know that Jane provided evidence against her husband and sister-in-law – that much is clear, in that, shortly after her death in 1542, her contemporaries gossiped about her involvement. Does her statement survive in the indictments? Let's examine the charges laid against Anne and George. Anne was accused of having 'procured and incited her own natural brother', George, 'to violate her, alluring him with her tongue in the said George's mouth, and the said George's tongue in hers, and also with kisses, presents and jewels'. George was accused of having then 'violated and carnally knew the said Queen, his own sister', which was 'sometimes by his own procurement and sometimes by the Queen's'. Such charges were, as yet, unproven statements as to the specific allegations that Anne and George would face at trial. They must, however, have been drafted in line with what little evidence that the prosecution were in possession of at that time, such as the depositions of Anne's ladies, her unguarded revelations in the Tower, or Smeaton's confession, all of which could be deliberately distorted to secure a conviction. A chance meeting with Smeaton on 29 April when Anne 'fond hym standyng in the ronde wyndo in [her] chambre' became, for the prosecution, a clandestine rendezvous 'incited' by the Queen[23]; that she had given to Norris 'certain medals' was apparently 'indicative that both were bound together' and that Anne had 'procured' him to 'violate her'[24]; her rather imprudent admission that she had on occasion 'given money' to Weston 'as she had often done to other young gentlemen' of the court was quite enough for them to levy the charge of Anne having encouraged 'several of the King's servants' by 'gifts, and other infamous incitations' in their 'illicit intercourse' until they 'grew jealous of each other' and 'yielded to her vile provocations'.[25]

Unfortunately, without transcripts of their depositions it is not possible to correspond the rest of the charges with any one eyewitness. Between the Middlesex and Kent indictments, exact dates and places were attached to four of the alleged offences involving Anne and George: 2 November 1535 at Westminster, 5 November 1535 at Westminster, 22 December 1535 at Eltham and 29 December at Eltham. The dates provided in the indictments have proven problematic, as many of them are highly improbable, on account of Anne being pregnant at the time, or theoretically impossible, as for more than a few of the alleged offences it can be established that either Anne, the men with whom she was accused, or even the entirety of the king's court were absent or situated elsewhere. This has led many historians to the conclusion that 'the detail was fabricated',[26] and that the charges in the indictment were wildly inaccurate, 'manipulated'[27] or 'manifestly invented'.[28] But as the only authoritative source for the charges laid against them, they cannot be so hastily dismissed. Crucially, the indictments contain a catch-all phrase: 'diversis aliis diebus et vicibus antea et postea' (in and on various other dates and places before and after), which suggests that the dates and places given were 'intended as specimen charges', i.e. that the dates and places may have been manufactured because such details 'had to be included', but that this did not necessarily mean that the charges levied themselves were fabricated.[29] It is quite plausible that Anne's ladies could remember more precisely exactly what had happened, but rather imprecisely on what date or in what chambers it had occurred.

What we do know, is that, on 4 May, having heard the news of his arrest, Jane sent to ask after her husband George. This would be communicated by Sir William Kingston in a letter to Cromwell: a 'gentilman ysshar came to me', he wrote, with a message for 'my [Lord of] Rotchfort from my lady hys wyf'. Although the letter is irretrievably damaged, it would appear that Jane wanted no more than to 'se how he dyd' and swore that 'she wold humly sut unto the kyngs hy[nes]... for hyr husband'.[30] How do we reconcile Jane's promise to petition the king on behalf of her husband with her betrayal? One clear explanation, perhaps the only explanation, is that Jane had not yet provided evidence. It was Anne's ladies who were apprehended,[31] isolated and interrogated as to her when and whereabouts. If any one was in a position to know the truth of the matter, it was the queen's servants. But Jane was not one of them. She was no longer serving in Anne's household, having been banished from court in 1534.

Jane likely provided her statement between the drafting of the Middlesex and Kent indictments on 10 and 11 May, when two separate juries met to rule on the alleged offences, and 15 May, when Anne and George stood trial. Let us suppose that, having made a promise to her husband to petition the king on his behalf, Jane solicited, not, Henry directly, but his secretary, Cromwell, as many seeking the king's favour often did. It was probably some time between 10 or 11 May, and 15 May, that Cromwell sent for Jane, and they met in private. If she was interrogated, we can infer from the indictments what questions she would have been asked. How often did George and Anne meet? On what days, and at what time, did they meet, and for how long? Was it in Anne's Presence chamber, or her Privy chamber? Did her husband ever go into the queen's bedchamber? Who was present on such occasions? Were they ever alone together, and if so, for how long? What did they talk about? And in what manner? Did she ever suspect that there was an unnatural or undue familiarity between her husband and her sister-in-law? Her deposition is not represented in the indictments; it would emerge only in the midst of George's trial that his own wife had given evidence against him.

Anne and George Boleyn stood trial on 15 May 1536, where their indictments would be presented to a grand jury and the accusations levied against them read aloud. They 'were tried separately'.[32] Anne went first. Before a jury empanelled with twenty-six peers of the realm, she was escorted by Sir William Kingston to 'the barre, where was made a chaire for her to sitt downe in'. 'Her indictment was redd afore her', and 'to all things layde against her', Anne, 'excusinge herselfe with her wordes so clearlie', it was felt, 'made so wise and discreet aunsweres'.[33] But it did not matter. She was found guilty. It could be said that the outcome of Anne's trial was something of a 'foregone conclusion' because, three days prior, when Norris, Brereton, Weston and Smeaton stood trial, the jury returned a guilty verdict. Smeaton plead guilty to the charge of 'violation and carnal knowledge of the Queen', while Norris, Brereton and Weston all plead not guilty.[34] The presumption then is that Anne was pre-judged: how could she possibly be found innocent of charges for which the men with whom she had been accused had already been found guilty? Spelman would note in his report that 'all the evidence was of bawdry and lechery, so there was no such whore in the realm'.[35] After the jury had returned their verdict, the Duke of Norfolk read aloud her sentence:

> Because thou haste offended our Sovereigne the Kinges grace, in committinge treason against his person, and here attaynted of the same, the lawe of the realme is this, that thou haste deserved death, and thy judgment is this : That thow shalt be brent here within the Tower of

London on the Greene, els to have thy head smitten of as the Kinges pleasure shal be further knowne of the same.[36]

It was reported that 'when the sentence was read to her,' Anne had 'received it quite calmly, and said that she was prepared to die'.[37]

George was next. He too was escorted by the Constable of the Tower to his chair, and his indictment read aloud in front of a jury of his peers who, only minutes earlier, had found his sister guilty of treason. This might mean that George too had been pre-judged, but all accounts of his trial indicate that the charges laid against him in the indictments alone would not have been enough to secure a conviction. This was because much of the evidence found against George was fragile, and at best, circumstantial. 'No proof of his guilt was produced', except that George had 'once passed many hours in her company', or 'had been once found a long time with her', wearing only his dressing-gown. Both Anne and George were accused together of 'having ridiculed the King', having 'laughed at his manner of dressing', mocking his poetry and, rather obscurely and tantalisingly, 'certain other little follies'. When the written statements in the indictments were read aloud, 'to all he replied so well that several of those present wagered 10 to 1 that he would be acquitted', Chapuys reported, 'especially as no witnesses were produced against him'.[38] 'Whereunto he made aunswere so prudentlie and wiselie to all articles layde against him, that marveil it was to heare,' Wriothesley observed, corroborating the ambassador's report, 'and never would confesse anye thinge, but made himselfe as cleare as though he had never offended'.[39] Just as it appeared to all who were in attendance that George would be acquitted of the charges, as the prosecution seemingly had little to no evidence to substantiate them, a folded slip of paper was produced and discreetly handed to the accused. He opened the slip of paper, and there was a written statement. It was Jane's statement, and George learned that his own wife had given evidence against him.

Of all the evidence laid against George, there is one damning statement which we know for a fact that Jane did make. It survives in the ambassador Chapuys' account of George's trial. 'I must not omit,' he reported, 'that among other things charged against him as a crime was, that his sister had told his wife that the King "que le Roy n'estait habile en cas de soi copuler avec femme, et qu'il n'avait ni vertu ni puissance...'", which, roughly translated, meant that Anne had told Jane 'the King had neither the skill nor the virility to satisfy a woman', or rather, that 'the King was impotent'. This statement could only have come from Jane, and the ambassador is clear in that it was not Anne but George against whom it was laid, meaning that the accusation itself must have been that sister and brother had discussed the king's sexual potency. This much was produced on a folded slip of paper and handed to George, and although he had been warned that, to answer the charge, 'he was only to say yes or no, without reading aloud the accusation', he was bold enough to 'read it aloud'. 'He immediately declared the matter,' Chapuys observed, 'in great contempt of Cromwell and some others'.[40] Cromwell would later remark that the depositions 'were so abominable that a great part of them were never given in evidence, but clearly kept secret'.[41] George was apparently 'unwilling' to incriminate himself or 'arouse any suspicion which might prejudice the King's issue' by not declaring it outright, suggesting he knew well the seriousness of the charge laid against him.

Before the trial, it was expected that Jane's husband, George, would be acquitted. The significance of Jane's evidence in this case thus cannot be overstated. It led to two interrelated charges: first, that he and his sister had discussed the king's sexual potency, and second, that George had questioned the paternity – i.e. the legitimacy – of the king's daughter Elizabeth. 'He was likewise charged with having spread the rumour or expressed a doubt as to Anne's daughter being the King's,' Chapuys noted, 'to which charge, however, he made no answer'.[42] Every precaution was taken to protect the king's lineage. Casting doubt on the legitimacy of Henry's own children, and on his sexual potency, amounted to treason, as it could be construed as attempting 'bodily harm' to 'the King's most royal person'.[43] It was also implied therein that if Anne could not have a child by Henry, she would look to father her child elsewhere, perhaps even with her own brother. Jane's evidence alone was more than enough to substantiate these charges, and it was only at the introduction of her statement that her husband's defense began to unravel.

George was clearly blindsided. We can be certain that Jane herself was not present at his trial as it was observed 'that no witnesses were called to give evidence against him... as is customary in such cases, when the accused denies the charge brought against him'.[44] There is no way that he could have known his own wife had turned against him. As a prisoner of the Tower, George, according to an ancient rule of law, was denied both assistance of legal counsel in matters of fact and, crucially, a copy of the indictment. This meant that he had no opportunity to prepare himself for trial, or any knowledge of specific charges, or evidence, and from whom it could and would be produced.[45] The delicate nature of Jane's statement – in that it contained rather sensitive remarks made as to the king's sexual potency – would surely have demanded discretion. Or perhaps the prosecution's strategy was to intentionally withhold Jane's evidence until that time at which they could introduce it mid-trial, and to great effect, knocking George off-balance. That his own wife had provided evidence against him must have struck a nerve, because his demeanour changed, and he lost all composure. He became agitated. Even if the charges laid against him had little to no substance, the jury would, as was the case in criminal trials resting on circumstantial evidence, recourse to judging George's character. His 'effrontery'[46] or disobedience in 'declaring the matter' aloud, to the 'great contempt of Cromwell and others', might have been a key factor in their deliberation, and ultimately, their decision to return a guilty verdict.

All of the gentlemen accused alongside Anne, Jane's husband among them, were executed at Tower Hill on 17 May 1536.

15

'Seche desyre as you have had to such tales hase browthe you to thys'
THE FALL OF ANNE BOLEYN

The most compelling evidence for Jane's role in the fall of Anne Boleyn is that which is now lost. Anthony Anthony, serving as a surveyor of the Ordinance in the Tower of London, kept a journal. Situated at the Tower, he was a probable eyewitness to what had taken place in May 1536. Although Anthony's journal cannot now be recovered, it was consulted by historian Gilbert Burnet. Writing in 1679, Burnet claimed that Jane 'carried many Stories to the King, or some about him, to persuade, that there was a familiarity between the Queen and her Brother, beyond what so near a Relation could justifie'.[1] Burnet explicitly identifies which sources were consulted for his 'just and faithful relation' of Anne's fall. He had seen 'a great many letters that were writ by those set about the queen' (the letters from Sir William Kingston to Thomas Cromwell), 'an account of it, which the learned Spelman, who was a Judge at that time, writ with his own hand in his Common-place book' (the report of Sir John Spelman), and 'another account of it writ by one Anthony Anthony, a Surveyor of the Ordnance of the Tower' (Anthony's journal). Neither Kingston nor Spelman identify Jane in their respective accounts, so unless Burnet substituted his own imagination in place of evidence it would seem fairly reasonable to conclude that it was on the authority of Anthony's lost journal that he determined that Jane had 'carried many Stories to the King'.[2] One of these 'Stories', Burnet noted, 'was only this: that he was one seen leaning upon her bed, which bred great suspition'. The other 'Stories' may be those which were reported by Chapuys and read aloud at George's trial: that Anne and George discussed the king's sexual potency, that they laughed at his dress, and mocked his poetry, that Anne had expressed that she was tiring of the king, and that

George 'had been once found a long time with her', along with 'certain other little follies'.³

The suggestion that Jane 'carried' many 'Stories' raises the question, was Jane's statement true, or false? And what was Jane's motive? It is hardly implausible that Anne would, albeit incautiously, discuss the king's sexual potency with her own brother, and later relate it to his wife when she was still at court and firmly on side.⁴ Before it was declared that he had been found guilty of committing treason, Jane's husband George appears to have refuted his wife's statement. 'On the evidence of only one woman you want to believe of me such a great evil', George exclaimed, turning to his peers, 'and on the basis of her allegations you determine my condemnation'.⁵ The 'one woman' to whom a clearly distressed and unnerved George was referring at this point was surely Jane. It could have been Elizabeth, Countess of Worcester, Anne's lady-in-waiting who was likely responsible for the initial accusations, but later 'when facing the case put before him' George would further remark that it was all 'nastily' or 'maliciously contrived lies'.⁶ Is it more likely that George had, not, the Countess in mind when he made such remarks, but his own wife, Jane, from whose testimony he and we can more plausibly infer 'malice'?

A letter written by an anonymous Portuguese gentleman visiting London in May 1536 to a friend in Lisbon, which contains an account of the executions of Anne and her fellow accused, claims 'that person' who 'did betray this accursed secret and together with it the names of those who had joined in the evil doings of the unchaste queen', did so 'more out of envy and jealousy than out of love towards the king'.⁷ Was Jane 'that person'? Burnet, probably informed by Anthony's journal, remarked that Jane was 'spiteful', and 'jealous of him'.⁸ Of all the particulars and details that emerged at trial, what made a more lasting impression, scandalising the court, was the betrayal of a wife to her husband, perhaps leading to such rampant – and irrepressible – speculation as to her true motives. Certainly many of Jane's contemporaries came to believe after her own conviction in 1542 that she her accusation was false. George Cavendish suggested that she was guilty of 'slaunder', and felt that she, 'beryng the name of an honest and chast wyfe', had acted 'without respect of any wyfely truthe'.⁹ John Foxe observed that it was 'reported by some' that Jane 'forged a false letter against her husband, and Queene Anne his sister, by the which they wer both cast away'.[10] Was this 'false letter' the folded slip of paper containing Jane's statement, indiscreetly handed to George mid-trial? Constantyne's account of Anne's fall also makes mention of a letter, again presented at trial: 'Her brother and she were examined at the towre. I heard saye he had escaped had it not byn for a Letter'.[11] George Wyatt believed that Jane, the 'wicked wife' and 'accuser of her own husband', fabricated the charges out of spite, 'more to be rid of him than of true ground against him'.[12] Writing in the reign of Elizabeth I, both Foxe and Wyatt were eager to vindicate Anne, the queen's mother. Yet crucially, their sources were women with whom Jane had served in the household of her sister-in-law, and who are likely to have witnessed Anne's fall first-hand.

Why did Jane reveal anything to Cromwell at all? It has been suggested that Jane 'found herself dragged into a maelstrom of intrigue, innuendo and speculation', and 'faced with such relentless, incessant questions, which she had no choice but to answer'.[13] Bewildered, frightened, and in peril, Jane was apparently forced to confess.[14] Jane seemingly had no idea what she was doing or saying, or how her words could and would later be 'maliciously interpreted', and as such she should be excused of any and all responsibility for her husband's death. This interpretation argues that 'Jane's main concern was for her husband', that she 'had not deserted him', or rather more explicitly, that she 'had no intention of harming her husband'.[15] In other words, there was no betrayal. 'The arrests had been so sudden and unexpected', we are told, 'that there was no time to separate out what testimony might be damaging, what could be twisted to become so, or what could only be innocuous no matter what the interpretation'.[16] The logic of such a scenario is unclear. Is there any conceivable way that Jane could not have been aware of the consequences of her testimony, particularly in claiming that her own husband and sister-in-law had discussed the king's sexual potency? No, and nor could she have been oblivious to the prosecution's intentions in mounting a case against George, as she was well aware he had been thrown in the Tower. To otherwise find that Jane was 'dragged' or 'forced' into admitting what she did is to diminish her role to little more than that of a hostage to the crown. Yet, there is no sign that she was in any danger in 1536. She was unlikely to have been implicated as an accomplice, as she was not at court when the adultery was alleged to have taken place. Even the use of the word 'interrogation'[17] is surely overstating it. If Jane was to face relentless questioning, or if the prosecution suspected at all that she could have been somehow involved, it seems strange that they did not send for her until at least a week after the initial arrests. If they did suspect anything of her, Jane certainly would not have been permitted to send a message to her husband, as she did on 4 May 'in the kyngs name', i.e. with the express permission of the king himself.[18]

Perhaps it was Jane who made the first move to divulge what she knew. We do not know for certain, but if Anthony noted that Jane 'carried many stories' to the king, he may have suspected that she herself took the initiative to testify and furnish the prosecution with damning evidence. As John Gostwick would urge his son in 1540,

> ...if your friend do open his mind and secret counsel to you, I charge you ... open [i.e. reveal] it not ... unless your friend should open to you felony or treason, then I charge you not to keep his counsel, but [if you are in the country] open it to two or three of the next [i.e. nearest] Justices of the Peace which dwelleth next to you, or else [if you are at court] one or two of the king's most honourable Council, if you may get unto them. But in any wise, utter it as soon as possible, for the longer you keep it the worse it is for you, and the more danger toward God and the king's majesty.[19]

The evidence suggests that Jane cooperated with the prosecution. If she was not responsible for the initial accusation of incest (this was probably the Countess of Worcester), she certainly lent credence to it. It is plausible that, upon hearing of her husband's imprisonment, Jane solicited Cromwell, not, to plead for clemency, but to inform the secretary of all that she knew, leaving no doubt as to her allegiance, for her own protection. If it was too late for George, she had a chance to save herself.

Were the charges of adultery and incest fabricated? Some remained sceptical of the charges laid against the queen. Constantyne observed that 'there was much muttering at Anne's death'.[20] Chapuys reported that 'although everybody rejoices at the execution of the putain [whore], there are some who murmur at the mode of procedure against her and the others, and people speak variously of the king'.[21] Alexander Alesius, later writing to Elizabeth I, remarked that 'no probable suspicion of adultery' could be substantiated by the prosecution, besides only circumstantial evidence like that 'the Queen's brother took her by the hand and led her into the dance among the other ladies', or that Anne wrote to George with news that she was pregnant.[22] If there was a 'conspiracy' against the queen, orchestrated by Cromwell, the involvement and cooperation of Jane and the queen's servants must be accounted for. Factionalism is unlikely, as the women who accused Anne were not aligned against the queen – quite the opposite. Why would they substantiate false charges against their mistress? Such a conspiracy could not have been executed without her women. If Anne was guilty, then her ladies and gentlewomen provided statements which condemned their mistress to death. But if Anne was innocent, these servants had 'turned' king's evidence. When Anne was first arrested, 'sundry ladies' were apparently thrown in the Tower with her, as, reportedly, they were 'acsesari to the sayme'.[23] One account suggests that Anne solicited an elderly lady-in-waiting, named Margaret, to facilitate her liaisons with Mark Smeaton. Anne 'ordered all her ladies to retire to their respective beds' and 'called the old woman' to 'bring [her] a little marmalade' (i.e. Smeaton) from the anteroom to her bedchamber.[24] This cannot be corroborated, and it would appear that no women were actually accused or executed alongside Anne, even though they must have been in some measure complicit.

None of the queen's servants were charged with Anne, but if the king's council suspected that her women, privy to the queen's most intimate affairs, were aware of her misconduct, they may well have been in danger. Certainly Alesius suspected that the king had his council 'watch her private apartments night and day'; 'they tempt her porter and serving man with bribes; there is nothing which they do not promise the ladies of her bedchamber'. This remark reveals what Alesius and his contemporaries believed to be possible – that Anne's ladies, and Jane too, may have accepted a bribe for their cooperation.[25] This claim is difficult to substantiate. There are no surviving depositions or statements taken from Anne's servants, meaning that it is difficult to discern the nature of their testimony. Yet there is some evidence that they would have been encouraged, and were likely spared, when they provided statements incriminating enough to secure Anne's conviction.[26]

The letters written from Sir William Kingston, constable of the Tower, to Cromwell, dating from 3 May, the day after Anne's arrest, to 19 May, the day of her execution, provide further insight into how the queen's ladies and gentlewomen became agents of the king. These letters are mutilated, some irreparably,[27] though they remain compelling, as they provide us with an insight into Anne's final days, and detail the nature of her interactions and candid conversations with her servants, which, otherwise, would not have been recorded or have survived today.[28] The day after Anne's arrest, Kingston reported to Cromwell that 'apon the kyngs counsell depart[*inge*] from the Towre [he] went before the queen in to hyr lodgyng, and [*then she*] sayd unto [him], Master Kyngston, shall I go in to a dungyn?' to which Kingston replied, 'No, Madam. You shall go into the lodging you lay in at your coronation.'[29] For the duration, Anne would occupy the queen's apartments in the Tower. Anne did not suffer her final days in a cold, dark and barren dungeon, cell or gaol. But a prison was a prison. She could not leave the Tower, and in her final days, Anne was likely restricted to her innermost lodgings: her Privy Chamber, closet and bedchamber. During her imprisonment, Anne was attended by four or five gentlewomen servants, and Kingston's letters provide us with some indication as to who these women were. The first was Mary Scrope, Kingston's wife. The 'lady Boleyn' can be identified as Elizabeth Wood, the queen's aunt, wife of Sir James Boleyn. The 'mistress Coffin' was Margaret Dymoke, wife of Sir William Coffin, gentleman of the king's Privy Chamber and the queen's master of the horse. One was a 'mistress Stonor', likely Isabel, the wife of Sir Walter Stonor, the king's sergeant-at-arms. Unfortunately, there is no record of the identity of the fifth, unnamed gentlewoman.[30] As Kingston observed, the Lady Boleyn and Mistress Coffin lay on the queen's pallet, that is, at the foot of her bed, whereas he and his wife lay at the door of her Privy Chamber. Like the constable, the gentlewomen, quite purposefully, kept Anne in the dark, as the queen remarked to Kingston, 'my lady Boleyn and Mestres [Cofyn]… cowd tell her now thynge of her father, nor nothynge ellys…'[31] In the Tower, the queen's Privy Chamber, where Anne would usually have retreated and relaxed in private, functioned, as it always did, by *restricting* access to the queen. Its attendant staff were responsible too for carefully regulating and controlling this access, though, instead of maintaining or preserving Anne's privacy, they now enforced it, and kept her in isolation. They were, effectively, her guards.

The gentlewomen attending upon the queen were instructed by Kingston to record and report back 'every thynge' that Anne said.[32] Certainly, the queen spoke unguardedly, as in the first few days of her imprisonment, she was manifestly nervous, increasingly anxious, desperately trying to make sense of her fall. Anne began rehearsing, in great detail, if indiscreetly, incidental conversations that took place in her chambers with the gentlemen with whom she was accused. Anne told Isabel Stonor of a conversation she had with Mark Smeaton, groom of the king's Chamber. On 29 April, a few days before her arrest, the queen had 'found hym standyng in the rounde wyndo in her Presence Chamber', and asked why he 'wase so sad'. He answered that 'it was now mater'. Here Smeaton's pitiful state must have vexed the queen, as she then she sayd scornfully, 'You may not loke to have me speke to you as I shuld do to a nobulle man, because you be an inferor [pe]rson.' To which he replied, panic-stricken, before taking his leave, 'No, no, madam, a loke sufficed me, and thus fare you welle.'[33] Anne was clearly taken aback by the familiarity with which Smeaton dared speak with her in public. Later that same day, Anne spoke with Henry Norris, gentleman of the king's Privy Chamber, a conversation which she confided to Margaret Coffin. She had asked Norris why he did not go through with his marriage to her cousin, Madge Shelton, to which he 'made ansure he wold tary [a time]'. '[Y]ou loke for ded men's showys,' Anne scolded, 'for yf owth ca[m to the King but good], you would loke to have me'. Norris was clearly horrified, fearing that 'yf he [should have any such thought] he wold hys hed war of'. Anne knew she had misspoke, and fearing that her words could be misconstrued, urged Norris to swear an oath to her almoner that she was a good woman.[34] She also recalled a conversation she had with Francis Weston, another of the king's servants; Anne says she spoke to Weston 'bycause he claimed he did not love hys wyf', but loved instead Anne's maid, Shelton. Weston then dared to add that '[h]e loved wone in hyr howse better then them bothe'. The queen asked, '[Who is] that?' 'It ys yourself', Weston said, and then 'she defyed hym'.[35] Unfortunately for Anne, her words were reported back to Kingston, and then to Cromwell, substantiating the charges of adultery and treason laid against her in a damning indictment.

Had Anne given rise to suspicions by her own conduct? Intriguingly, Pizan wrote at length on the readiness of women at court to 'whisper scandal to each other'. 'If they see their lady or mistress merely speaking quietly to a person once or twice, or showing some sign of intimacy or of friendship, or if they see some laughter or some merriment', these women might 'jump to the wrong conclusion', or even 'embroider the story with invented details'.[36] Anne's interactions with her gentlewomen in the Tower reflects more broadly on how and why a queen, any queen, might yet feel isolated and alone *even* within such an institution as her own household, surrounded by her servants. A queen's Privy Chamber in itself could be a prison if it were under the control of the sovereign. 'I thynke [moche onkindnes yn the] kyng to put seche women abowt me as I never loved', the queen said to Kingston, 'bot I wold have had [of myn owne prevy cham]bre, weche I favor most'.[37] Anne longed for the presence of those women whom she knew well, liked and cared for, could confide in and whom she felt would serve her loyally and faithfully. Crucially the gentlewomen who were attending upon the queen were chosen by the king, not by Anne herself. More than an 'onkindnes', it was calculated, and deliberate. These gentlewomen were the king's spies, as Kingston says:

> Wher I was commaunded to charge the gentelwomen that give thayr atendans apon the Quene, that ys to say thay shuld have no commynycasion with hyr in lese my wyf ware present.
> Notwithstandynge it canot be so, for my lady Bolen and Mestrys Cofyn lie on the Quenes palet, and I and my wyf at the dore with yowt... I have every thynge told me by Mestrys Cofyn that she thinkes meet for you to know.

Kingston acknowledged further 'that tother ij. gentelweymen lay without him, and requested to know t[he] Kynges plesure in the matter.[38] Anne reiterated again days later that 'the Kyng [knew] what he dyd w[hen he put such] ij.

women abowt hyr as the lady Boleyn and Mestres [Cofyn]'.[39] Kingston assured her that Henry 'took them to be honest and gud wemmen', or, in other words, that these women could be trusted to watch and inform against her.[40] At least one of the gentlewomen watching Anne readily provided information for Chapuys, a known adversary of the queen. Chapuys acknowledged that 'the lady who had charge of her has sent to tell me in great secrecy' that Anne 'before and after receiving the sacrament, affirmed to her, on the damnation of her soul, that she had never been unfaithful to the King'.[41] His reports were able to penetrate the Tower's walls because, from the first day of the queen's incarceration, as he claimed, 'the lady under whose custody and keeping she was has not concealed a single thing from me'.[42]

Why did Anne incriminate herself? She knew herself to be 'creuely handeled' by the king, and yet confessed to, or confided in, women whom she, in her own words, had 'never loved'. Perhaps it was her fragile, nearly hysterical state of mind that saw her unravel. Kingston's letters provide an almost unprecedented insight into the mental and emotional state of the queen during her imprisonment. Anne was understandably strained and shaken. On the night of her arrest, she declared, 'Jesu, have mercy on me', before she knelt down 'wepyng a [*great*] pace, and in the same sorow fell in to a great laughing, as she hathe done [*so*] mony tymes syns.'[43] Kingston reiterated that, during her imprisonment, at times Anne was 'mery', and at others she wept, or even laughed uncontrollably. As the constable observed 'for one hour she ys determyned to die, and the next hour meche contrary to that'.[44] Later, when Kingston visited her again, Anne said that she had 'heard say the executioner was very gud, and I have a lyt[el neck, and [she] put he]r hand abowt it, lawynge hartely.' 'I have seen many men and women executed,' Kingston reported, 'all of them in gre[at sorrow, [but] to my knowle]ge thys lady hasse mech joy and plesure in dethe.'[45] The terrifying vulnerability of her position might have left an otherwise astute queen desperate, achingly lonely, and incautiously candid.

Were these gentlewomen servants merely the king's spies, lying in wait to strike the queen at the slip of her tongue? Certainly her aunt, Elizabeth, Lady Boleyn, was unsympathetic. As Kingston recorded, she sayd to hyr niece, 'Seche desyre as you have h[ad to such tales] hase browthe you to thys...'[46] It may be suggested that these women were guilty of almost baiting Anne into revealing more than she should. Margaret Coffin appears to have eagerly obliged and abided by the instructions of the king. On the other hand, it could be that she and the rest of Anne's gentlewomen reported back only that which they thought or felt was necessary. Their interactions, as they survive in these letters, are incomplete, and distorted by the hand of Kingston, recording too only what he felt was pertinent, or in other words, what was *political*. Nor were Anne's gentlewomen likely to have rehearsed for the constable any interactions in which they had shown her any empathy or compassion. We hear little from mistress Stonor, for instance, who, by this account, spoke only a few words in seventeen days, and initially, neither she nor the unnamed gentlewoman were chaperoned by Kingston or his wife when they attended to Anne.

Perhaps there was agency in their silence, in what they did not disclose, in what remains undocumented, and what is now, unfortunately, impossible to trace. Albeit speculative, it is far from implausible that their loyalty to, or affection for Anne, as their mistress, could have frustrated the efforts of the investigation. Margery Horsman, Anne's maid-of-honour, had shown herself reluctant under interrogation to provide evidence. Sir Edward Baynton, the queen's vice-chamberlain, cooperated directly with the king's council, and was tasked with extracting testimony from Anne's servants. On 3 May 1536, in a letter to Sir William Fitzwilliam, the king's treasurer, Baynton admitted that he struggled to wrest a confession from her maid. 'I have mewsed myche at ...mastres Margery,' Baynton wrote, 'whiche hath used her[self] strangely toward me of late being her fry[nd] as I have ben'. 'But no dowte it cann... but that she must beof councell therewith', and, Baynton observed, there 'hath ben great fryndeship betwene the Q[ueen and] her of late'.[47] Although the queen's vice-chamberlain and her maid had been familiar, the arrest of their mistress had created a rift between them, reflecting then the divergence of their allegiances and interests. The 'strange' conduct that Horsman was exhibiting, as Baynton reports, was her reluctance to implicate Anne, because of the 'great fryndeship' she had with her mistress. To comply, to conform, or to resist, in all measures, embodied a choice made by Anne's women. The queen's servants did not obey, or refuse, orders, without making a decision, though it must be observed that such a decision may have been, in some way, intimidated, or coerced, by the threat of incurring the king's wrath, thus constraining their agency. When Cromwell remarked that 'her ladyes of her privy chambre, and her chamberers' could 'not conteyne it within their brestes', he rather suggests that they, loyal to the queen, would have kept the information to themselves if they could have.[48]

The gentlewomen who attended upon Anne in the Tower are often characterised as one-dimensional, uncaring and indifferent to Anne's torment. It was these same women who, on 19 May, accompanied the queen from her lodgings to a nearby scaffold. Accounts of Anne's execution vary slightly, but at least three of them record the presence of her gentlewomen. Lancelot de Carles, secretary to the French ambassador residing in England, says they were 'nearly dead themselves', describing them as 'bereft of their souls, such was their weakness'. Mere moments before death, the queen 'consoled her ladies several times', as one of them 'pouring forth continuous tears', came forward and 'veiled her face with linen'.[49] This last detail is corroborated by an Imperial ambassador, who said that Anne 'knelt down, fastening her clothes about her feet, and one of her ladies bandaged her eyes'.[50] Another eyewitness to Anne's execution observed that her gentlewomen 'then withdrew themselves some little space, and knelt down over against the scaffold, bewailing bitterly and shedding many tears.'[51] Turning to the crowd, she gave a speech on the scaffold:

> Good Christen people, I am come hether to dye, for accordyng to the lawe and by the lawe I am judged to dye, and therefore I wyll speake nothyng against it. I am come hether to accuse no man, nor to speake anythyng of that wherof. I am accused and condempned to dye, but I pray God saue the king and send him long to reigne ouer you, for a gentler nor a more mercyfull prince was there neuer: and to me he was euer a good, a gentle, & soueraigne lorde. And if any persone will medle of my cause, I require them to judge the best. And thus I take my leue of the worlde and of you all, and I heartely desyre you all to pray for me. O lorde haue mercy on me, to God I comende my soule.

Then Anne knelt down, saying, 'To Christ I commende my soule, Jesu receiue my soule', until her head was stricken off with a sword.[52] Once the executioner had done his duty, Anne's ladies on the scaffold, 'fearing that their mistress might be taken and touched unworthily by the hands of discourteous men', wrapped her head and body in a white cloth and carried her to the chapel of St Peter ad Vincula, where she was to be buried.[53] Another account reveals that, in her final moments, before she knelt down to meet her fate, Anne apparently addressed her servants:

> ...my damsels, who, whilst I lived, ever shewed yourselves so diligent in my service, and who are now to be present at my last hour and mortal agony, as in good fortune ye were faithful to me, so even at this my miserable death ye do not forsake me. And as I cannot reward you for your true service to me, I pray you take comfort for my loss... forget me not ; and be always faithful to the King's Grace, and to her whom with happier fortune ye may have as your Queen and Mistress...[54]

Certainly these heart-wrenching scenes could have been exaggerated. Neither chronicler Hall or Wriothesley corroborated them, as they did not record the presence of her gentlewomen, though we do know that they were in attendance. This aside to her ladies is touching, but it is likely fabricated. These words, especially her last, pointed and strikingly magnanimous allusion to her rival and successor, Jane Seymour, would surely have been recorded by other eyewitnesses.[55] Though it remains implausible that Anne ever spoke these words, such reports from the scaffold do, however, serve to remind us that the queen's servants were not merely pawns of the king. Servants had complex, often overlapping, obligations, and emotions. Their empathy here needs not be reconciled with their political allegiance. Politically, Anne's gentlewomen were necessarily aligned with the king, their sovereign. Yet emotionally, they shared in this most harrowing experience of the queen, and may even have provided their forsaken mistress with genuine emotional comfort in her final days, easing her loneliness and isolation. Although the king could perhaps command the allegiance of men and women who served his queens, he could not always dictate how they thought and felt.

This distinction serves us to assess Jane's position too. No matter how she felt about her husband and sister-in-law, if she wanted to protect her own interests, she had little or no choice but to betray their trust. And betray their trust she did. Her statement placed her, strategically, on the side of the king, and as we shall see, facilitated her transition to the new queen's household, in spite of how her loyalties had previously aligned with the Boleyns. And Jane was not the only one. At least six women who were appointed to serve the queen's successor, Jane Seymour, gave evidence against Anne.[56] These women do not appear to have been necessarily pressurised, or 'bullied', by the crown, into providing damning evidence against their mistress. A more accurate, or nuanced, reading is that they were anxious about their own survival. By demonstrating their loyalty to the king, these women survived the scandal with their careers intact.

Confronted with the dilemma of either informing against the queen, and in her compliance demonstrating her loyalty to the crown, or otherwise refusing to conform to and cooperate with their agenda, Jane did not, and arguably, could not hesitate in her treachery.

16

'A power desolat wydow wythoute comffort'
WIDOWHOOD

Jane was left in a precarious state following George's execution in 1536. As was customary practice for convicted criminals in this period, her husband's property was confiscated. At his trial, upon hearing his sentence, George 'begged the King that his debts, which he recounted, might be paid out of his goods'.[1] When Jane and George were first married, all of Jane's property was transferred and put under the control of her husband. Jane had no legal right to the possessions that they had together carefully accumulated. All land, estates and personal items, had been seized by the crown, and Jane depended on the king's favour to claim it back. Unfortunately for Jane, her relationship with Henry was uneasy, having so far upset the king in 1534 that he had her banished from court. Still stuck in exile, Jane had little more to rely upon other than her jointure. Although she was in receipt of an annuity of one hundred marks, this was not enough to sustain her, or, in Jane's own words, 'to schyffte the worldd wythall' as a 'power desolate widow wythoute comffort'. To put that figure into perspective, 100 marks amounted to £66 13s. 4d.; on one occasion Jane's husband spent £50 on a cup of gold, and the privy purse expenses for 1529 to 1532 reveal that George regularly gambled large sums in pastime with the king.[2]

The king, and her father, Lord Morley, had settled her jointure with Sir Thomas Boleyn, Earl of Wiltshire and Ormond, upon her marriage to his son George 'to the some off too thowsand Marks'. Jane complained that she was 'assuryd of no more' than 'one hundredth Markes' for each year of her father-in-law's life. She may have petitioned Sir Thomas directly for an increased allowance, but if she did, she was unsuccessful. It would hardly have come as a surprise to Jane that her father-in-law had no interest in helping her, as will have been aware of her role in bringing his son and daughter to the scaffold. Jane remained estranged from the Boleyns, and as such, required the intervention of the king's secretary, Thomas Cromwell.[3]

Shortly after her husband's execution, Jane wrote to Cromwell for his help in easing her financial troubles. As her only surviving letter, it is worth quoting in full:

> Mayster Secretory, as a power desolat wydow wythoute comffort, as to my specyall trust under God and my Pryns, I have me most humbly recommendyd unto youe; prayng youe, after your accustemyd gentyll maner to all them that be in suche lamentabull case as I ame in, to be meane to the Kyngs gracyous Hyghnes for me for suche power stuffe and plate as my husbonde had, whome God pardon; that of hys gracyous and mere lyberalyte I may have hyt to helpe me to my power lyvyng, whiche to his Hyghnes ys nothynge to be regardyd, and to be schuld be a most hygh helpe and souccor. And farther more, where that the Kyngs Hyghnes and my Lord my father payed great soms of money for my Joynter to the Errel of Wyltchere to the some off too thowsand Marks, and I not assuryd of no more duryng the sayd Errells naturall lyff then one hundredth Marke; whyche ys veary hard for me to schyffte the worldd wythall. That youe wyll so specyally tender me in thys behalff as to enforme the Kyngs Hyghnes of these premysses, wherby I may the more tenderly be regardyd of hys gracyous persone, youre Worde in thys schall be to me a sure helpe: and God schall be to youe therfore a sure reward, whyche dothe promes good to them that dothe helpe powere forsaken Wydos. And bothe my prayer and servys schall helpe to thys duryng my naturall lyff, as most bounden so to doo, God my wyttnes; whoo ever more preserve you.
>
> Jane Rocheford[4]

If Cromwell sent Jane a letter in response to her own, it has not survived. Although her 'self-abasement', as one author put it, might have been 'galling', it was successful.[5] We do know that Cromwell approached the king, and that they would both take up Jane's cause and put pressure on her father-in-law to increase her allowance from her jointure settlement. Thomas received letters from them both, as he observed, 'consernyng an augmentacon of lyvyng to my dowghtyr of Rochford'. It was in his interests to comply with their requests. He wrote directly to Cromwell to negotiate a new settlement proposing an increase to the existing annuity of 100 marks a year of '50 marks a year more in hand', and adjusted the 200 marks a year Jane could expect after his death to 300.[6] He was explicit in that he did this, not, for his daughter-in-law, Jane, but 'alonly to satysfye the kynges desyre and plesur', and even that he did begrudgingly, scornfully remarking on Jane's childlessness: 'When I married I had only 50*l*. a year to live on for me and my wife as long as my father lived,' the Earl grumbled, 'and yet she brought me every year a child'.[7] It is clear that Jane, a childless widow who had betrayed the Earl's only surviving son, was little more to him than a financial burden.

In addition to his help in securing an increased allowance, Jane asked that Cromwell 'be meane to the Kyngs gracyous Hyghnes for [her]' so that she might secure moveable property in 'stuffe and plate as [her] husbonde had', which she observed 'to his Hyghnes ys nothynge to be regardyd', but to her 'schuld be a most hygh helpe'.[8] The inventory taken when George's possessions would have been confiscated, listing 'parcelles of Stuff' that did 'remayne a chest beyng in the chambr over the kechen', probably at Grimston Manor, does however suggest that some attempt was made to distinguish between his and her most personal property. Various gowns and garments, rich sleeves, satins and silks, 'prymers', 'bokes' and 'bedes' were identified as 'the Lady Rochefords'.[9] An inventory taken shortly after her death in 1542 of property belonging to 'the late Lady Rocheford' indicates that Cromwell had, in 1536, managed to secure for Jane some of her husband's moveable property: therein was recorded 'oone bed stede of wodd painted & gilt with burnished golde' with 'bases of white Satten alover embrandered with trayles of tawny cloth of golde... with the lorde Rochfordes knottes upon the seames'.[10] A few years later, in 1539, probably as a result of Sir Thomas Boleyn's death in March, Parliament passed an Act which confirmed Jane's jointure, securing her the manors of Swavesey, Blickling, Calthorpe, Filby, Stiffkey and Postwick.[11] Shortly thereafter the Court of Augmentations granted to 'Lady Joan Rocheford, widow' the manors of Ultecote and Loxley in Warwickshire.[12]

Perhaps the most astonishing of miracles that Cromwell performed for Jane was that, less than a year after her husband's execution, she was reinstated to her position in the queen's household, to serve Jane Seymour, Henry's third wife, as a Lady of the Privy Chamber. On 13 May 1536, less than a week before Anne's execution, the king sent Sir William Fitzwilliam and Sir William Paulet to Greenwich, where they 'deposed and brooke upp the Queenes househoulde... and so discharged all her servantes of their offices clearlye'.[13] When a queen's household was discharged, all of her servants gave up their offices, and there was no guarantee that they would be reappointed to serve her successor. On the day of Anne's execution, John Husee reported that 'most of the late queen's servants are set at liberty to seek service elsewhere',[14] whereas a poem written shortly after described her servants as 'sheep without a shepherd'.[15] Servants who owed their appointments to the queen, like her family, friends and clientele, whose ties were strictly to their mistress, had their careers cut short. Lacking any claim to office, these servants had been firmly aligned with the fallen queen, and thus they could not properly attend upon her rival and successor. None of the Boleyn kinsmen and women survived the scandal, though one exception was George Taylor,[16] Anne's receiver-general, who, it was observed, was 'merry', for he had clearly been given some assurance of his place. 'I trust the King's Highness will be good and gracious lord unto me', he remarked, shortly after being discharged, 'and so I have a special trust in his Grace.'[17] And he was not the only one. Husee had heard that 'the King's Highness of his goodness hath retained, as is said, some of them'.[18] Perhaps Jane too had been given some assurance of her place.

Households were established for queens consort before, upon, or shortly after marrying the king. Henry VIII and Jane Seymour, for instance, were married at Whitehall on 30 May 1536, and within a few days, Sir John Russell reported that Jane was being 'served by her own servants'.[19] The chronicler Charles Wriothesley recorded that, on 4 June, Jane was 'proclaymed Queene at Greenewych, and went in procession, after the King, with a great traine of ladies following after her'. She 'began her howsehold that daie, dyning in her chamber of presence under the cloath of estate'.[20] We do not know when, how or why Jane, Lady Rochford, was reinstated, but of all the ladies and gentlewomen who must have been vying for a position with the new queen, extraordinarily, it was Jane who was appointed.

It has been suggested that Jane won her appointment on merit, due to her years of experience at court.[21] This however, is unconvincing, in light of her position in 1536. The 'Boleyn' name had been tarnished, and their stronghold at court had been eradicated. Jane was careful to renounce her husband in her letter to Cromwell, tacitly acknowledging the justice of his fate in asking that God pardon him. She did not survive the scandal unscathed, but she faired better than her father-in-law, who was deprived of certain lands and was forced to resign his office as Lord Privy Seal to Cromwell.[22] As the poor widow of a disgraced courtier and convicted traitor, her prospects were few. Estranged from her kith and kin, and exiled from court, Jane should have faded quickly into relative obscurity. Her resurgence begs an explanation. Although the king was fickle, it is staggering that he would have concerned himself at all with her perilous state. Cromwell was likely her patron.[23] It was only by Cromwell's hand that Jane felt she, in her own words, 'may the more tenderly be regardyd of hys gracyous persone'.[24] As the king's secretary, Cromwell was inundated with letters, petitions and bribes. At times, he was keen to act as their patron; at others, he was not. Why did he act on Jane's behalf? Evidently he busied himself in her interests and probably urged Henry to reconsider her exile after he had banished her from court nearly two years before. The almost unavoidable conclusion is that Jane had 'turned' king's evidence. Her role in securing a conviction against her husband and sister-in-law demonstrated her loyalty to her sovereign. It was irrefutable proof of her allegiance. For her cooperation, she was owed something in return. It was a royal show of gratitude.

17

'No meet suit for any man to move such matters'
POLITICS

What distinguished Jane's position as a Lady of the Privy Chamber from her previous role as a Maid-of-Honour was her 'nearness' to the queen. The queen's Privy Chamber created an atmosphere which encouraged familiarity and the forming of close bonds between mistress and servant. The nature of the service they provided to the queen as her 'body servants' meant that they were in regular and close proximity, facilitating their own interactions, be it polite but opportune exchanges with her person, or hushed, self-seeking whispers in her ear that led to their own advancement. This extended to a servant's family, friends and clientele when they acted on their behalf to secure the queen's favour. Power, and influence, lay in access to, and intimacy with, their mistress. This potential for Jane and other servants in the queen's household to engage in politics is illustrated in the *Lisle Letters*, the surviving correspondence of a sixteenth-century English gentry family.

Servants in the queen's Chamber and Privy Chamber acted as patrons who were solicited by would-be clients as a 'way in' to their mistress. Each of the queen's chambers were closely guarded, allowing fewer and fewer people access, and the right of entry was restricted to her servants, who were often responsible for regulating who and what came through them. Those who visited the court were received by the queen's servants in her Guard and Presence chambers. Thomas Warley, Honor Grenville, Lady Lisle's servant, met in Anne Boleyn's Presence chamber with Margery Horsman, her maid-of-honour, who had arranged for Warley to receive a kirtle from the queen. When Warley returned there later to thank her, he found that Horsman had 'returned into the Privy chamber, so that since I could not speak with her'.[1] On another occasion, when

Thomas Wynter, Archdeacon of York, arrived to meet with the queen, she had kept him 'a long time', and he was sent for only upon 'being reminded by her attendants', who received him 'very kindly'.[2]

Persons and petitions alike had to go through the queen's attendants, whose authority and status was derived from their intimacy with their mistress. In this, women had the advantage. Access to the queen's Privy chamber was strictly for her most intimate servants, who necessarily had to be women, and the queen's innermost chambers constituted a strictly *female* space. John Husee, Lady Lisle's agent in London, advised her that, to find preferment for her daughters, Anne and Katharine, to the queen's household, it was 'no meet suit for any man to move such matters, but only for such Ladies and women as be your friends'.[3] On 6 June 1536, Husee wrote to Lady Lisle promising to move 'the preferment of your ladyship's daughter unto the Queen'.[4] The agent had to petition Eleanor Paston, Countess of Rutland, a lady of the queen's Privy chamber, and Margery Horsman and Mary Arundell, both maids-of-honour: 'I shewed my Lady Rutland that your ladyship would gladly have one of your daughters with the Queen, and so I showed Mrs. Margery and Mrs. Arundell in like manner, but I am sure none of them never motioned the Queen's grace therein'.[5] Upon hearing that the matter for her daughters' preferment had not been moved, Lady Lisle began courting the queen's servants more aggressively for their favour. She was exhaustive in her efforts to secure them as her patrons, petitioning them through Husee, with whom she kept close correspondence and by whom she conveyed various gifts, tokens and sums of money: the Countess of Rutland received 'cherries and peasecods', a token 'heart of gold' and later 'a pipe of Gascon wine and two barrels of herring'; Elizabeth Harleston, Lady Wallop, received a 'little diamond'; Sir William Coffin, Master of the Horse, received a hawk; Margery Horsman, received a 'casket of steel and flower', and a 'a ring of gold', and John Powes, a yeoman usher, received 20*s*.[6] Tokens could be a personal, treasured possession of the sender, not often kept by the recipient but accepted in recognition of their relationship and returned in due time.[7] After receiving such a token from Lady Lisle, Margery showed her gratitude to Husee, Lisle's agent, before closing the exchange. 'I ensure you, madame, she sets not a little by it', reported Husee, 'and she delivered to me a cramp ring of gold for your ladyship, which ye shall receive herein closed.'[8]

Patronage, or the use of influence to bestow privilege, honour or financial aid, was 'ubiquitous, normal and unavoidable' in the Tudor era.[9] The queen's servants did not always have their own axes to grind, but their position meant that they were often solicited by those who wished for them to act as intermediaries on their behalf. In 1534, John Grainfield, who was later sergeant-at-arms to Henry's queens, promised Lord Lisle, 'I have moved a friend of mine about the Queen in Haward's matter'.[10] That same year, Elizabeth Staynings, whose husband had been imprisoned, asked Lady Lisle 'to write to any lady she knows at Court who is familiar with the Queen, that she may resort to her sometimes'.[11] In 1537, Thomas Raynolds too wrote to Lady Lisle, who was responsible for securing his appointment as chaplain to Jane Seymour, asking, 'if lord Lisle or she have any other friends about the King or Queen, as he is sure they have many now, a good word may do him great pleasure'.[12]

Thus the patron-client system shifted to their advantage. Upon learning that Thomas Culpeper, a gentleman of the king's Privy Chamber, was to be given a hawk by Lady Lisle, Mary Arundell, Countess of Sussex, now a lady of the queen's Privy chamber, intervened, suggesting that Culpeper 'should not have the hawk, saying that he can do your ladyship small pleasure'.[13] 'By her advice', Lady Lisle then gifted the hawk instead to the Countess' husband, Robert Radcliffe, Earl of Sussex. Shortly after Jane became queen, Husee was informed that she 'had appointed all her maidens already'.[14] Lady Lisle's agent reported any potential vacancies from within the queen's household. On 30 April 1537, Husee reported that Jane Ashley, one of the maids, was shortly to be married, and that if one of her daughters 'had been now here she might have chanced to have furnished her room, but she must first be seen or known ere she be taken into the Queen's service'.[15] Margery Horsman, her faithful patron, had contrived a way for one of her daughters to be 'seen or known' by, or to be near to her mistress, promising to 'receive her and lay her in her chamber, or else with young Mrs. Norris',[16] and to 'bring her with her into the Queen's chamber every day'. 'Madam, your ladyship is not a little beholding unto this gentlewoman,' wrote Husee, in recognition of the young Margery's labour in the suit.[17] Within a year, Husee was able to assure Lady Lisle that her patrons in the household promised that one of her daughters 'shall be immediately preferred unto the Queen's service at the next vacant, which is thought shall be shortly'.[18] The opportunity to advance this suit would arise when Eleanor, Countess of Rutland, and Mary, Countess of Sussex learned that the queen, who was heavily pregnant, was craving quails. Of this they promptly informed Husee, before receiving and conveying a delivery of two dozen quails to the queen on 9 May 1537.[19] Her ladies, seeing that the queen was unsatisfied with them, then warned the agent to inform Lady Lisle, rather bluntly, that 'those that your ladyship shall hereafter send, let them be very fat, or else they are not worth thanks'.[20] Two months, and presumably, many quails later, 'the Queen at dinner, while eating the quails,' her agent reported, 'spoke of your ladyship and your daughters before my lady Rutland and my lady Sussex'.[21] 'Such communication was uttered by the said ij ladies', it was observed.[22] 'The matter is thus arranged that you shall send them both over', reported Husee, 'that her Grace may see them herself, and take which she pleases'.[23]

In this suit 'for her preferment', the queen's servants, in the words of Husee, provided 'counsel'.[24] By 'counsel', Husee meant that they, as her servants, were in a position to know and advise Lady Lisle in the process on how she might ensure a successful outcome to her suit. Later Elizabeth I's gentlewomen would fulfil the same role by advising courtiers and councillors when to broach their business with the queen. As Robert Beale, clerk of the Privy Council, urged the principal secretary in 1592: 'Learne, before your accesse, her majestie's disposicon by some in the privie chamber with whom you must keepe creditt, for that will stande you in much steede'.[25] There can be no doubt that servants of a queen consort fulfilled the same function, acting as a channel to their royal mistress. Jane Seymour's servants too would have known when the queen was in good humour, and how and when she might be approached or solicited for favour. And thus they facilitated the process by which one of Lady Lisle's daughters would be appointed by giving Husee explicit instructions as to 'the Queen's pleasure': both Anne and Katharine 'must be sent over about vj weeks hence';[26] that they should arrive 'before the Queen takes her chamber, because her Grace would see them before then';[27] that 'the Queen will be at no more cost with her but wages and livery';[28] that the queen had to know their 'manners, fashions and conditions';[29] that they had to be 'apparelled according to their degrees' with 'ij honest changes they must have, the one of satin, the other of damask, and that whichever of her daughters would be appointed 'must have a servant to wait on her and the Queen will give her but 10*l.* a year'.[30] By 17 September, Anne Basset 'was sworn the Queen's maid'.[31]

Like many others, Lady Lisle was anxious to remain in the queen's favour. The queen's servants, knowing her disposition or state of mind, could assure their client of her position: 'I promise you, madame,' George Taylor, Anne Boleyn's receiver-general, wrote to Lady Lisle in the summer of 1532, 'as far as I can perceive, she favours you very well, and I trust it shall always continue more and more'.[32] A few years later, Husee reiterated that 'all your ladyship's friends in the Court are merry and commendeth them heartily unto your ladyship'. 'It hath been shewed me by one or ij of the Queen's servants', he wrote, 'that her Grace hath spoken of your Ladyship divers times since departing from Dover'.[33] Richard Dauncy, the queen's gentleman usher, later assured Lady Lisle in a letter on 22 July 1537 that Jane would show her the same goodwill as did Anne. 'Ye thought the Queen's grace did not favour you', Dauncy wrote, 'I ensure you Madam it is not so for I have heard her Grace speak of you, and wish for you divers times since your departing'.[34] By their privileged access, the queen's servants were apt to gather, facilitate and 'broker' information to which they alone were privy. Husee clearly had a back-and-forth with servants in the queen's household, as is reflected further in his close reports on the progress of Jane's pregnancy: on 9 May 1537, 'it is said the Queen is with child 20 weeks gone. God send her a prince'[35]; on 23 May, 'the Queen is great with child, and will be open-laced with stomacher between this and Corpus Christi Day'[36]; the queen was 'in good health and merry' on 10 June[37]; and further that 'the Queen takes her chamber in 20 days' on 1 September.[38] The queen's servants were often central to a system of communications – networks – which ran through the wider court, and by which all manner of messages, letters, petitions and suits, rumours and gossip were transmitted.[39] The most politically astute of these servants kept their eyes and their ears open at all times for information which was potentially useful or relevant, either to them, the queen or their clientele at court.[40]

In all, these politics might be thought to be fairly inconsequential, but in the view of the wider court, particularly when an aging and ill king was increasingly impatient and inaccessible, queens and their servants could be vital in matters highly personal, political, and even religious. On 26 October 1536, Christopher Askew, gentlemen usher to the king, was examined by his 'moste honorable counsaill'.[41] Some three weeks earlier, Askew had been sent by Cromwell to Lincolnshire to gather intelligence on a popular uprising against the dissolution of the monasteries.[42] On his journey, Askew was urged by the abbess of the Benedictine nunnery of Clementhorpe in York to move the queen, Jane Seymour, to prevent its dissolution, promising him £30 'for his labor if the mater were brought to'.[43] Jane was known to be strictly orthodox, and there is evidence that the queen was committed to monasticism.[44] Thus the abbess of Clementhorpe had Christopher Askew act as a go-between to solicit the queen for her protection. In this Askew could not go immediately to the queen; he had to go through her servants at her 'outward' chambers, and rely on them to move the request on his behalf. This the abbess must have known, as the insurgents in Yorkshire, working alongside her, urged Askew to bring the matter to 'the Quenes counsaill' and 'bade hym offer... money to theym'. On 25 October, Askew travelled to Windsor Castle and arrived at the queen's chambers. This was the occasion on which Askew was examined by the king's council. A transcript of Askew's testimony survives, though the document is mutilated. On 26 October, Askew told the council how he had went the day before 'into the Quenes chamber within the Castell of Wyndesore, and there mett with' Sir Edmund Bedingfield, the queen's chancellor, and William Paget, her secretary, and 'shewed vnto theym' the matter of Clementhorpe. He told them that the abbess would give 300 marks to the queen, which 'she may yet have if ye think... mete for her grace to take them'. When Askew advised how the insurgents might convey the 300 marks safely from York, assuring them of their bribe, the queen's servants 'p[ro]missed to move the Quenes g[ra]ce'. Askew told 'the same tale... after to Margerie Horsman, the Quenes gentlewoman', who 'asked of hym what co[mmuni]cation he had with the Quenes counsaill'.[45]

An intensely personal faith shared by queens and their servants could attract the attention of the wider court and kingdom. After the Pilgrimage of Grace, Jane Seymour was solicited by Sir Robert Constable, one of the leading Yorkshire rebels, to move the king for his pardon. Constable wrote to his son, Marmaduke, begging him 'to entreat my lord of rutland', Thomas Manners, Earl of Rutland, the queen's lord chamberlain, 'to be meane vnto the queyn hir grace of petye to sew vnto the kynge his majesty to p[ar]don me my lyff w[i]th as as poor a lyvyng as may be to thentent that may all my lyff tym lament myne offencis'. The rebel trusted that the queen's lord chamberlain would, like Jane, be sympathetic to his cause and move the matter. In this he was quite clear: 'yf he canne get my lord of rutland and hym both to labor vnto hir grace than... al shalbe well'. 'I entend to lyve by god's grace who levyth noe good deid unrewardid', 'if ye offer a some of money', Constable added, 'ye shalbe no losser'.[46]

It is unknown if the queen or her servants intervened or attempted to intervene, but the Benedictine nunnery of Clementhorpe in York was dissolved in 1536, and Sir Robert Constable was executed for treason in 1537. Discerning and determining the nature – and relative success, or failure – of these interactions is crucial in establishing what necessarily, or potentially, lay within the jurisdiction of queens as consorts (and thus, by extension, what lay in the jurisdiction of their servants). 'At the beginning of the insurrection', Jane, profoundly upset, apparently 'threw herself on her knees before the King and begged him to restore the abbeys, but he told her, prudently enough, to get up', warning her 'not to meddle with his affairs'.[47] The matter would be quite different when it was the king who wished to meddle in his queens' affairs.

By surveying the *Lisle Letters* and other documents from 1536 to 1537, the period of Jane Seymour's brief tenure as queen, it would at first appear that Jane, Lady Rochford, lacked the influence of her fellows in the new queen's household. Her name appears only once or twice, whereas Eleanor, Countess of Rutland, and Mary, Countess of Arundell, both recur frequently throughout the correspondence. Margery Horsman too appears to have been a favourite of the queen. The limitations of this evidence are obvious; Jane did receive the gift of a gold tablet from the new queen, but it is not difficult to conceive of how or why Jane Seymour might have been wary of a Boleyn in her ranks. As we shall see, if Lady Rochford lacked influence in the queen's household, this does not necessarily mean that she was not influential at court. Perhaps it was the Lisles who lacked Jane's favour, as there is some evidence to suggest that Jane acted as a patron for others. Certainly Cromwell saw her as a useful agent, so much so that he would ensure her appointment to serve not only Jane Seymour, but her successor too.

18

'...sume of your speciall frendes nygh aboute the kynges highnes'
PATRON

The queen's household was, once again, discharged, when Jane Seymour died on 24 October 1537.[1] 'All the ladies and gentlewomen' who were in attendance at her funeral 'knelt about the hearse during mass afore noon', struck with grief, before all of the late queen's servants was disbanded.[2] It is difficult to measure the impact of this on their lives, as they often disappear from the record. Some would have retired to their estates, whereas others struggled to find preferment. Anne Basset, Jane's maid-of-honour, was sent to stay with her kinswoman and one of the queen's ladies, Mary Arundell, Countess of Sussex: 'I perceive my lord and you have taken my daughter Anne', Lady Lisle wrote to the Countess on 14 November, 'until, by your good suit, she may obtain place again'.[3] During these years when there was no queen, Jane, Lady Rochford, probably lived in Grimston, or, by 1539, once she had acquired it, Blickling, in Norfolk (an inventory of her belongings taken in 1542 indicates that she left considerable property there). Either of these two manors are likely to be where she went whenever she was not in attendance at court.[4]

Deconstructing the queen's household, and, again, breaking down its composition, reveals that the period from 1527 to 1547 was, for its servants, characterised by instability. On no less than five occasions, the queen's household had to be discharged, its servants disbanded, and many of their careers cut short. When the household was reshuffled between queens, a patron, or lack thereof, could be decisive in determining who kept their office, and who did not. John Croft, who served his cousin, Jane Seymour, struggled to find a foothold at court for many years after her death in 1537. Sir Wymond Carew, the late queen's receiver-general, wrote on Croft's behalf to Anthony Denny and John Gates, of the king's Privy Chamber, so that he might be appointed as a gentleman waiter to Prince Edward, Jane's son, 'even without wages'. 'I am bound to do for this gentleman, Mr. Croft, all I can', Carew began, before reminding them that Croft had served Jane 'honestly', and the queen 'did favour him well'.[5] When their mistress was divorced, beheaded, or if she died in the midst of their service, many such servants lost their claim to office. Yet the households of Henry's queens ran almost consecutively. This meant that there was an opportunity for the queen's servants to retain their offices and secure their position by transitioning between households. Unlike Croft, Anne Basset was, by the king, 'promised she shall have her place whensoever the time shall come'.[6] 'I trust we shall have a mistress shortly', Anne wrote to her mother at the end of 1539, anticipating the arrival of Anne of Cleves, Henry's fourth wife.[7]

Servants who kept in the king's favour were strategically well-placed to find preferment not if, but when, he remarried. There was no queen to attend upon, nor was there a household in which to serve in the intervening period, yet surviving accounts which were kept by Sir Wymond Carew, Anne's receiver-general, begin with a list of wages 'payde at Mydsomer quarter In the xxxi[th] yere of the Reigne of our Soverayne Lorde Kyng Henry theyght' (24 June 1539, more than six months prior to Anne's arrival in England), indicating that, after her death, Henry retained some of Jane Seymour's household,[8] and kept them at court. At a banquet held at Westminster by the king on 19 November 1538, for instance, many of the late queen's servants 'lay all night in Court and had banquets in their chambers, and the King's servants to wait upon them,' and reportedly, 'did not take leave till four o'clock after dinner next day'.[9] The most politically astute of the queen's servants kept up their familiarity with the king by exchanging gifts and sending correspondence.[10] On 4 August 1539, shortly after visiting Henry's fleet of ships at Portsmouth, the late queen's ladies and gentlewomen servants wrote a letter to the king to express their awe, wonder and gratitude. The letter is so unsubtle in its purpose that it is worth quoting at length:

> Most gratiouse and benigne sovraigne Lorde, please it your Highnes to understonde that wee have seene and beene in your newe Greate

Shippe,[11] and the rest of your shippes at Portismowth, wiche arr things so goodlie to beeholde, that, in our liefs wee have not seene (excepting your royall person and my lord the Prince your sonne) a more pleasaunt sight; for wiche, and the most bountiful gifts, the chere and most gratiouse enterteignment, wich your Grace hath vouchsavid to bestowe upon us your most unworthie and humble servaunts and bedewomen.[12]

It was outright flattery of this nature that appealed to Henry's own sense of majesty and self-image, assuring that he would remember them.

At the end of 1539, Cromwell, who engineered the king's fourth marriage, personally administered the new queen's household, and had control over its appointments. On 8 October, Anthony Denny, for instance, wrote to Cromwell, advising that the king intended for Susan, 'late mystres parker now mystres Gylmyn', to serve his new queen, 'to have hyr in hyr chamber'. 'The pouertie of the woman wyllyd me to geve you knowledge of hys plesure,' Denny noted, 'that he thought yt mete to sett hyr for the as ap[er]teynyth to suche a oon'.[13] The household of Anne of Cleves was prepared in advance of her arrival in England. She began her journey on 26 November 1539, setting off from Düsseldorf to Cleves, and thereafter to Calais, before travelling by sea to Dover, where the Englishmen and women appointed to serve in her household were gathered, waiting anxiously to receive and welcome their new queen.[14] When Anne arrived in Calais on her journey to Dover, the appearance of the German maids in her retinue of over 300 caused quite a stir. 'She brings from her brother's country 12 or 15 damsels', reported Charles de Marillac, the French ambassador, 'inferior in beauty even to their mistress and dressed so heavily and unbecomingly that they would almost be thought ugly even if they were beautiful'.[15] Henry intervened and ordered that arrangements be made for the 'strange maidens' to return to Cleves. The king may have been concerned with the potential cost or financial strain of subsidising them, or perhaps he suspected these 'strangers' could, as they often did, exercise undue influence on his new bride, or even act as spies for their homeland. Most of the gentlemen and women identified by Nicholas Wotton in December 1539 as those who 'came with the Queen's grace to England', and who intended 'to continue with her', were promptly sent back.[16]

Henry VIII's marital instability created an ever-shifting 'inner circle' in the queen's household. Eleanor, Countess of Rutland, was an intimate of Jane Seymour, and as such was able to facilitate the preferment of Anne Basset to be her maid-of-honour. But a few years later, when Eleanor, now in the service of Anne of Cleves, was solicited again, on this occasion to advance Lady Lisle's younger daughter, Katharine, the Countess, regrettably, could not move the suit. She wrote to Lady Lisle on 17 February 1540, after receiving 'a pipe of Gascon wine and two barrels of herring' to 'move her Grace in that behalf', to advise her then to 'make some means unto Mother Lowe, who can do as much good in this matter as any one woman here, that she may make some means to get your said daughter with the Queen's said Grace'. The Countess reiterated this to the young Katharine herself. 'For my Ladye of Rutland sayth, that Mother Lowe, the Mother of the Dowche Maydes, maye do muche for my Preferment to the Queen's Highness,' Katharine wrote to her mother, 'so that your Ladyship wold sende her my good Token, that she myght the better remember me'. The Countess knew well that Mother Lowe, one of her native-born servants who had known the queen for much longer, and was in her confidence, would be better fit for the purpose.[17]

The queen's servants were reluctant to advance suits without the king's knowledge or approval. The Countess did not want to approach the king for the appointment of Katharine Basset, as she knew Henry wished 'that no more maids shall be taken in'.[18] When Anne Basset approached the king on behalf of her mother, Lady Lisle, to find preferment for her sister, Katharine, she found that 'divers other hath spoken to his Grace for their friends', but that the king 'sayd a wolde nott grant me nor them as yte', and that 'hys grase sayd that a wollde have them that showlde be fayre and as he thoght me[e]tt for the rome'.[19] Like the queen's servants, the king's servants too were inundated with petitions for preferment to the new queen's household. When Lord Lisle petitioned Cromwell in 1539 to be appointed as lord chamberlain to the queen, he was informed by his agent, Husee, that 'no suit will profit in that behalf', as Cromwell admitted that it 'lay in the King's disposition and not in his'.[20] The office of lord chamberlain to the queen was apparently far too important, and lay outside of even Cromwell's jurisdiction.

It is not difficult to conceive of when or where Jane, as one of the queen's attendants, might have interacted with the king. Henry treated his queens' chambers as an extension of his own. Unlike the king's chambers, however, wherein Henry often transacted affairs of state, his queens' chambers were a place of comfort, for the king to relax and take solace. This distinction is reflected in the arrangement and architectural layout of many royal palaces, in which there was to be a 'large passage' between the king and the queen's chambers.[21] Wherein the 'outward' chambers of a queen were a stage for court ceremonial, her 'inward' chambers were 'less permeable than those of the king', with greater seclusion, and often, and almost without exception, more 'isolated from public buildings and from ceremonial routes'.[22] In preparing the king's and queen's lodgings, John Norris, Henry's gentleman usher, wrote that 'where the kinge and the Quene be in one house the kinges pleasure is that the Quene shall have the ffayreste and the largest romes for the kinge woll alwaie resorte unto the Quenes Chamber for his comfort pastime solas and disporte'.[23] The king frequently dined in his queens' chambers, and if a queen met, dined or slept with the king in his own chambers, her servants would often accompany her there.[24]

As their sovereign, the king demanded due respect and overt displays of subservience and humility from the servants in the households of his queens. Yet Henry, as a monarch, could also be affable, friendly, cheerful and gracious in his manner,[25] more accessible, and in his demeanour more approachable, particularly in the relaxed atmosphere of his queens' chambers. Of all his queens' servants, it was clearly their ladies and gentlewomen in whose company the king was known to take the most pleasure in, affording them unprecedented access to their sovereign. When 'the kyng was yong and lusty, disposed all to myrthe and pleasure', he was known to be 'more given to matters of dancing and of ladies' than his predecessors.[26] At a banquet held in the queen's chambers on 24 February 1533, 'the King was so much engaged in play and conversation with the ladies that he scarcely talked to the rest of the company'. Henry was reportedly 'so much occupied with mirth and talk that he said little which could be understood'![27] When the king received Chapuys in the queen's Presence chamber in 1536, the Imperial ambassador observed that, while he was congratulating Jane Seymour on her marriage, the king busied himself 'talking to the other ladies'.[28] Even as late as 1546, a year prior to his death, though his health was deteriorating quickly, Henry was 'still inclined to pay his court to ladies',[29] and continued in 'banqueting and huntinge, and rich maskes everie night with the Queene and ladies'.[30]

Knowing that Henry retained ultimate authority as sovereign, the queen's servants often circumvented the queen and appealed directly to the king in their pursuit of preferment. It was observed that the king might be more receptive to female petitioners: 'be not idle', Sir Thomas Wyatt urged and advised gentlemen at court, 'thy niece, thy cousin, thy sister or thy daughter, if she be fair, if handsome by her middle, if thy better hath her love besought her, advance his cause, and he shall help thy need'.[31] Politics in the queen's chambers mirrored politics in the king's chambers; indeed, they were the same, they were 'court politics'. This often represented a marked deviation in reality from the formal, or the institutional. The Eltham ordinances of 1526 stated that no servant shall attempt to 'advance himself further', 'nor presse his Grace in makeing of sutes, nor intermeddling of causes or matters, whatsoever they be'.[32] That the queen's servants did approach him, and often, is clear, so much so that the king's Privy council in 1540 had to reiterate and command 'the Vicechambrelains of the King's and Quenes syde w[ith] diverse other gent[lemen of] the King's and the Quenes s[e]rvants... from hensforth in no wise molest his personne w[ith] any maner [or] sute'.[33]

In his later years, Henry had to be approached cautiously. Shortly after Anne Basset was appointed to serve in the queen's household, her mother began advising her closely on how to remain in Henry's good graces. 'I have declaryd vnto the kynges highenis all thynges, as your ladeship wyllyed me to dow,' Anne wrote to her on 22 December 1539, acknowledging and expressing her gratitude 'for the good and motherly counsell your ladiship dothe gyve me, concernyng my contynuans in the kyngs ffavor'.[34] The king could also be ruthlessly cynical, suspicious, and fickle in his favour. Servants of the queen may have been wary of interaction with Henry for fear of incurring the king's wrath. This became worse still when his health deteriorated, and a 'humour' had fallen upon his leg, leaving it swollen, causing him so much pain that he became irritable and often cruel.[35] Certainly Anne Basset had shown herself reluctant to approach him on account of his ill-temper. 'Ffor I knowlyge myselff most bounde to his Highenes of all creatures', Anne wrote to her mother, 'if I shold, therfor, in anny thing offende his Grace willingly, yt were pitte I sholde lyve.'[36] Lady Lisle sent to her various gifts and tokens for her to convey to the capricious king: 'Madam, the kyng dothe sowell lyke the conserves you sent hym last,' Anne observed, 'that his grace comandyd me to wrytte vnto you for more of the codynack of the clerest makyng, and of the conserve of damessyns, and this assone as may be'.[37] Anne wrote again to her mother on 19 February 1540 to inform her that she had received and presented the cognac to the king, and that 'hys grace douse lyke hyt wondyrse well'. When the king 'had tastyd' his cognac in her presence, Anne was urged to 'move hys grace for to send you some tokyn of rememrans'.[38] 'And whereas you do wrytte to me that I showlde remembyr my syster', Katharine, for her preferment to the queen's household, Anne assured her mother, 'I have spokyn to the kyngs hyghenes for her'.[39]

The king received petitions and granted requests from the queen's servants in all manner of suits, demonstrating their potential to engage in the wider network of patronage and clientelism. In 1522, Henry granted a pardon to, and restored all the 'forfeited goods, chattels and lands' of Gawin Lancaster, 'on the supplication' of Maud Parr, who was serving in the household of Catherine of Aragon.[40] When Thomas Cranmer, Archbishop of Canterbury, in 1534 sought to move the suit of one of his servants, he wrote, not, to the king himself, but to Agnes Howard, Dowager Duchess of Norfolk, lady-in-waiting to Anne Boleyn, asking her explicitly to 'cause sume of your speciall frendes nygh aboute the kynges highnes' for his preferment'.[41]

Service in the queen's household provided an opportunity to build one's own prestige, reputation, and standing with the crown, which in itself drew in clientele from the wider court and kingdom. Jane, Lady Rochford, as one of the queen's servants, could be solicited to act as a patron on account of her relationship with not only the queen, but the king and his courtiers and councillors too. In 1536, William Forster, a cleric and scholar, described Jane as a 'most special patroness of my stody'. He regarded her too as a potential patron in his suit with Cromwell for the advowson of an ecclesiastical benefice in

Swaffham, Norfolk. In a letter to Cromwell, Forster acknowledged and expressed his gratitude for the secretary's 'gret favoors and singuler goodnes' in the matter, which was first moved by 'my laydy of Rechforthe', who Forster noted had 'traveled to yow for me'.[42] Clearly Jane had already petitioned Cromwell on his behalf; that Jane was being petitioned at all for her favour suggests that her relationship with Cromwell was perceptible, and seen as something to exploit. Unfortunately, the surviving source material is so fragmentary that we cannot determine the success of the suit, or discern how frequently Jane herself was petitioned or solicited as a patron.

19

'Those with the queen are guards and spies, not servants'
SPY

Why did Thomas Cromwell ensure Jane's appointment to the queen's household? Was it simply in recognition of her role in the fall of her husband and sister-in-law in 1536, or did the king's secretary have more to gain? In her letter to Cromwell, Jane curiously remarked

> God schall be to youe therfore a sure reward, whyche dothe promes good to them that dothe helpe powere forsaken Wydos. And bothe my prayer and servys schall helpe to thys duryng my naturall lyff, as most bounden so to doo, God my wyttnes; whoo ever more preserve you.[1]

It has been suggested that, in the 1530s and 1540s, Jane acted on Cromwell's behalf as his spy in the queen's household and the wider court.[2] Although there is no actual evidence to prove this, it is less absurd than it may at first seem. Households were politicised by their intimacy. Whereas politics within the household were characterised by trust, integrity and loyalty to their mistress, politics *at court* were characterised by pride, envy, flattery, lust, avarice, intrigue and corruption. 'It is hard trusting this wyllye worlde', one man sighed, '...every man here is ffor himsylff'.[3] Self-interest and profit-seeking was well-documented by the king's servants. Sir Anthony Denny, some time in 1548, regarded the court as 'a place so slipperie ...where ye shall many tymes repe most unkyndnesse where ye have sown greatest pleasurs, and those also readye to do yow moch hurt, to whom yow never intended to think any harme'.[4] Thomas More remarked that it was 'hard for any person eyther man or woman, in great worldly welth & rich prosperitie, so to withstand the suggestions of the devill and occasions given by the world, that they kepe them selfe from the desier of ambiciouse glorye'.[5] Sir Edward Neville uttered that 'the King keepeth a court of knaves here that we [dare no]ther loke nor speak, and I were able to live I wolde rather [live any] lyfe in the world than tary in the pryvye Chamber'.[6] Integrated fully with the wider court, the queen's servants were not invulnerable to these tensions, and it is not difficult to conceive of how dangerous the most trusted and intimate of these servants could be when it became in their interests to make the personal, political.

Servants in the queen's Chamber and Privy Chamber could act as agents, or *double* agents, for the king, his courtiers, councillors, even ambassadors. When Henry began seeking an annulment from his marriage to Catherine of Aragon in 1527, Cardinal Wolsey was meticulous in his efforts to secure for Henry what he desired. The king's 'Great Matter' was to be conducted and kept in utmost secrecy, and for this purpose, Wolsey intended to prevent the queen from communicating with her nephew, Emperor Charles V, 'so all objection which might be urged by the Queen might be avoided'.[7] But when the matter 'reached the ears of the Queen', Catherine immediately dispatched Francis Phillip, her sewer, to the Emperor.[8] It is apparent from Wolsey's letters that Catherine conspired with her sewer to communicate secretly with her nephew. Phillip requested a license to visit Spain to see his mother, who was apparently 'verai sore syke'. To avoid suspicion, Catherine feigned her disapproval and 'refused to assent unto his goyng', and even 'laboured unto the Kinges Highnesse to empeshe the same'. Henry, however, 'knowyng grete colusion and dyssymulation betwene theym', came to suspect that 'the Queene is thoonly cawse of this mannys goyng into Spaigne'.[9] The king and Wolsey thus attempted to 'turn' Phillip, with a view of manipulating and exploiting him as an agent on their side. In the summer of 1527, granting Phillip his license to visit Spain, Henry arranged for the queen's sewer to 'be taken by ennymyse' on his journey through France, so that the king might then 'pay his rawnesome' and bring him 'in more ferme confidence'.[10] A few days later, these orders were made more explicit: Henry wanted Phillip 'secretly to be stopped and molested in some part of France, that he may not reach Spain'. The king intended to stage his arrest so that he might gain his trust. Henry was also quite clear 'that it be not in anywise known that the said let, arrest, or deprehension' of Phillip came by his own hand.[11] Phillip, Henry acknowledged, 'hath bene allways prive unto the Quene's affaires and secretes'; it was clearly felt by the king to be to his advantage to have him on side. It appears, however, that Phillip's allegiance could not be won, as a few years later he too had to be discharged from Catherine's service. As Chapuys observed, it was 'very strange that out of four Spanish servants whom she had they should take away her maître de salle', as Phillip 'had followed her from Spain and had now nothing to live on'.[12]

But not all of the queen's servants were as loyal as Phillip. In 1528, Wolsey met with the queen's almoner, Robert Shorton, who had previously served in the cardinal's Chapel, and asked him 'to let him know what were the Queen's intention and purpose in this matter', urging him 'to keep their communication secret'. In this Wolsey 'adjured him, on his fidelity', reminding him of 'his obligation to be true and faithful' not to the queen, his mistress, but to Henry. He even invoked and reminded Shorton of the preferment he had enjoyed at the hands of the king.[13] The almoner was reluctant,[14] but 'protesting his devotion', duly informed Wolsey of all he had heard in the queen's chambers. The cardinal 'marvelled not a little at her indiscreet and ungodly purposes and sayings, which caused him to conceive that she was neither of such perfection nor virtue as he had once thought her to be'.[15]

William Tyndale accused Wolsey of having 'gathered unto himself the most subtlewitted' of the queen's servants who were 'fit for his purpose', and 'made her sworn to betray the Queen, and tell him what she said or did'.[16] These servants were apparently susceptible to the cardinal's influence, and could be bribed with gifts, financial rewards or other inducements: 'whosoever of them was great, with her he was familiar, and gave her gifts... by these spies, if ought were done, or spoken in Court against the Cardinal,' Tyndale observed, 'of that he had word within an hour or two'.[17]

Tyndale's accusation alone does not substantiate a network of spies in the queen's household. He was an enemy of the cardinal and opposed to the king's Great Matter.[18] The difficulty with proving the existence of a spy network is obvious, seeing as its existence should not have been known in a public forum like the court, and Wolsey would have been too careful, shrewd or untrusting to mention it in his own correspondence. Yet it must be remembered that Wolsey was criticised for manipulating the structure and makeup of personnel in the English royal household to his advantage. In a satirical pamphlet written in 1529, John Palsgrave wrote that the cardinal 'put about the Kyng *and Quene*' men and women 'such as wol[d] never [be] contra[r]ye' to him, and of having 'weryeed and put away... all syche officers and counseillours as would do or try any thing frely'.[19] Similarly, Tyndale remarked that one of the queen's servants was known to have 'departed Court for no other cause, but for that she would no longer betray her mistress', indicating that Wolsey had the authority to dismiss them.[20] On at least one occasion, six servants on 'the quenes syde' were 'put out of there Rowmes', and their offices redistributed, under Wolsey's administration.[21] Tyndale too observed that the cardinal, with the king's men (and the queen's women 'in like manner'), would prefer and advance those who had sworn to be faithful to him before admitting them to royal service.[22] It is clear too that Wolsey often liaised with the queen's servants. In 1518, the cardinal was informed by Richard Pace that 'the quenes servants have made vnto her grace' a 'goodde reaporte' for the 'favour shewn... for here sake, vnto them in all there causis'.[23] Taken together, the evidence amounts to more than mere suspicion. Wolsey was powerful, but he did not have immediate access to the queen's chambers. The queen's servants, however, did have access, and thus, to consolidate his hold on the court and its politics, the cardinal solicited them to act as his agents.

Conceptually, what the Wolseyian spy network illustrates is how conflicting allegiances, or interests, could destabilise the relationship between mistress and servant. The stability of this relationship rested on the obligations of both queens and their servants being met. But queens could not always match the king's individual magnetism, presence and authority, nor could they rival his ability to bind, or oblige, servants, and their loyalty, by rewarding and advancing them. Service 'did not displace' the interests of the servant, but rather 'coexisted with them, and it was able to do so because service largely entailed obedience to *specific* commands'.[24] All servants had their own interests, obscured or altogether concealed by the 'performance' of service. Such interests more often coexisted and were aligned in harmony with the interests of their master, or mistress. If, or when, that loyalty was in doubt, however, when the interests of the queen and the king, or, perhaps, more accurately, the queen and her servant, did not align, when servants had a choice, it politicised them, destabilising the relationship between mistress and servant, and the 'functioning' queen's household.

This is reflected in anxieties concerning the potential 'doubleness' of servants. Henry himself was suspicious, even paranoid, urging Wolsey in 1519 to 'make good wache on the duke of Suffolke, on the duke of Bukyngham, on my lord off Northecomberland, on my lord off Darby, on my lord off Wylshere and on others whyche yow thynke suspecte'.[25] A decade later, Thomas Alvard, a servant of Wolsey, who had by 1529 himself fallen out of favour, expressed this concern in a letter to Cromwell: 'My lord of Suffolke, my Lord of Rochford, maister Tuke, and Master Stevyns', Alvard reported, 'did as gently [be]have theymselfs, with as moche observaunce and humy[lyte to] my Lords Grace', Wolsey, 'as ever I saw theym do at any [time] tofor'. 'What they bere in ther harts,' he warned, cautiously, 'I knowe n[ot]'.[26] The French ambassador Charles de Marillac remarked in 1540 that 'the ministers seek only to undo each other to gain credit; and under colour of their master's good, each attends his own. For all the fine words of which they are full, they will act only as necessity and interest compel them'.[27] Nor were the women at court altruistic in their motivations, as they too operated on self-interest. Christine de Pizan warned that women in the service of a queen 'may well curtsy respectfully to her, with one knee touching the ground, and make deep bows and flatter her', even 'agree with and support her', and yet 'laugh at her and talk about her behind her back', and 'betray the one to whom they are outwardly pleasant and obedient'.[28] Rarely would servants publicly oppose, criticise or betray their mistress, and their performance of routine duties, tasks and functions might conceal their duplicity or inauthenticity. On 4 February 1529, the ambassador Inigo de Mendoza, in a letter to Charles V, suggested that the queen should protest a tribunal investigating the legitimacy of her marriage to the king, but then acknowledged that such a task would only be done 'with great difficulty', fearing that 'the Queen is surrounded by spies in her own chamber'.[29] A few years later, Montfalconet, Charles' envoy, reported that Catherine was 'surrounded by vile persons devoted to the king'.[30] The fact that Catherine would be forced to contrive a way of communicating with ambassadors, cloak-and-dagger, indicates that 'those with the Queen' were indeed 'guards and spies, not servants'.[31]

Evidently Catherine was surrounded, as is testified by Chapuys, who acknowledged in his correspondence that he found it difficult to communicate with her. Chapuys reported in 1534 that he was restricted from visiting Catherine at Kimbolton. Her lord chamberlain and steward had been explicitly instructed by the king not to let the ambassador see or speak with her.[32] Fortunately, Chapuys had his own informants with the Princess Dowager, one of whom urged the ambassador and his party to visit outside of the castle, which they did, to the 'great pleasure' and 'consolation' of Catherine and her ladies, 'who spoke to them from the battlements and windows'.[33] In 1535, Chapuys received a letter from Catherine's physician, who felt that she was in grave danger, having learned that the king intended to 'propose the oath to our mistress, and if she will not take it she will be put in perpetual prison or beheaded'.[34] Chapuys visited Catherine at Kimbolton again in 1536, and reported on 9 January that the king had sent a man (described by Chapuys as 'a friend of Cromwell's') to 'spy and note all that was said and done'. Notwithstanding the king's orders, Chapuys was left alone with Catherine and her physician for 'nearly an hour'. Sir Edmund Bedingfield, Catherine's steward, inquired as to the nature of their meetings, but regrettably, 'no one was present except the persons mentioned and her old trusty women'. 'If the matters were of importance', Bedingfield wrote to Cromwell, 'we should get... knowledge by them'.[35] Thereafter Chapuys was informed by 'one of her chamber' that she had slept better, and her physician told him that he was in 'good hope of her health'. The ambassador was assured that 'if any new danger arose, he would inform me with all diligence'.[36]

Outwardly, the queen's servants would have been loyal, necessarily concealing their innermost convictions, and any competing claims on their allegiance. In 1540, when the king obliged Sir Wymond Carew, Anne of Cleves' receiver-general, to intercept the letters addressed to and received from her brother, William, Carew was to read them and report back to the king, which he did. Carew was instructed by the Duke of Suffolk to spy on his mistress, but when Anne learned of this, she became, in the words of Carew, 'bent with her women to do me dyssplesure'.[37] She began to mistrust him, 'for as I suppose she hath had knowlige how I procured... suche letters as was sent to her', Carew reported. He must have felt that he had lost any trust or faith that Anne had in him, and even asked to be discharged from her service.[38]

Perhaps Jane acted as Cromwell's eyes and ears within the queen's household. Like Wolsey, he did not have the right to freely roam and access the queen's chambers, but Jane did. How else would Cromwell have known that Jane Seymour died in childbed 'by the neglect of those about her who suffered her to take cold and eat such things as her fantasy in sickness called for'?[39] It was likely Cromwell who ensured that his spy was reappointed to serve Anne of Cleves. Henry married Anne at Greenwich on 6 January 1540,[40] but 'ever since the King saw the Queen, he had never liked her', and reportedly 'often as he went to bed with her, he mistrusted the Queen's virginity'.[41] The king himself confided in Cromwell that, 'I liked her before not well, but now I like her much worse', after having 'felt her belly and breasts', Henry came to believe that she 'was no maid'.[42] Cromwell, who was responsible for arranging the match between them, resolved to approach the queen. But 'lacking opportunity' himself, Cromwell twice 'spoke with her lord Chamberlain', the Earl of Rutland, urging him 'to induce her to behave pleasantly', or, in other words, make herself more attractive to the king. Perhaps Cromwell solicited Jane too, as she would eventually tackle Anne and broach the subject of her relations with the king in her Privy Chamber.

Anne would confide in Jane, Lady Rochford, Eleanor, Countess of Rutland, and Katherine, Lady Edgecombe, of her Privy chamber, all of whom later journeyed from Richmond to Westminster on 7 July 1540, swore to and signed a deposition relating their conversation with the queen. Anne's servants maintained that the queen herself admitted to them one night the truth of the king's contention that the royal marriage had not been consummated:

> First, Al they being together, they wished her Grace with child. And she answered and said, She knew wel she was not with child. My Lady

Edgecomb said, How is it possible for your Grace to know that, and ly every night with the King? I know it wel I am not, said she. Than said my Lady Edgebomb, I think your Grace is a mayd stil. With that she laughed. And than said my Lady Rocheford, By our Lady, Madam, I think your Grace is a mayd stil, indede. How can I be a mayd, said she, and slepe every night with the King? There must be more than that, said my Lady Rocheford, or els I had as leve the King lay further. Why, said she, whan he comes to bed he kisses me, and taketh me by the hand, and byddeth me, Good night, swete hart: and in the morning kisses me, and byddeth me, Farewel, darlyng. Is not thys enough? Than said my Lady Rutland, Madam, there must be more than this, or it wil be long or we have a Duke of York, which al this realm most desireth.[43]

All this might seem like idle chatter, but their impertinent questions had wider political significance. This conversation, supporting the claim that Henry and Anne had not consummated the marriage, would secure for the king his annulment. It is almost incredible that Anne would have spoken so openly with these ladies, having met them only six months prior. Perhaps in the intimacy of her chambers, and at the mercy of the incessant, almost insolent questioning of her attendants, Anne was caught off-guard. Or perhaps not, it seems, as 'these words', the deposition records, 'she hath said to them altogethers, and to eche of theym apart divers and sondry tymes'. Should we doubt the validity of their testimony? It is possible that they might have 'conspired together to create fictitious conversations with her'?[44] Some find it extraordinary that Anne would have been so ignorant of conception and sexual intercourse as to think that merely sharing Henry's bed was enough. It has been suggested that the king's commissioners, seeking grounds for an annulment, fabricated the detail of the conversation so that it was fit for purpose – curiously, the three ladies signed one deposition, as opposed to providing their own, individual accounts. Others raise the issue of whether the conversation could have taken place at all, questioning if Anne was able to speak English clearly, as the Earl of Rutland once remarked that he could not understand her when they spoke and called upon her receiver-general, Carew, to act as an interpreter.[45] The Countess of Rutland wondered if the queen had confided in Mother Lowe, her native-born servant, but Anne was mortified by the thought, supposedly saying 'Mary, fy, fy, for shame, God forbid'.

Knowledge of the personal, and the intimate, lay in the hands of the servant, and possession of this knowledge made servants, like Jane, at once powerful, and dangerous. There is no doubt that Jane knew well the significance of her deposition for securing Henry's desired annulment. She would claim that the queen had declared to her 'how the King used her the four first nights: which was to theffect afore written', leaving no doubt as to her allegiance.

On 6 July 1540, the queen sent for the Earl of Rutland. She informed him that the king's council stated that her marriage to Henry was unlawful, and that they required her consent for an annulment: 'she called us into her chambre and dec[lare]d by the Imbassador that the Kynges highnes had sent to her a c[ertai]n message which required awnswer agayn'.[46] The marriage was declared null and void a few days later, as Anne consented and signed in the presence of Charles, Duke of Suffolk, and, to bear witness, her ladies, with Jane among them.[47] Thomas Wriothesley, of the king's council, arrived at Richmond 'to discharge the officers and servants who attended on her as Queen, and appoint and swear others to serve her as the King's sister'.[48] Anne would no longer be known as queen, but 'the Lady Anne of Cleue', and in addition would be kept 'in honourable estate', receiving a generous settlement. The king's councillors were dispatched once again a few days later 'to see her household fully established', with its size and status appropriately reduced.[49] On 12 July, the king's councillors visited her at Richmond and presented her with a settlement for the annulment. They 'went straight to the Lady Anne's chamber' to discuss 'matters of her household', reporting later that 'it seemeth she can n[ot but be conte]nt to have such as your M[ajesty by your] commandment shall app[oint her]', though she did ask on behalf of her gentlewomen servants that they should remain.[50]

Serving 'the king's sister' was not nearly as prestigious nor as advantageous as serving the king's wife. On 4 December 1541, Jane Rattsey and Katharine Basset were apprehended and examined by the king's Privy council.[51] Jane and Katharine were servants to Lady Anne, who was now residing with her household at Richmond Palace. Jane hoped that Anne might be reinstated as queen.[52] 'What if god workith this worke to make the ladie Anne off Cleves quene again?' Jane asked Katharine, who herself presumed 'that she sholde shortly se a chawnge, whiche she gatherid for that she saw the mayds room sadly downe'.[53] 'What a man is the king, how many wifys will he have?' Jane uttered, rather incautiously, to Katharine. All this Jane later maintained was no more than 'idle convercacion', yet it is clear from her deposition that she and Katharine aspired to serve in the household of a queen.

When Anne of Cleves died at Chelsea Manor in 1557, her last will and testament, dictated to, and witnessed by, her household servants, would take the form of an appeal to 'our most dearest and entirely beloved sovereign lady queen Mary', that is, Mary Tudor, Henry's daughter, now Queen of England. Her appeal began, 'beseeching her highness that our poor servants may enjoy such small gifts and grants as we have made unto them in consideration of their long service done unto us'. Anne pleaded with Mary for her favour, on behalf of her servants, invoking her father's memory. The king had appointed them, and he 'said then unto us, that he would account our servants his own, and their service done to us as if done to himself'.[54]

Henry VIII's queens came and went, yet the king was a constant. The succession of a new queen did not necessarily require an overhaul in personnel, as many of them were kept firmly in his favour. This transition became crucial, and ties to the king, or those near about him, essential, in surviving Henry's marital instability.

20

'...you wyll com whan my lade Rochforthe ys here'
BAWD

Shortly after marrying Anne of Cleves, Henry became infatuated with the young, diminutive but vivacious beauty, Katherine Howard, the queen's maid-of-honour.[1] There were rumours that the king was seen crossing the Thames to visit Katherine, and before long he began seeking an annulment.[2] Henry and Katherine were eventually married on 28 July 1540, and preparations began for the new queen's household.[3] The French ambassador Charles de Marillac later reported that one of Katherine's sisters, Margaret or Mary Howard, who was initially chosen to serve the new queen in her household, 'had been dismissed from her sister's chamber in favour of lady Rochefort'.[4] Jane's faithful patron, Cromwell, had fallen with Anne of Cleves. He was executed mere weeks after the royal marriage was annulled. Jane may thus have petitioned Katherine's uncle, Thomas Howard, Duke of Norfolk,[5] though more likely it was the king who assured her place as a holdover from the previous queen's household. 'The booke of Certayne of the Quenys Ordynary as yet to no place appoynted', probably drawn up at around the time of Katherine's accession as queen on 8 August, identified Jane as a Lady of the Privy Chamber, whereas Margaret was only to serve Katherine infrequently when she required a greater entourage for state occasions.[6] Perhaps Katherine, upon learning that the king intended to marry her, got a bit carried away and, rather prematurely, promised an appointment to her sister, and others, before the king necessarily intervened on behalf of those women who had served her predecessor and whom he had already assured of their place. Margaret was unceremoniously dumped from the queen's Privy Chamber, and replaced with Jane, a far less obvious candidate for the position. Jane must have known that she was not the new queen's first choice; Katherine would surely rather have been served in this capacity by her own sister. Jane was only distantly related to Katherine, and she was much older.

Henry's marital instability meant that, through the 1530s and 1540s, there was a revolving door of queens, each with their own personality and temperament to please. Katherine's predecessor, Anne of Cleves, was judged to be 'lowly', modest and homely, and had an amiable, relaxed temper.[7] On 22 December 1539, Lady Lisle, informed her daughter, Anne, who had been appointed to serve the new queen as one of her maids-of-honour, 'of her Grace, that she is so good and gentle to serve and please'. This reassured Basset, who herself acknowledged 'it shall be no little rejoicement to us, her Grace's servants here, that shall daily attend upon her'.[8] But the young, frivolous, often juvenile and quick-tempered Katherine was reportedly 'more imperious', 'commanding', 'troublesome', and could be 'difficult to serve'.[9] Dorothy Josselin, who appears to have been retained by Katherine as her silkwoman, remarked in 1541 that 'the Queen's work troubles me so much and yet I fear I shall scant content her grace'.[10] While Anne of Cleves was known to 'occupieth her time most with the needle', Katherine Howard 'did nothing but dance and rejoice'.[11] Unsurprisingly, her household was so unruly that, on 18 September 1540, to restore 'sobre and temperat ordyr', the Privy council had to summon Sir Edward Baynton, Katherine's vice-chamberlain, among other servants in her household, to reprimand them for their behaviour in the queen's Presence chamber, and towards the king's own servants.[12]

The opportunity for Jane to endear herself to the new queen arose when she was approached by Thomas Culpeper, gentleman of the king's Privy Chamber. Culpeper was born the son of a gentry family in Kent, and was sent to court at a young age to serve as a page. He became a royal favourite;[13] his proximity and intimate access to the king was noted by Lady Lisle, who, in 1537, had hoped to cultivate him as a patron.[14] He received a number of awards and grants 'in consideration of his true and faithful service',[15] and he may even have been protected from the rigid brutality of the law if, in 1539, he was, in fact, guilty of having 'violated the wife of a certain park-keeper in a woody thicket while… three or four of his most profligate attendants were holding her at his bidding'.[16] 'For this act of wickedness', it had been observed that Culpeper 'was, notwithstanding, pardoned by the King'.[17] Handsome, elegant, athletic, passionate and, as Cavendish recalled, somewhat arrogant and 'proud out of measure',[18] by the time Culpeper met Katherine in around 1540 he was in his mid-twenties and a man of considerable wealth and status.[19] Culpeper pursued Katherine while she 'tarried still in the maidens' chamber', but at that time, he would later recall, he had 'found so little favour at her hands' that 'he was then moved to set by others'.[20] Certainly she was charmed by him, perhaps even had already begun to have feelings of love for him. However Katherine had no choice but to spurn his advances, having already caught the eye of her sovereign, who, in contrast, was much older than her, ate and drank to excess, and suffered with an ulcerated leg. In spite of her feelings for the young gallant, Henry intended to marry her, and this, 'when she was a maiden', apparently left Katherine in such 'grief' and heartache that she 'could not but weep in the presence of her fellows'.[21]

As a lady of the queen's Privy Chamber, Jane could recommend Culpeper to her favour, which she did. Katherine later told her examiners that it was Jane who encouraged her to meet with Culpeper: 'my lady Rocheford', she claimed, '...made instans to her to speke with Culpeper declaryng hym to beare her good wyll and favour'.[22] Although at first Katherine was reluctant to renew their acquaintance, she 'did at the last graunte he shuld speke with her' when Jane 'durst swere uppon a booke he ment nothyng but honestye'.[23] This is probably how Culpeper's renewed interest in Katherine first came to her attention, with Culpeper approaching Jane, who then moved her mistress.

In April 1541, while the court was at Greenwich and some eight months after Katherine married Henry, the queen sent for Culpeper by her gentleman usher, Henry Webbe, and, in 'the entry between her Privy Chamber and the Chamber of Presence', she 'gave him by her own hands a fair cap of velvet garnished with a brooch and three dozen pairs of aglets and a chain'.[24] 'Put this under your cloak', Katherine warned him, '[and let] nobody see it!' 'Alas, Madam,' Culpeper sighed, 'why did not you this when you were a maid?'[25] His words alluded to their brief but flirtatious past, and to her gift as a token of her love for him which, now that Katherine was queen, she did not dare speak of. She was agitated, even disturbed, and took her leave. 'Is this all the thanks ye give me for the cap? If I had known ye would have spoken these words', Katherine later said angrily, 'ye should never have had it'. Exactly what reaction Katherine had intended to provoke in him is unclear. She could not have been unaware of how her actions might be taken by Culpeper, or by others misconstrued: why else did she exhort him to conceal her gift under his cloak? Culpeper's words were foolhardy, and Katherine, reminded of her station, kept her distance from him.

A few weeks later, Katherine heard that Culpeper had fallen ill. At this time, she became anxious to see or hear from him, but the queen could hardly visit him herself without arousing suspicion. She dispatched the lowly and unsuspecting Morris, her page, with food, served in her chambers or prepared especially in her kitchens, to aid his recovery.[26] Morris may be the same 'pore felowe' who she sent thereafter with a letter to Culpeper: 'on of the grefes that I do felle,' the queen wrote, 'is to departe from hym for than I do know noone that I dare truste to sende to you'. Clearly Katherine exercised caution in judging which of her servants could be trusted to undertake this sensitive, if otherwise menial task.[27] In her letter to Culpeper, Katherine would also explicitly identify Jane as someone who was in her confidence:

> Master Coulpeper, I hertely recomend me unto youe prayng you to sende me worde how that you doo. Yt was showed me that you was sike, the wyche thynge trobled me very muche tell suche tyme that I here from you prayng you to send me worde how that you do. For I never longed so muche for [a] thynge as I do to se you and to speke wyth you, the wyche I trust shal be shortely now, the wyche dothe comforthe me verie much whan I thynk of ett and wan I thynke agan that you shall departe from me agayne ytt makes my harte to dye to thynke what fortune I have that I cannot be always yn your company. Y[e]t my trust ys allway in you that you wolbe as you have promysed me and in that hope I truste upon styll, prayng you than that you wyll com whan my lade Rochforthe ys here, for then I shalbe beste at leaysoure to be at your commarendmant. Thaynkyng you for that you have promysed me to be so good unto that pore felowe my man, whyche is on of the grefes that I do felle to departe from hym for than I do know noone that I dare truste to sende to you and therfor I pray you take hym to be wyth you that I may sumtym here

from you one thynge. I pray you to gyve me a horse for my man for I hyd muche a do to gat one and thefer I pray sende me one by hym and yn so doying I am as I sade afor, and thus I take my leve of you trusting to se you s[h]orttele agane and I wode you was wythe me now that yoo maitte se what pane I take yn wryte[n]g to you.

Yours as long as lyffe endures
Katheryn

One thyng I had forgotten and that hys to instruct my man to tare here wyt[h] me still, for he sas wat so mever you bed hym he wel do et.[28]

Even a brief analysis of this document reveals that it is, unmistakeably, a love letter. Correspondence from this period often reads as detached, lacking a personal touch. The composition of letters was such that the author would surely have always been aware of how and by whom it would be read, meaning it is difficult to discern their true feelings.[29] Although this letter adheres to many traditional literary conventions of the period, its tone is strikingly heartfelt, urgent and somewhat desperate, which is to be expected given the circumstances in which it was written. Upon learning that Culpeper had fallen ill, Katherine admits that she was troubled by the news and soon became anxious to hear from him ('Yt was showed me that you was sike, the wyche thynge trobled me very muche tell suche tyme that I here from you praying you to send me worde how that you do'). She tells Culpeper that she desires to see him ('trusting to se you s[h]orttele agane'), and expresses the great comfort that it would bring her ('wyche dothe comforthe me verie much whan I thynk of ett'). Finally, Katherine solicits him to meet her in her chambers. 'Y[e]t my trust ys allway in you that you wolbe as you have promysed me and in that hope I truste upon styll,' she wrote, 'prayng you than that you wyll com when my lade Rochforthe ys here, for then I shalbe beste at leaysoure to be at your commarendmant'. Perhaps singular expressions of queen's, such as 'I hertely recomend me unto youe' and 'yours as long as lyffe endures', were purely rhetoric in line with contemporary linguistic conventions; others, such as 'ytt makes my harte to dye to thynke what fortune I have that I cannot be always yn your company', or 'I never longed so muche for [a] thynge as I do to se you and to speke wyth you' are more affectionate and were sufficiently incriminating. It is clear from her letter that she felt for him deeply.

Although Katherine's letter to Culpeper is undated, it was likely written between either 12 and 31 May or 4 and 18 June, while the court was at Greenwich, during which time we know that Culpeper had fallen ill.[30] It may be significant that in her letter Katherine explicitly instructs Culpeper to 'com whan my lade Rochforthe ys here for then I shalbe beste at leaysoure to be at your commarendmant'; surely redundant if the letter were, in fact, written during the summer progress, by which time Jane was already intimately involved. It was of utmost importance that the letter be kept confidential. If the queen was reluctant to entrust her secretary to scrawl it out, we can speculate, as it was written in two different hands, that she may have solicited Jane to write or finish it on her behalf.

Shortly thereafter Culpeper did liaise with Jane and, at that time, he recalled, 'took a cramp-ring off my Lady Rochford's finger, which, she said, was the queen's'. When Jane told Katherine, she 'took another cramp-ring off her own finger and bade the Lady Rochford carry it to Culpeper', and with it the message that 'it was an ill sight to see him wear but one cramp-ring and therefore she did send him another'.[31] It probably wasn't until the royal progress to the north in the summer of 1541 that Katherine and Culpeper took their association a step further, exchanging fairly innocuous gift-giving for clandestine trysts in her chambers.

That Katherine urged Culpeper to come when Jane was present is indicative of her intimate role as a Lady of the queen's Privy Chamber. Royal palaces were labyrinthine, often crowded, essentially public spaces. Privacy in the early-modern period was rare.[32] Like the king's Privy Chamber, the queen's Privy Chamber functioned by restricting access to, and maintaining the privacy of, it's mistress. All of the queen's Privy Chamber servants had to be circumspect and discreet. 'All such persons as be appointed of the privy chamber' were explicitly sworn to 'keeping secret all such things as shall be done or said in the same, without discloseing any parte thereof to any person not being for the time present in the said chamber'.[33]

Jane would facilitate the queen's late night rendezvous with Culpeper, not unlike Sir William Compton, Henry VIII's groom of the stool, who, from the king's accession in 1509 until Compton's death in 1528, acted as an intermediary between the king and his mistresses, often arranging and accommodating their trysts.[34] The Groom of the Stool was chief gentleman of the Privy Chamber, serving in the king's bedchamber and in 'other privey places'.[35] He slept on a pallet mattress or folding bed placed on the floor at the foot of the king's bed, and his own lodgings were adjacent to the king's chamber by a private staircase. Perhaps Jane, as a lady of the queen's Privy Chamber, fulfilled for the queen the same duties as the king's Groom of the Stool. Like Compton, Jane had her own lodgings adjacent to the queen's bedchamber by a staircase, and arranged the queen's trysts with Culpeper, even, on more than one occasion, perhaps coincidentally, in her 'close stool'![36]

When the summer progress of 1541 arrived at Lincoln, Jane 'appointed' Culpeper 'to come into a place under her Chamber being, so he thinketh, the queen's stool house'.[37] Jane and Katherine 'stood waiting at the back door for Culpeper' until 'one of the watch, having a light in his hand, came that way'. Panicked, they immediately withdrew to the queen's chambers, as the king's watch 'pulled to the door' through which Culpeper was expected to make his entrance 'and locked it, and so departed'.[38] Shortly afterwards, 'about at eleven of the clock in the night', Culpeper arrived at the stool house where he 'found the queen and the Lady Rochford and no other body'.[39] Both ladies 'marvelled [at] how he came in', and Culpeper told them he and his servant 'did pick the lock'.[40] Until 'three of the clock in the morning or thereabout', Katherine and Culpeper spoke 'of themselves and of their loves before time'. As the hours went by, they rekindled their affection for one another: 'Now she must indeed love him', Katherine declared, to which Culpeper replied that 'she had bound him both then and now and ever that he both must and did love her again above all other creatures'. Upon leaving, he took her hand and kissed it gently, 'saying he would presume no further'.[41]

Thoroughly unnerved by the incident with the king's watch, Katherine became increasingly cautious. The queen would, according to Culpeper, 'in every house seek for the back doors and back stairs herself', and often 'started away and returned again as one in fear lest somebody should come'.[42] It was at this time that Jane began accommodating Katherine and Culpeper in her own bedchamber. We know that they met on at least two more occasions before the court set off for Pontefract. Katherine Tylney, the queen's chamberer, was later examined as to 'whether she knows and deposes that the Queen went out of her chamber any nights or night whenever it was late at Lincoln and where she went and who went with her'. 'She saith,' her examiners noted, 'that she remembers at Lincoln the Queen went two nights out of her chamber when it was late to my Lady Rochford's chamber, which was up a little pair of stairs by the Queen's chamber'. On the first night, Tylney, with Margaret Morton, another of Katherine's chamberers, followed her up the stairs, 'but were sent back'. Shortly after, Morton went back up and did not return until 'about two of the clock'. 'Jesus', Tylney exclaimed, 'is the Queen not a-bed yet?'[43] On the second night, Tylney accompanied Katherine up the stairs and sat at one side outside of the bedchamber with one of Jane's own servants, and as such 'never saw who came unto the Queen and my lady Rochford, nor heard what was said between them'.[44] Still at Lincoln, one night Jane left Katherine and Culpeper 'secretly together' and slept in an adjoining room 'until the queen did call her to answer Lufkyn', i.e. Maude Lovekyn, yet another of the queen's chamberers.[45] That Jane slept in an adjoining room on occasions during their liaisons corresponds with Katherine's testimony that her lady 'wold many tymez, beyng ever by, sytt sumwhatt farre of or turn hyr bak', for which the queen would apparently reprimand her, uttering 'for Goddes sake, madam, even nere us'.

It is not surprising that the queen's chamberers were curious, as on many occasions through the summer progress, Katherine, indiscreetly, and rather incautiously, sent them to and from her confidante, Jane, with various 'secret' messages. While the court was visiting Lyddington on its way to Lincoln, Morton carried from Katherine to Jane a sealed letter without superscription, and in response from Jane to Katherine with the explicit instruction for 'her grace to keep it secret'.[46] Tylney remembered that at Grimsthorpe the queen had 'bade her go to the Lady Rochford and ask her when she should have the thing she promised her', to which Jane replied that she had 'sat up for it and she would next day bring her word herself'.[47] A similar if not identical message was later conveyed from Katherine, through Tylney, to Jane at Hampton Court. This 'thing promised' by Jane could have been jewels, money, items of clothing, food or otherwise, but the ambiguous nature and timing of her request, and the fact that Jane had 'sat up for it', indicates that the 'thing promised' was Culpeper.

Through the summer progress Katherine remained thoroughly unsettled and ever-vigilant, trapped in an interminable state of dread, fearing that her late night rendezvous with Culpeper would be detected. On one occasion the queen warned Jane, 'alas madam this wol by spyed oon day and then we be all undone', to which she replied, steadfast, 'feare not madam let me alone I warraunt yowe'.[48] At Pontefract, Katherine and Culpeper kept up their affair 'in her bedchamber', but not without some difficulty. On the first night, Jane hastily sent word to Culpeper that he should have come 'if [only] there [had] been any place that would have served'. 'The Queen feared lest the king had set a watch' at the back door to her bedchamber, 'which way he should have come'.[49] Jane had one of her own servants 'watch the door one night and the next to see if any of the watch or any other went in or out', and when it was apparent that no watch had been set, the queen gave her a note to hand to Culpeper which read, 'as ye find the door, so to come'. In the meantime, Culpeper, who it seems was unashamedly promiscuous, had publicly shown some affection for another woman, and when he arrived that night at Katherine's bedchamber, she scolded him for his philandering: 'I marvel', Katherine said, 'that ye could so much dissemble as to say ye loved me so earnestly and yet would and did so soon lie with another', namely Anne Herbert, a gentlewoman of the queen's Privy Chamber. He retorted that she 'was married afore he loved the other', and that he 'found so little favour at her hands at that time that he was rather moved to set by others'. Katherine continued to tease him: 'if I listed I could bring you into as good a trade as Bray hath my lord Parr in', that is Dorothy Bray, her maid. To this Culpeper remarked that there was 'no such woman as Bray was'. 'Well', Katherine replied, 'if I had tarried still in the maiden's chamber, I would have tried you'.[50]

This was not the first time that the queen, actuated by her own jealousy, had concerned herself with Culpeper's love life. At Lincoln, 'fond communication of... their loves before time' led to talk 'of Bess Harvey', Culpeper's former mistress. He must have mistreated Besse in some respect, thoughtlessly and indiscreetly deserting her, as Katherine even took it upon herself to send Jane to give Besse 'a damask gown', and relate to Culpeper that 'he did ill to suffer his tenement to be so ill repaired and that she for to save his honesty had done some cost of it'. In other words, Katherine was mocking them both, likening Bess to a rented building (tenement) which had been ill-maintained and abandoned by Culpeper.[51]

'Every night' at Pontefract it was observed that 'the queen being in her bedchamber having no nother with her but my Lady of Rochford, did not only lock the bedchamber door but also bolted it on the inside'. A gentleman of the king's Privy Chamber, Sir Anthony Denny, 'found it bolted himself'.[52] At Hatfield, Morton had her suspicions raised when she saw the queen 'look out of her chamber window on Mr. Culpeper after such sort that she thought there was love between them.' That night Morton and Lovekyn were prying again, and this time, when caught, having explicitly forbade their attendance in her bedchamber, the queen became 'angry' and threatened to 'put them both away', or, in other words, to dismiss them from her service.[53]

Then, at York, Katherine and Culpeper met once again 'in the lady Rochford's chamber' where the queen continued to flirtatiously tease and taunt him, remarking that 'she had store of other lovers at other doors as well as he', to which he replied in jest, 'it is like enough'.[54] While the progress took a brief excursion to Sheriff Hutton, 'the queen sent him two bracelets with this message that they were sent him to keep his arms warm', her implication being that he should not then have to keep them warm in the embrace of another woman. On another occasion at York, he 'spoke with the queen at the back stairs', where she told him 'how well she loved him'.[55]

Shortly after their meetings at Lincoln, Pontefract and York, the court returned to London, at which time Katherine, appearing to have come to her senses, attempted to end their acquaintance. Jane saw no reason why the affair should end with the summer progress, and continued to search the backstairs for herself, even scouting an 'old kechyn' at Greenwich 'wherin she myght well speke with hym'.[56] The next time Jane 'moved her for hym', Katherine told her, exasperated, 'alas madam woll this never have ende? I praye yowe, byd hym desier no more to troble me or send to me'. 'His aunswer', Katherine later told the king's council, 'was that he besought me to send hym no such word for he wold take no suche aunswer', at which time she called him her 'lytle sweete foole'. Later, Katherine warned Jane 'to troble hir no more with suche light matters', to which Jane replied, 'yet must yow gyff men leave to looke for they woll looke uppon yowe'.[57]

Clearly Katherine was hesitant, and anxious, in meeting with Culpeper. Although these clandestine meetings were conducted in her privy lodgings, her words betray a sense of vulnerability. Her fear was, and is, palpable. Katherine knew her relationship with Culpeper would 'be spyed oon day and then we be all ondone'.[58] She even warned him that 'whensoever he went to confession he should never shrive him of any such things as should pass betwixt her and him', for, 'if he did', the king would have knowledge of it.[59] Incessant interruptions by busy nights-watchmen and ever-curious chamberers could only have inflamed her paranoia. The separation of male and female in the queen's chambers often encouraged gossip, fostering an atmosphere of mistrust. The first entry in the miscellany the 'Devonshire Manuscript', an anthology of courtly verse circulated by the women in Anne Boleyn's household, is a poem by Sir Thomas Wyatt, which warned a lover of his indiscretions, and concerns the lack of privacy and unrelenting surveillance at court:

> Take hede be tyme leste ye be spyede
> yor lovyng I yee can not hide
> at last the trwthe will sure be tryde
> therefore take hede.[60]

In the words of William Latymer, Anne's chaplain, 'nothing canne longe escape the percinge eyes of princes, esspecially in their awne pallacies'.[61] Pizan warned women at court that they 'ought not to defame' their mistress, 'either among themselves or elsewhere, for words can never be said privately enough that they may not be reported'.[62] Was it Katherine's infatuation with, and overwhelming desire for Culpeper, that led to her to abandon caution? Or should it be asked, rather, who led the queen to abandon caution? It was Jane who reassured the queen to 'feare not' and 'badd the quene hold her own'.[63] Queens could be drawn in by the presence of servants whom they trusted, but who actually facilitated only the *illusion* of privacy, feigning an atmosphere of intimacy, and leading, in this instance, to the recklessness of an adulterous affair between a queen and her husband's servant. Unlike the king's Privy Chamber, which, for the king, established a clear distinction between his public and his private lives,[64] the queen's Privy Chamber in this period more often failed in this most essential function.

By November 1541, it had emerged that, before her marriage to the king, Katherine committed, and later concealed, sexual indiscretions with Henry Mannox and Francis Dereham, two male attendants with whom she had served as a chamberwoman in the household of her step-grandmother, Agnes Howard, Dowager Duchess of Norfolk, at Horsham and Lambeth. Mary Hall, who had served alongside Katherine at Lambeth, disclosed her knowledge of these indiscretions to her brother, John Lascelles, who in turn approached and related what he had been told to Thomas Cranmer, Archbishop of Canterbury. Cranmer 'reported the matter to the King in writing', and Henry, 'thinking the matter forged', commissioned an investigation.[65] On 5 November, Mannox and Dereham were arrested, and under interrogation, they both confessed to having had 'carnal knowledge of' and 'familiarity with the Queen', establishing the truth of Hall's accusations.[66] Henry was devastated: 'his heart was so pierced with pensiveness', his council reported, 'that long it was before his Majesty could speak and utter the sorrow of his heart unto us'.[67] Katherine and her ladies were promptly confined to her apartments at Hampton Court. Marillac reported that 'she has taken no kind of pastime but kept in her chamber'. 'Whereas, before, she did nothing but dance and rejoice,' the ambassador wrote, 'now when the musicians come they are told that it is no more the time to dance'.[68] The following day, the king and his council set out in the middle of the night for Whitehall. Katherine would never see him again, but legend has it that before the king left Hampton Court she broke free of her guards and ran down a gallery towards the Chapel Royal, where Henry was attending mass, in a last, desperate attempt to beg him for mercy. Her guards intercepted her and Katherine, hysterical, was dragged screaming back to her chambers.[69]

A delegation of councillors later confronted Katherine, and Cranmer procured her full written confession. Among other faults, Katherine admitted that, before marrying the king, Dereham, whom she had since appointed as her gentleman usher,

> by many persuasions procured me to his vicious purpose and obteyned first to lye uppon my bedde with his doblett and hose and after within the bed and fynally he lay with me nakyd and used me in such sorte as a man doith with his wyff many and sondry tymez but howe often I knowe not.[70]

The king's councillors had no difficulty in extracting further proof of the queen's premarital misconduct from various other witnesses. Katherine Daubeney, Alice Restwold, Joan Bulmer, Agnes Howard, her step-grandmother, and Margaret Gamage, her aunt, were apparently examined and all 'agreed in one [tale]'.[71] The Howard stronghold at court collapsed, as it was judged that her family, whose fortunes were closely aligned with Katherine as queen, had 'falsely concealed' knowledge of her indiscretions; for this they were shown little mercy. Many of them were thrown in the Tower and charged with 'misprision of treason'.[72] Having sufficiently proven that Katherine was 'not of pure and honest living before her marriage', preparations were made to move her to the monastery of Syon, 'there to remain, till the matter be further resolved'.[73] Chapuys reported that 'she would be shut up in the cloister of a late nunnery near Richmond, guarded by four women and some men'.[74] Unlike Anne Boleyn, Katherine was able to choose the gentlewomen who would attend upon her in her final days, with the exception 'always that my lady Baynton be one, whose husband the king's pleasure is should attend the queen and have the rule and government of the whole house'.[75] The Bayntons' custody of Katherine here echoes that of the Kingstons, William and Mary, who watched over Anne on behalf of the king. Katherine would remain at Syon until she was escorted to the Tower of London on 7 February 1542.[76]

For now the council investigated the matter of the queen's prior indiscretions with Mannox and Dereham. Katherine and her ladies, among them Jane, were effectively placed under house arrest and kept to the queen's chambers at Hampton Court. At first, the queen must have feared that her confinement meant that the king had somehow learned of her late night rendezvous with Culpeper because, 'three or four times daily since she was in this trouble', she would ask Jane if she had heard from him: 'if that matter came not out', Katherine, visibly shaken, murmured, 'she feared not for no thing'.[77] Seeing that she was beginning to panic, and her emotions probably erratic, Jane feared that the queen might crack under the psychological pressure of interrogation, and, speaking of the king's councillors, advised the queen that 'they wold speke feire to yowe and use all weyes with yowe but... if yowe confesse yowe undo both your selff and others'. 'And for my parte,' Jane promised, 'I woll never confesse it to be torne withe wylde horsez'.[78] She must have been at least a little concerned, but Jane remained steady, and tried to calm her mistress. 'She badd the quene hold her own for Culpepir was yesterday mery a hawkyng', yet Katherine remained in a state of dread, urging Jane that 'it wold out, what hold your own I warraunt yowe, be yowe afrayd'.[79]

And Culpeper was not 'mery a hawkyng' for long. In a report dated 12 November, the king's council wrote abroad: 'Now may you see what was done before the marriage, God knoweth what hath been done sithence'.[80] On account of there being 'an appearance of greater abomination in her', and the fact that Katherine had retained in her service both Dereham and Tylney, who was privy to her prior indiscretions, the king's councillors were convinced that she had continued her affair with Dereham even after her marriage to Henry.[81] When they approached Dereham and questioned him, he denied it outright, and 'to show his innocence since the marriage, said that Culpeper had succeeded him in the Queen's affections'.[82] On 13 November, Wriothesley was sent to visit the queen at Hampton Court,

> and called all the ladies and gentlewomen and her servauntes into the Great Chamber, and there openlye afore them declared certeine offences

that she had done in misuing her bodye with certeine persons afore the Kinges tyme, wherefore he there discharged all her howsehould.[83]

It is likely that Jane too, as one of her ladies, had been summoned to be discharged from her office. As yet she had not been implicated in the investigation; indeed at this stage she knew more about the affair than the king's council. One wonders how Jane held her nerve, as she will surely have known that it was only a matter of time before her name would surface.

21

'My lady of Rochford was the principal occasion of the queen's folly'
THE FALL OF KATHERINE HOWARD

Jane, Katherine, Culpeper, and the queen's chamberers, Tylney and Morton, were all interrogated by the king's council. All of their testimonies are suspect. Under interrogation, their every word would be scrutinised. Faced with the reality of severe punishment, it seems almost inevitable that they would have played right into the council's hands. In some instances, it is entirely possible, perhaps even likely, that the accused could have lied, while in others, imagination may have supplemented memory. Undoubtedly their depositions could be manipulated and further distorted. None of them refused to admit that the queen and Culpeper met late at night, but the nature of those meetings, and how or why they came to happen in the first place, was contested. Reconciling, as far as possible, the inherent conflicts found in their depositions, what emerges is an altogether damning tale of intrigue, passion and persuasion; a clandestine love affair conducted right under the king's nose, and at the centre of it all, was Jane.

Culpeper was arrested on around 12 or 13 November 1541 and taken immediately to the Tower, where he would be interrogated by the king's council. Protected from the duress or coercion of physical torture, Culpeper's account was fairly balanced, in that he was prepared to acknowledge his own feelings for Katherine and – rather extraordinarily – that 'he intended and meant to do ill with the queen and that in like wise, the queen so minded to do with him'.[1] To his credit, Culpeper admitted to their flirtatious conversations at Greenwich, Lincoln, Pontefract and York, even in instances where he risked incriminating himself. Throughout his deposition, Culpeper appears to have been plain, direct and remarkably nuanced; indeed it is difficult to imagine how he could even have begun to fabricate the specifics as to when, where and exactly what they had spoken about. During his trial, Culpeper 'persisted in denying his guilt', and maintained 'that he never solicited or had anything to do with her'. He reportedly 'said it was the Queen who, through lady Rocheford, solicited him to meet her in private'. Culpeper even added that 'she pined for him, and was actually dying of love for his person'.[2] That it was Katherine who sent for him in the first place is surely obvious. The initiative for nocturnal trysts in the queen's chambers, where he alone had no right of admission, had to have come from her. Katherine is otherwise represented by Culpeper as flirtatious, yet cautious, playful, but sincere, a girl very much in love, so much so that at times she was noticeably insecure, even at times jealous of her love rivals, something which she often seems to have masked with witty retorts and overcompensated for with gifts. In a sense, this Katherine is very real, and the details of Culpeper's deposition are, for the most part, quite plausible.

When Katherine was visited by the king's council at Hampton Court on 12 November and examined on 'the matter now come forth concerning Culpeper', she would admit that she had met with him on three occasions through the summer progress: at Lincoln at 'about ten or eleven of the clock an hour or more' she spoke with him 'in a little gallery at the stair head'; at Pontefract 'in her bed chamber'; and 'another time' at York 'in my lady Rochford's chamber'. Although Katherine made no mention of their earlier engagement in the entry between her chambers at Greenwich, she did acknowledge that on one occasion she gave him 'a fair cap of velvet garnished with a brooch and three dozen pairs of aglets and a chain'. 'As for the act,' her examiners noted, 'she denied upon her oath, or touching bare of her but her hand'.[3] She claimed that Jane had assured her 'he desiered nothyng elles but to speke with her'. While Culpeper gave full, frank statements, Katherine plead ignorance and quite consciously evaded the subject of their late night rendezvous, relating not even a word of their conversations together. Her account was not convincing; indeed it was scarcely believeable. Her examiners must have pressed Katherine for more, particularly on the nature of her relationship with Culpeper, but she refused to admit the truth of her feelings for him. The king himself felt that 'she hath not, as appeareth by her confession, so fully declared the circumstances of such communications as were betwixt her and Culpeper'.[4] 'He desires them to essay again to get more from her,' Sir Ralph Sadler, the king's secretary, informed his council, but only 'if her wits are such that they may do so without danger to her'.[5] In other words, Henry did not believe that Katherine was telling the whole truth, and nor should we.

Yet there are historians who maintain, as she did, that her rendezvous with Culpeper were 'from her part innocent'. Is there any evidence with which to corroborate Katherine's defence? It has been suggested that their interactions must be seen in the context of the 'courtly love' tradition.[6] As the presiding queen, Katherine was altogether unattainable, but nonetheless commanded male attention. Culpeper remarked that the queen was 'dying' of love for him, but her deposition does not admit to a romantic or even an affectionate relationship, representing Culpeper to the council as her 'little sweet fool' in love, whose pursuit of her was relentless, but apparently futile. Culpeper was, to Katherine, her kinsman, and while his attentions were flattering they were 'ultimately of no interest to her'.[7] Katherine's gifts represented her 'desire to become better acquainted with him', and their exchanges essentially platonic, later misrepresented or misconstrued out of context.[8]

It is, however, unconvincing to suggest that their liaisons, together alone, late at night, most often in her bedchamber, met social conventions. On one occasion at Lincoln, Katherine and Culpeper met in 'the queen's stool house', that is, her lavatory. Hardly an appropriate stage for the rituals of courtly love! Was it in her lavatory that Katherine, as one author has claimed, cultivated Culpeper's friendship?[9] If her rendezvous with Culpeper were 'from her part innocent', it begs the question, why were they conducted in secret? If Culpeper 'desiered nothyng elles but to speke with her', why did Katherine not receive him in her Presence Chamber as she did other visitors, like foreign ambassadors? If her gifts to him were not intended as love tokens, why in April did she insist that he conceal the velvet cap under his cloak? Any attempt to reconcile Katherine's words with her actions proves problematic, and requires some stretch of the imagination. Was Culpeper 'an aggressive, dangerous suitor' who 'had come into sensitive information about her past' and 'was using it to blackmail her'; an unscrupulous man who having 'established some form of threatening control over the queen's life' then 'manipulated' her into clandestine meetings in her own chambers, which were from her part little more than a 'misguided attempt at appeasement'?[10] No, there is no proof for such a claim; nor is there any evidence that Culpeper bribed or blackmailed Jane to facilitate their first meeting.[11] Not even Katherine represented Culpeper as dangerous or manipulative (and surely, if he were blackmailing her, it would have served her defence to admit that, but she said no such thing). The surviving depositions attest to lively flirtation between Katherine and Culpeper, invalidating any interpretation that maintains that the queen was an innocent, that she met with him reluctantly, or that she felt obliged to do so to placate him in his pursuit of her.[12]

Although Culpeper's admission that 'he intended and meant to do ill with the queen and that in like wise, the queen so minded to do with him' was quite enough to condemn them both, the king's council, working as they often did on the presumption of guilt, might have had their suspicions that it had already gone much further. Both Katherine and Culpeper denied this, and relying entirely upon the confessions of the accused, the council were lacking proof. To uncover the truth of the matter as they suspected it, what they were missing was a compelling eyewitness. In this respect, the testimony of the queen's chamberers, Tylney and Morton, lacked substance, in that neither of them could provide first-hand accounts of what actually occurred at, or even who Katherine was meeting, at her late night rendezvous. Tylney, for one, admitted that 'she never saw who came unto the queen and my lady Rochford, nor heard what was said between them', while Morton was clear about the fact that she had been forbidden to enter her bedchamber.[13] Tylney and Morton were questioned as to 'whether the Queen went out of her chamber any night late'.[14] At Pontefract, Morton would recall that Katherine, 'being alone with Lady Rochford, locked and bolted her chamber door on the inside' and insisted that 'neither Mrs. Lofkyng nor no nother should come into her bedchamber'.[15] Tylney corroborated Morton, adding only that, at Lincoln, they 'were sent back' on two occasions when the queen went to Lady Rochford's chamber.[16] They insisted that they had 'heard or saw nothing of what passed', though their accounts meant that the prosecution could convincingly levy the charge of the queen having held 'illicit meeting and conference'.[17] Wriothesley later acknowledged that Tylney 'hath done us good service',[18] indicating that she may have been offered a reprieve for her cooperation. Hall, the chamberwoman who first brought Katherine's indiscretions before her marriage to the king's attention, was not only spared: she was protected. 'She is, as an encouragement to others to reveal like cases,' the council assured, 'not to be troubled'.[19]

The depositions of the accused, and that of eyewitnesses, directed the council to Jane. Katherine and Culpeper had both given their own accounts of the affair, but Jane, as their accomplice, was the key witness. Her testimony was 'regarded a specially cogent evidence' and could be 'admitted without corroboration'.[20] She was the missing link. The crux of Katherine's defence was that she had Jane accompany her to act as her chaperone. Jane 'would many times, being ever by, sit somewhat far off or turn her back', and the queen sighed, 'for God's sake, madam, even near us'. Jane was probably nearly twice her age, and her presence as a mature widow was apparently meant to protect the young queen and, if necessary, swear to her reputation and innocence.

Jane was not interrogated until 13 November, by which time the king's council were in possession of enough evidence to arrest her. She was taken to the Tower, where she told them that, although she was often in attendance at their rendezvous, 'the queen and Culpeper talked so secretly that she heard not their conversations'. At Lincoln, Jane maintained that while Katherine and Culpeper were 'secretly together' she slept in an adjoining room 'until the queen did call her to answer Lufkyn', her chamberer.[21] She admitted that she had kept watch one night at Pontefract, while 'Culpeper stood upon the stairs ready always to slip down if noise came and the queen stood upon the uppermost step afore him where they might speak and do together', but as to their conversations she was 'never the privier' because she had kept her distance from them.[22] So much for the star witness. It would appear that Jane was careful not to incriminate herself, representing her actions as those of an unwilling but compliant servant who was merely following the orders of her mistress. In other words, Jane, like Katherine, plead ignorance. 'For my parte,' Jane promised Katherine, 'I woll never confesse it to be torne withe wylde horsez'; and it appears at first that she meant to keep that promise. But either the council pressed her for more information, or it became apparent to Jane that they were not satisfied, nor were they convinced, by her answers, because she abandoned her defence and, at the end of her interrogation, made one last, brief, but damning statement: 'she thinketh that Culpeper hath known the Queen carnally', Jane told her examiners, 'considering all things that she hath heard and seen between them'.[23]

Was Jane 'frightened into telling a much more damning story', or was she, in fact, telling the truth?[24] Had Culpeper 'known the Queen carnally'? Certainly they were attracted to one another, flirted with one another and felt deeply for each other, but Katherine insisted that she and Culpeper had not committed the 'act' of sexual intercourse, and nor was there 'touching bare of her but her hand',[25] while Culpeper maintained until his death that he had 'not passed beyond words', though 'he confessed his intention to do so'.[26] The king and his council were not convinced that Katherine had 'fully declared' the extent of her relationship with Culpeper. Surely they pressed Jane on this point.[27] In the words of one author, 'the repeated confessions of clandestine meetings between a man notorious for his gallantry and a woman who was already sexually awakened really do not admit of any other explanation'.[28] That it was Henry's unsatisfactory performance as a lover which drove a 'silly, feckless and oversexed'[29] Katherine into adultery may be too simplistic, though the king was an ageing, corpulent man, who had an ulcer on his leg which regularly oozed pus.[30] One of his contemporaries remarked in 1538 that 'the King is full of flesh and unwieldly, and that he cannot long continue with his sore leg'.[31] He was hardly a fit mate for Katherine. Henry could give his wife as many jewels, garments, money, land and status as she desired, but for Katherine their relationship was probably lacking if not in physical attraction then a genuine, emotional or romantic connection between them, which she sought elsewhere. Whether or not Katherine was guilty of committing adultery remains a mystery, for not even Jane had witnessed the lovers *in flagrante*, admitting only that what she had heard and seen between them meant she could not think it otherwise.

Let us consider the case against Jane. It consisted of statements made by Culpeper, Katherine, her chamberers and, eventually, by Jane herself, which, taken together, identified her as playing a crucial role in the affair. Katherine mercilessly threw her confidante to the wolves. It was Jane who 'made instans to her to speke with Culpeper, declaryng him to beare her good wyll and favour', and did 'swere uppon a booke' that 'he ment nothyng but honestye'. It was Jane who dispelled her fears that it would 'by spyed oon day', telling her to 'feare not', and Jane who, totally lacking in moral sense, instead of chaperoning their late night rendezvous would 'sytt sumwhatt farre of or turn hyr bak'. It was Jane who 'moved her for hym', and Jane who 'wold at eevery lodging serche the bak doors & tell hir of them if there were eny, onasked', the critical word here being 'unasked'. More curious yet is Katherine's claim that the two bracelets Culpeper thought he had received from the queen 'to keep his arms warm' while at Sheriff Hutton were, in fact, bought and sent by Jane: 'my lady Rocheford prayed hir she myght bye sumwhat to send hym', Katherine told her examiners, 'and of hir own choyse bought a payer of brayselettz to send hym'. If it was Jane who sent Culpeper the bracelets, does that mean it was also she who wrote the corresponding message, supposedly written from the queen, that they were 'to keep his arms warm' so that he should not have to keep them warm in the embrace of another woman?

Culpeper told them that Jane was privy to their late night rendezvous; indeed she had, according to him, even acted as a go-between to contrive the meetings at Lincoln, Pontefract and York, often accommodating them in her own chambers. He was also explicit about her role in that he had 'at divers time sent many familiar messages to the Lady Rochford and that she was the conveyer of all messages and tokens between himself and Katherine'. Somewhat more ambiguous was his claim that it was Jane who 'provoked him much to love the queen', and worse still that it was Jane who told him 'how much the queen loved him by which means he was tricked and brought into the snare which blind youth hath no grace to foresee'.[32] Tylney and Morton corroborated his testimony as to Jane's whereabouts late at night in their chambers, and admitted to various 'strange' messages which were exchanged, including a sealed letter without superscription from Jane to Katherine, with Jane's instruction for 'her grace to keep it secret'.[33]

What should be made of all this? Some statements – such as that Jane would often 'sytt sumwhatt farre of or turn hyr bak' – are readily believeable, while others – such as that it was Jane 'provoked' or 'tricked' Culpeper into loving the queen – seem odd and require more rigorous analysis. The evidence is inherently confusing, even contradictory. No doubt Culpeper wanted to absolve himself of any responsibility for the affair, but it is entirely possible, perhaps even likely, that, however embellished or exaggerated, he was essentially telling the truth and, not necessarily shifting the blame to Jane, but casting her as he saw fit.

As far as the facts are concerned, shortly after Katherine was reacquainted with Culpeper in around April 1541, Jane became her chief confidante in the affair and began carrying letters, tokens and gifts between them. When Culpeper fell ill and Katherine became anxious to see him, Jane would contrive a way for them to meet in private, late at night, usually in the queen's innermost chambers. During their liaisons at Lincoln, Pontefract and York, Jane would chaperone. She often excused herself, and would sit far off with her back turned or sleep in an adjoining room, but by her own admission had heard and seen much of what occurred between them. It seems reasonably well-established that Jane was actively encouraging Katherine to meet with Culpeper, and when Katherine began to lose her nerve, Jane remained steadfast and went to great lengths to alleviate her fears and calm her mistress, from setting a watch of her own to accommodating them in her own chambers.

Whereas the case against Katherine and Culpeper could not be proven, the evidence against Jane was overwhelming. In fact, it is difficult to see how the affair would have lasted through the summer, or have taken place at all, if it were not for Jane's connivance. That Jane 'tricked' Culpeper into loving the queen at first seems implausible, and perhaps should not or cannot be taken too literally. But in a very literal sense, Jane *was* deceiving Culpeper when she sent him two bracelets and told him they were from the queen, and with it a decidedly flirtatious message that they were 'to keep his arms warm'. This one recorded instance of Jane acting independently of her mistress invites some speculation in asking, exactly how many love tokens or flirtatious messages had Jane herself sent to Culpeper, or, at that rate, to Katherine? Culpeper stressed that he 'at divers times sent many familiar messages to the Lady Rochford', and that Jane 'was the conveyer of all messages and tokens' between himself and the queen.[34] Crucially, Jane effectively controlled all communication between them and could, if she was so inclined, subtly inflame their passion for one another. In any case, Jane was determined to keep that flame burning. When Katherine expressed her desire to end her acquaintance with Culpeper, Jane seemed almost reluctant to let her, telling her that 'yet must yow gyff men leave to looke for they woll looke uppon yowe'. It seems that Jane was pulling many strings, as she would remind Katherine that Thomas Paston, another of the king's gentlemen who had previously rivalled Culpeper in pursuing the queen, did still 'bear her favour'.[35]

The unknown Spanish chronicler frequently invokes the devil in their imaginative account of the queen's downfall: 'the devil tempted her'; 'the devil being strong in her'; Katherine 'let the devil overcome' her, etc. In other words, it was the 'devil' who brought Katherine to ruin by her insatiable lusts. It would appear from the evidence that the real devil was Jane. Cavendish, lamenting in Jane's name, would acknowledge her integral role in the affair:

> And when my beautie began to be s[p]ent;
> Not with myn owne harme sufficed or content,
> Contrary to God, I must it nedes confesse,
> Other I entised by ensample of my wredchednes.[36]

Jane was not merely obeying orders. Far from maintaining a sort of dignified detachment from the whole affair, the meddlesome Jane, by persuasion, and deception, recklessly, but quite deliberately, endangered the queen, her lover, and herself.

The only question which remains, is why? What was her motive? We lack conclusive evidence, but many have speculated. Some interpretations are thought-provoking, while others inventive and far-reaching, if not a little absurd. A popular theory is that Jane, an ageing widow whose life had been 'starved of affection', obtained a vicarious thrill or voyeuristic pleasure from arranging and observing their illicit affair, and was 'living out in Katherine the romantic fantasies that she had never known'.[37] Perhaps Jane, supposedly sexually frustrated, even 'harboured some affection for Culpeper'.[38] Similar assessments of her character find that a mischievous Jane 'relished' in her role: she had a 'love of scandal and intrigue', and 'an addiction to palace life' that 'predisposed her to participate in its plots'.[39] Or maybe Jane was simply a 'romantic', 'sympathetic' to Katherine and kept her secret 'out of loyalty to her mistress'.[40] All of these theories are plausible. Less plausible is the suggestion that Jane, 'unhinged by malice', sought revenge against Henry, and encouraged his wife to commit adultery if only to make a cuckold out of the king and embarrass him publicly.[41]

Other theories are inconsistent with the evidence that we do have. It has been suggested that Jane was 'financially straitened' and as such had no choice but to contrive late night rendezvous for Katherine and Culpeper, presumably in exchange for regular payments from her mistress.[42] Certainly following the execution of her husband in 1536, Jane was left in a precarious state, but by the time she was serving in Katherine's household she had obtained her jointure settlement.[43] Alternatively, Jane is supposed to have been 'the queen's pawn', who did not dare refuse direct orders from Katherine in the first instance and was oblivious to the danger she was in until it was much too late. To imagine, in spite of the overwhelming evidence to the contrary, that Jane was merely an obedient servant, and that she did her best 'to minimise the dangers' after being dragged into 'a deadly vortex of deceit and intrigue', an impossible situation from which she 'could not extricate herself', is altogether misleading. Not even Jane kept that charade up, and the testimonies of her contemporaries identify her as a leading participant, not an unwilling pawn.[44] Jane was no casualty; she could have gone immediately to the king, or dissuaded the queen from danger. She could not have been unaware of the risks involved, nor could she have been oblivious to the severe consequences which awaited all three of them if they were caught, remembering the fate of her own husband and sister-in-law in 1536. On this account Jane has been regarded as an imbecile, potentially 'insane',[45] and her behaviour often described as 'foolish'.[46]

But Jane was no fool. There had to have been a method to her madness. We can only guess, but there is a clue in the evidence as to her motive. It lies in the testimony of Margaret Morton. Morton kept a close eye on Jane and Katherine. She was inquisitive, and their behaviour aroused her suspicion. On one occasion at Pontefract, she and Lovekyn went to the queen's bedchamber and began prying when their mistress threatened to 'put them both away'. Later, under interrogation, Morton grumbled that if she and Lovekyn had, in fact, been dismissed from her service, then the queen would have 'taken other off my lade off rochfordes pouttyng'.[47] In other words, Katherine would have taken two women into her service at Jane's recommendation.[48] Jane's ascendancy in the queen's affections had clearly provoked the jealousy of those less fortunate servants who did not share in her mind and favour.[49] Rivalry, infighting and conflict were rife at court, as patrons and clients alike vied for advantage. As Pizan acknowledged, favouritism in the court of a queen was almost inevitable, and 'however great a lady may be, if she sees or notices or if it is drawn to her attention that her mistress shows someone else more favour than she does her, or often confides in another person and prefers her to know her secrets and be around her more', the 'vice of envy' might 'overcome her'.[50] Queens could not advance all of their servants equally. Nor could their favour be distributed evenly or fairly. When Katherine appointed Dereham to serve in her household, she 'had him in notable favour above others', and 'gave him divers gifts and sums of money'.[51] This was escalated by the irreverent Dereham, who felt that 'men dispised hym by cause they perceyved that the quene ffavored hym'.[52] An incident occurred one evening at supper in the queen's chambers when Dereham was sat at the table 'after all other were rysen', the custom being that strictly the queen's council were to remain after supper. Henry Johns, gentleman usher of the queen's Chamber, sent a messenger to take Dereham away, who retorted, 'go to Mr. Johns and tell hym I was of the quenes cownsell beffore he knew her and shalbe when she hath fforgotten hym'.[53]

In the queen's court, Jane was the favourite. The relationship between 'mistress' and 'servant' had been upturned, and it was Jane who was felt to be in control. Morton is unlikely to have been alone in feeling that Jane had acquired undue power and influence over the queen. Her unrelenting, domineering hold over Katherine kept her hostage as she schemed and determinedly encouraged, even manipulated the affair, to her own advantage. Her motive was thus political – it was power. Exploiting the queen's trust, Jane's place as her close confidante was guaranteed with a carnal secret. In the words of Katherine's chamberer, 'my lady of Rochford was the principal occasion of the queen's folly'.[54]

22

'wt goodly wordes and stedfast contenance'
EXECUTION

Upon learning of Katherine's infidelities, Henry was, at first, incredulous, believing the matter to have been 'forged'. He refused to accept the truth that he had been cuckolded, to the detriment of his ego, honour and masculinity. Eventually, the king was convinced of her guilt, and it was reported that he had 'changed his love for the Queen into hatred, and taken such grief at being deceived that of late it was thought he had gone mad, for he called for a sword to slay her he had loved so much'.[1] Henry cried that she 'should have torture in her death', lamenting 'his ill luck in meeting with such ill-conditioned wives'.[2] Lacking proof, the king and his council proceeded against Katherine, Culpeper, Dereham and Jane on the basis of intent. No overt act of adultery could be proven; to 'construct' a damning case against them, all that was required by law was to infer from their own words that the accused intended to commit treason. The Treasons Act of 1534 declared that to 'maliciously wish, will, or desire by words or writing, or by crafty images invent, practise, or attempt any bodily harm to be done or committed to the King's most royal person', including any attempt 'to deprive' the 'heirs apparent' of their 'dignity, title, or name of their royal estates' to which they were entitled constituted treason.[3] In other words, the presumption to commit treason alone was quite enough to secure a conviction. Culpeper would maintain that, in his late night rendezvous with Katherine, they had 'not passed beyond words', but he had already confessed his intentions 'to do ill with the Queen' and 'his confessed conversation, being held by a subject to a Queen,' it was felt, 'deserved death'.[4] As the chronicler Hall observed, sithe her Mariage, she was vehemently suspected with Thomas Culpeper, whiche was brought to her Chamber at Lyncolne, in August laste, in the Progresse tyme, by the Lady of Rochforde, and were there together alone, from leuen of the Clocke at Nighte, till foure of the Clocke in the Mornyng, and to hym she gaue a Chayne, and a riche Cap.[5]

As has been demonstrated, the private activities of women, concealed in the cloistered chambers of a queen, often provoked male anxieties of the unknown. The king's council could not prove Katherine had committed adultery, but from their view, it was damning that the queen had met Dereham 'in her secret chamber and other suspect places', and Culpeper, 'five or six times in secret and suspect places' where 'they were closetted together'.[6] The queen's Privy chamber was designated as 'secret' and 'suspect', concealing limitless indiscretions, untold acts and motives which could, and would, be misconstrued.[7]

On 1 December 1541, Dereham and Culpeper were escorted by Sir John Gage, Constable of the Tower, to Guildhall, London, where they would be arraigned for treason for their 'mysdemeanour with the Quene, as appeared by theyr inditements'.[8] Upon hearing the accusations, both men plead 'not guilty'; Culpeper in particular reportedly 'persisted in denying his guilt',[9] but 'after sufficient and probable evidence had been given on the King's part', both Dereham and Culpeper changed their plea to 'guilty'.[10] The grand jury returned a guilty verdict, and sentenced them both 'to be taken back to the Tower and thence drawn through London to the gallows at Tyburn, and there hanged, cut down alive, disembowelled, and (they still living) their bowels burnt, beheaded, and quartered'.[11] The chronicler Wriothesley's account recorded that, on 10 December, both Dereham and Culpeper were 'drawne from the Tower of London to Tyburne'; while Dereham was brutally 'hanged, membred, bowelled, headed, and quartered', Culpeper's noble heritage meant he was spared the full penalty for treason. 'After exhortation made to the people to pray for him,' it was observed that Culpeper 'there standinge on the ground by the gallows, kneled downe and had his head stryken of'.[12]

Jane was accused of having 'falsely and traitorously aided and abetted' Katherine and Culpeper 'in their illicit intercourse'. She was retained, as the prosecution saw it, for 'the better and more secretly to pursue their carnal life'.

'When the Queen and Culpeper were alone in such chambers she, the Lady Rochford', the indictment read, 'watched at the doors to prevent their being surprised'.[13] Jane was expected to stand trial alongside Dereham and Culpeper on 1 December, and 'would have been sentenced at the same time', but 'on the third day of her imprisonment' Jane reportedly 'went mad'.[14] She was taken from the Tower and, according to the ambassador Chapuys, was sent at the king's orders to stay at Russell House in London, placed in the custody of the Lord Admiral, Sir John Russell, and his wife Anne, Lady Russell.[15] His report is corroborated by Wriothesley's account which noted that Jane was taken to the Tower on two separate occasions: first, on around 14 November 1541, and second, in the middle of the night on 9 February 1542, when he observed and recorded again that 'the Lady Rochford was had to the Tower'.[16]

Jane had no trial. She was proceeded against by Act of Attainder, a statute declaring both Jane and Katherine guilty of high treason. It was introduced to the House of Lords on 21 January 1542 and received several readings laying out the treasonous crimes committed, all through which Lord Morley, Jane's father, was duly in attendance.[17] It was essentially Jane's death warrant, taking the form of a petition to the king requesting his consent or 'royal assent' to her conviction, and for the Act itself to be passed into law, which was received by commission on 11 February. The Act begins by laying out the indiscretions committed by Katherine prior to her marriage to the king, before stating that she,

> not satisfied with thies abhomynable carnall desyres, the ende wherof how perillous it was and might have been to your Majestie and psone were harde to expresse, hathe allso synnes that tyme most traytorouslye confederated herself with the Ladye Jane Rocheford wydowe, late wief of George Boleyn Knight late Lorde Rocheforde, to bring her vicious and abhomnyable purpose to passe with Thomas Culpeper Esquier late oon of the Gentlemen of your Grace's privye Chambre, by whose meanes the Quene brought to passe that the saide Culpeper and she mett in a secrett and vyle place, and that at an undue hower of a xj a Clocke in the night, and so remayned there with him till three of the Clocke in the morninge, none being with them but that Bawde the Ladye Jane Rocheford, by

> whose meanes Culpeper came thither, and there they all three and at other conference togyther afterward most falselie and traiterouselye comytted and ppetrated many detestable and abhomynable treasons, to the most fearefull peril and daunger of the distruccon of your most royall pson and to thuttre losse disheryson and desolacon of this your Realme of England, if God of his infinite goodenes had not in due tyme brought the saide treasons to light...

The legal context to characterising Jane as 'that bawde the Ladye Jane Rochforde' in 1542 is clear. It was a statement as to her amoral character, from which the prosecution – or, in this case, Parliament – could show her intent to commit treason. It was essential that they prove manifestly the malice or evil of the offender, so that juries and contemporaries believe that due justice had been served. To demonstrate that Jane was capable of committing the act of which she was accused was proof enough that she was culpable in the act itself. The Act continues as such before ultimately declaring

> the saide Quene Katheryne and Jane Ladye Rocheford, for theyre saide abhominable and detestable treasons by theym and every of theym most abomynablie and trayterouslie comytted and doon against your Majestie and this your Realme, shalbe by thaucthoryte of this present parliament convicted and attainted of Highe Treasone...

As punishment, Jane and Katherine were condemned to

> suffre paynes of Death losse of goods catalls debts fermes and other things as in cases of Highe treason by the lawes of this your Realme hath been accustumed graunted and given to the Crowne; And also that the saide Quene Katheryne Jane Ladye Rochford... shall lose and forfaite to your Highnes and to your heyres all suche right tytle interest use and possession... or to all suche theyre Honours manours meases lands tenements rents reversions remaynders uses possessions offices rights condicions and all other theyre hereditaments of what names natures or qualities soever they be...[18]

Jane, as a suspected traitor to the crown, had been subjected to the pressure of interrogation and the isolation of imprisonment. She may have suffered a nervous breakdown, collapsing under the strain of her situation. It is also possible that she was feigning her illness. Chapuys reported that Jane 'had shown symptoms of madness' up until her execution, when 'they told her she must die', suggesting that perhaps she was faking it.[19] She must also have known that, in her fragile state, she could not legally stand trial, nor was it legal to execute the insane. If Jane lost her mind, she might yet keep her head. The king sent his own physicians to Jane on daily visits, 'desiring her recovery', but not, Chapuys felt, out of any concern for her welfare but, rather chillingly, to ensure that she was fit enough to climb the scaffold steps and 'have her executed as an example and warning to others'.[20] Henry was altogether unforgiving and was determined that Jane should suffer, irrespective of her mental state. There was a statute introduced to the House of Lords at around the same time as the Act of Attainder which condemned Katherine and Jane, namely the 'Act for due proces to be had in High Treason in cases of Lunacy or Madnes'. It acknowledged that, to interpret in the case of any one person whether or not their 'lunacy or madnes' was real or feigned was 'a thinge almoste ympossible to judge or trye', and as such the Act provided for 'mad' persons charged with treason to be proceeded against by the same laws as sane persons. This statement indicates that there was some concern that those accused of treason could feign madness in order to avoid punishment. There is no question that this Act was directed at Jane, with, at least, its immediate purpose, to facilitate her execution. On the same day, 11 February 1542, that the Act of Attainder against Jane and Katherine received royal assent, so too did the 'Act for due proces to be had in High Treason in cases of Lunacy or Madnes'.[21] It effectively meant that pleas of insanity could not act as Jane's defence, or protect her from suffering the full penalty for committing treason, thus securing her fate. The timing of this new Act cannot be a coincidence, and must have been felt necessary to ensure that Jane would face punishment.

She was unquestionably guilty. Facing the brutal reality of punishment by decapitation, perhaps Jane's 'fits of frenzy'[22] were improvised in hope of obtaining a reprieve. If Jane was feigning insanity, it was a performance she kept up until the very last. Chapuys observed she had 'had shewn symptoms of madness until the very moment when they announced to her that she must die'.[23] There could be nothing quite as sobering as the thud of the axe as it struck off the head of her former mistress. Perhaps Jane knew her time had come and finally accepted her fate, notwithstanding all that she had done to escape it.

The day had come. At 'about nine o'clock in the morning' on 13 February 1542, Jane sat quietly in her room while, a few hundred yards away, Katherine was escorted by Sir John Gage to the scaffold on Tower Green and began climbing the steps amidst a small crowd of onlookers. Many citizens of London, together with members of the king's council had turned out to witness their executions within the precinct of the Tower. She turned to them and, reportedly, with courage, patience and constancy, began to speak:

> Brothers, by the journey upon which I am bound I have not wronged the King, but it is true that long before the King took me I loved Culpeper, and I wish to God I had done as he wished me, for at the time the King wanted to take me he urged me to say that I was pledged to him. If I had done as he advised me I should not die this death, nor would he. I would rather have him for a husband than be a mistress of the world, but sin blinded me and greed of grandeur, and since mine is the fault mine is also the suffering, and my great sorrow is that Culpeper should have to die through me.

The headsman knelt before her and asked for her pardon. Katherine spoke, defiantly, 'I die a Queen, but would rather die the wife of Culpeper. God have mercy on my soul. Good people, I beg you pray for me.' This account of Katherine's final words is extraordinary, but if she dared to say this on the scaffold it would surely have been preserved elsewhere. Other eyewitnesses made no mention of it, but to the contrary, observed that Katherine was utterly repentant in her final moments, and 'with goodly words and steadfast countenance' acknowledged her faults and the justice of her sentence.[24] Alternatively, the ambassador Marillac later reported second-hand that Katherine 'was so weak that she could hardly speak, but confessed in few words that she had merited a hundred deaths for so offending the King who had so graciously treated her'.[25] Her ladies bandaged her eyes, and after she handed the headsman a purse containing some coins, she fell to her knees and prayed solemnly for her soul and for the king's welfare. Katherine positioned herself carefully on the block, as she had rehearsed.[26] The headsman struck off her head with a single blow.[27] Jane may well have heard the cries and gasps of the crowd as the young Katherine was beheaded. It was only a matter of time before Gage arrived to conduct her from her lodging within the Tower to the nearby green.

Jane mounted the scaffold and, turning to face the crowds of onlookers who had gathered to witness her execution. Perhaps she met the eyes of those with whom she had once shared in the splendour of court life: men with whom she had dined and danced, or women with whom she had laughed and cried. Jane was to die in front of them. There is no verbatim transcript of Jane's scaffold speech. One account records that, when Jane addressed her audience, she made a last, almost astonishing confession:

> God has permitted me to suffer this shameful doom as punishment for having contributed to my husband's death. I falsely accused him of loving, in an incestuous manner, his sister, Queen Anne Boleyn. For this I deserve to die. But I am guilty of no other crime.[28]

It was an extraordinary revelation to make in her final moments. Unfortunately, this version of Jane's scaffold speech, albeit rather bold and instantly memorable, is almost certainly fictional, and cannot be corroborated.

More plausibly, Jane gave 'a long discourse of several faults which she had committed in her life',[29] and, adhering to convention, rather straightforwardly confessed her sins and 'died repentaunt'.[30] Her public execution, with Jane acknowledging her guilt, would speak to the justice of her condemnation and legitimise the authority which sanctioned it. It was felt important to die well and make a good end. In her last moments Jane had to speak and act with quiet, self-effacing dignity and a show of sincere repentance, for the sake of her own soul and salvation, but also to leave as good an impression in the eyes of her contemporaries. Otwell Johnson, a London merchant and eyewitness to the executions, felt that Jane's soul would surely be with God. He observed that she, alongside Katherine, was altogether sincere in her repentance:

> I se the quene & the Lady of rotcheford suffer wt in the tower whos sowles (I doubt not) be wt god, ffor thay made the moost godly christyans ends, that ever was hard tell of (I thinke) sins the worldes creation, uttering thayer lyvely faeth in the blode of Christe onely, wt wonderfull pacience & costancy to the death, & wt goodly wordes & stedfast contenance they desired all christen people, to take regard unto thayer worthy and just punisshement wt death for thayer offences, agenst god heinously from thayer youth upward, in breaking of his comandements, and also agenst the Kinges Royal maiesty, very daungerously: wherfor thay being justly condempned (as thay sayed) by the lawes of the realme & parlement, to dye, required the people (I say) to take example of them, for amendement of thayer ungodly lyves, & gladly to obey the kinge in all thinges, for whose preservation they did hartely pray, and willed all people so to do comending thayer sowles to god, & ernestly calling for mercy uppon him: whom I besieche to geve us grace, wt suche faeth, hope and charitie at or departing owte of this miserable world, to come to the fruition of his godhed in joy everlasting. Amen.
> Your loving brother
> Otwell Johnson[31]

Jane's servant-women slipped off her cloak, caught her hair in a white linen coif and bandaged her eyes. She knelt down on the scaffold and, again, with a single blow of the axe, it was done. Jane was beheaded. Her women then faithfully stepped forward and did their last act in covering her body which, alongside that of her former mistress, was carried to and interred in the Chapel of St Peter ad Vincula in the Tower, where her husband and sister-in-law had been buried beneath the altar some six years earlier.

On 22 February, just over a week after Jane's execution, the king's Privy council ordered her property to be packed up and sent to Sir James Boleyn, her uncle by marriage who was residing at Blickling.[32] Much of her belongings remained in the custody of the crown; among the rich bedding that 'was the late Lady Rocheords and hereafter delivered in charge by the kinges comaundement', received by the royal wardrobe, were 'thre bases of white Satten alover embrandered with trayles of tawny cloth of golde' which had 'the lorde Rochfordes knottes upon the seames'.[33] A year later, Mary Boleyn was granted the lands which had belonged 'by way of jointure' to Jane, her sister-in-law.[34]

At New Year in 1543, less than a year following Jane's execution, her father Henry, Lord Morley, translated Boccaccio's *De Claris mulierbus* from Latin to English and presented it to the king. Not so coincidentally, the book chronicles the lives of historical women, in all espousing the need to control and govern their behaviour. One narrative concerns Semiramis, a queen who, 'in usynge hirself moste unhappely in fleshly lustes', acted 'more beastly then womanly in the company of corrupte bawdes'.[35] Morley suggests that the translation might function as a conduct book, as Boccaccio intended: 'he dyd it to a good entente, that all ladyes and gentlewomen, seynge the glorye of the goode, may be steryde to folowe theym, and seynge the vyce of sum, to flee theym'.[36] Morley continues

> And for asmuche as that I thoughte howe that your Hyghnes, of youre accustomede mekenes and pryncely herte, wolde not disdayn it, so dyd I imagyne that if by chaunce it shulde cum to the handes of the ryght renomyde and moste honorable ladyes of your Highnes most tryhumphaunte courte, that it shulde be well acceptyde to theym to se and reede the mervelouse vertue of theyr oune sexe, to the laude perpetuall of theym.[37]

Morley makes no mention of his daughter, but this translation has been interpreted as a response to her misdeeds and a tacit acknowledgement, or acceptance, of the justice of her fate.[38] Alternatively, it has been argued that Morley, albeit rather subtly, defended his daughter. In his account of Polyxena, in which the princess is sacrificed to atone for the sins of an adulterous Helen of Sparta, Morley diverts from the translation to remark, 'so sweet a maiden should be devoured by the hands of Pyrrhus for to satisfy for another woman's offence'.[39]

During the 1876 restoration of the chapel of St Peter ad Vincula, set within the Tower of London, it was observed that, where Jane had been buried, 'the pavement had sunk very considerably on the south as well as on the north side of the chancel, and it had therefore been decided to lift the stones of that portion'.[40] What they found upon examination was the skeleton 'of a woman of probably forty years of age' at the time of her death.[41] Perhaps this was Jane. She may have been buried beside Katherine.[42] In the portion of the chapel where their bodies were said to have been interred, only one skeleton was found. Examining the age and size of the bones ruled out the possibility that this was the late queen, who was only around twenty years old when she was executed, and who was known to have been very small in stature. Katherine's remains, it became clear, 'had already become dust'.[43] The bodies of those who were executed on the scaffold were judged as being 'beyond all possible means of identification', and in some instances it was even found that their bones had been 'much disturbed' and their coffins 'designedly broken up and their contents scattered'.

23

THE INFAMOUS LADY ROCHFORD

In recent years, historians have claimed to deconstruct the myth and legend of the infamous Lady Rochford, and have sought to vindicate Jane. They maintain that she was a 'scapegoat' and innocent of any wrongdoing. This interpretation distorts the evidence, and misrepresents Jane as a victim of circumstances far beyond her control. Certainly she was no statesman, councillor, or architect of royal policy, but she could not have been so naïve, unconscious or altogether oblivious to the nature of conspiracy and court intrigue which governed the very world she lived in. As a woman, her impression on the surviving source material would be expected to be rather more informal, subtle, even hidden; the recurrence of her name in state papers and ambassadorial reports is thus quite striking.

In the historical record, the court is where Jane's life begins, and it is the court where her life ends. One author characterised the Tudor age as one wherein 'men played the risky game of politics with their lives and women were hapless pawns in the complex scheme of dynastic ambitions'.[1] But Jane was not hapless, nor was she a pawn. Her career is a compelling case study to challenge the view that the early Tudor court was a male-dominated society, and that court politics were strictly a *masculine* preserve. Drawn into the lives and affairs of the mistresses she served, Jane, like many of the king's servants, engaged in politics of intimacy; indeed the very intimacy of her position meant that Jane often became involved in the politics of extricating the king from one marriage, and projecting him into another. She negotiated the expected traits of woman, as a daughter, and a wife, with the ruthless pragmatism of a politician, subtly redefining the formal constraints put upon her. Jane was a servant, courtier, companion, confidante, patron, client, broker, agent and informant. Her actions often directly shaped the course of her life and career, of which there is a definite sense that she was aware, astute and in control. Undoubtedly, Jane had a hand in determining her own fate.

Jane forged a career through the 1520s and 1530s, when the court was dangerously volatile. Caught up in the machinations of monarchy, serving the queen could be unpredictable, precarious, even perilous. The queen's household had to be discharged, its servants disbanded, and many of their careers cut short on no less than five occasions. Some could and did, like Jane, transition between households, and this transition became crucial, and ties to the king and his court essential, in surviving what his wives did not. It has been shown that the careers of the queen's servants in this period were not inextricably caught up with the fate of their mistress. When the household of Katherine Howard was discharged in 1541, the king's Privy council declared that 'order must be taken with the maidens, that they repair each of them to their friends, there to remain', acknowledging 'any of the Quenes servants unprovided for, whereof they think the Kings Highness should have consideration'.[2] Many of these servants were appointed to the new queen's household when Henry married Katherine Parr in 1543. Remarkably, Jane had served five of Henry's wives throughout her career; she would not live to see his sixth.[3]

Henry's marital instability led to conflicting loyalties in his queens' households, with disastrous consequences. Faced with complex, often unprecedented crises, the outcome of which would impact her career directly, Jane was forced to act, or react, in one way or another, to align, or realign her loyalties, and in some instances, betray those who were once near to her, to survive. Some careers in the queen's household were made in professionalism, honour, obedience, loyalty and obligation to their mistress, but others, like Jane's, were made in treachery, and opportunism. Of course, there were women who did not, or refused to, engage in court politics. There were also women who did not have a choice. Whereas the king often commanded the allegiance of men and women who served his queens, he could not always dictate how they thought and felt. Jane has left so little behind that we cannot know how she thought or felt, and so it is easy to presume that she was unfeeling or lacking in emotional depth. Some historians mean for us to like Jane, and yet, the impression left by the evidence is that she was not particularly well liked by those who knew her. She may have won the trust of the queens whom she served, but in 1534, during her exile, it seems no one at court, not even her family, spoke out for her; in 1541, at her fall, all those involved, without exception, did not hesitate to turn on her. She died unlamented.

Jane may be described as cold, calculating and devious, or perhaps, more fairly, clever, and ambitious. Certainly she was conniving, meddlesome, and an inveterate plotter and schemer. There is something admirable, even intoxicating, in her talent for intrigue: that Katherine and Culpeper's late night rendezous went undetected for as long as they did is impressive. Her story captures the fickle fortune and grim, cut-throat nature of court politics. The evidence speaks of a woman quite capable, and merges into a coherent narrative held together by her instincts for calculated servility and self-survival. It is this for which Jane should be remembered. Under scrutiny, most historical myths and legends fall apart. In the case of Jane, the infamous Lady Rochford, perhaps the legend, and her place in history, should remain intact.

NOTES

For quotations taken from manuscripts, the original spelling has been retained. If the meaning is ambiguous, explanations are in square brackets.

All institutions and departments of the English royal household (Chamber, Privy Chamber, Household, Wardrobe, etc.) are capitalised, whereas physical spaces (chamber, the queen's chambers, Presence chamber, Privy chamber, court, etc.) are not.

In Tudor England, money was calculated in pounds, shillings and pence. One pound ('li' or £) was twenty shillings. One shilling (s.) was twelve pennies. One penny (d.) was two halfpennies (ob).

Chapter 1: 'My slaunder for ever shall be ryfe': Who was Jane Boleyn?

[1] *LP* XVII 100.

[2] *LP* XVI 1366.

[3] Sleidan, f. cxl (f. 140). Echoed by English chronicler Richard Grafton in 1569. Grafton, vol. 2, p. 456.

[4] Cavendish, *Visions*, pp. 71-74. Albeit exaggerated with a didactic tone, Cavendish's *Metrical Visions* are of definite interest, as his words, 'Whom I oons knew, Jane, Vicountess Rocheford', establish him as her contemporary.

[5] Foxe, vol. 4, p.462n. This marginal note may have been written by John Day, Foxe's printer.

[6] Wyatt, *Boleigne*, p. 447.

[7] Gilbert Burnet, *The History of the Reformation of the Church of England*, 3 vols. (1679), vol. 1, p. 189.

[8] Agnes Strickland, *Lives of the Queens of England*, 8 vols. (1851), vol. 4, pp. 197-198.

[9] Peter Heylyn, *Ecclesiae Restaurata, or the History of the Reformation of the Church of England* (1660), p. 92. Edward Herbert of Cherbury, *The Life and Raigne of King Henry the Eighth* (London, 1649), p. 36.

[10] Sharon Turner, *The History of England, From the Earliest Period to the Death of Elizabeth*, 12 vols. (London, 1839), vol. 10, p. 451.

[11] Thomas Carte, *A General History of England*. 4 vols. (London, 1752), vol. 3, p. 163.

[12] S. Hubert Burke, *Historical Portraits of the Tudor Dynasty and the Reformation Period* (London, 1880), vol. 1, p. 429.

[13] Burnet, *History*, vol. 1, p. 313. Many historians echoed Burnet's judgment of Jane. T. G. Smollett, *A Complete History of England, from the Descent of Julius Caesar, to the Treaty of Aix la Chapelle*, 11 vols. (London, 1758-1760), vol. 6, p. 35. David Hume, *The History of England, from the Invasion of Julius Caesar to the Revolution in 1688*, 5 vols. (London, 1789), vol. 4, pp. 154, 221. Thomas Birch, *The Heads of Illustrious Persons of Great Britain* (London, 1747), p. 26. P. Rapin de Thoyras, *The History of England, as well Ecclesiastical as Civil*, 2nd edition (London, 1732), vol. 1, p. 831. Edward Stone, *Remarks upon the History of the Life of Reginald Pole*, 2nd edition (Oxford, 1766), pp. 247-8. Charles Coote, *The History of England*, 9 vols. (London, 1791), vol. 5, p. 79. Charles Granville, *A Synopsis of the Troubles and Miseries of England, during the Space of 1800 Years*, 4 vols. (London, c. 1747), vol. 1, p. 108.

[14] Jennifer Ann Rowley-Williams, 'Image and Reality: the Lives of Aristocratic Women in Early Tudor England' (University of Wales, Unpublished Ph.D. thesis, 1998); Elizabeth Norton, *The Boleyn Women: The Tudor femmes fatales who changed English history* (Gloucestershire, 2009); Sylvia Barbara Soberton, *Ladies-in-Waiting: Women Who Served Anne Boleyn* (2022).

[15] Antonia Fraser, *The Six Wives of Henry VIII* (London, 2009) p. 349.

[16] Gareth Russell, *Young and Damned and Fair: The Life and Tragedy of Catherine Howard at the Court of Henry VIII* (London, 2017).

[17] Anthony Martienssen, *Queen Katherine Parr* (London, 1973), pp. 141-2.

[18] Lacey Baldwin Smith, *A Tudor Tragedy: The Life and Times of Catherine Howard* (London, 1962), p. 161. See also Alison Weir, *The Lady in the Tower: The Fall of Anne Boleyn* (London, 2000).

[19] Dakota L. Hamilton, Review of Jane Boleyn: The True Story of the Infamous Lady Rochford by Julia Fox, *The Sixteenth Century Journal*, 40, 3 (2009), pp. 828-829.

[20] Julia Fox, *Jane Boleyn: The True Story of the Infamous Lady Rochford* (New York, 2009), p. 326. In spite of the evidence to the contrary, this interpretation has proven to be highly influential. Clare Cherry and Claire Ridgeway, *George Boleyn: Tudor Poet, Courtier & Diplomat* (2014). Charlie Fenton, *Jane Parker: The Downfall of Two Tudor Queens?* (Hampshire, 2021).

[21] Hilary Mantel, 'Frocks and Shocks', Review of Jane Boleyn: The Infamous Lady Rochford by Julia Fox, London Review of Books, 30, 8 (2008).

[22] Joanna Denny, *Katherine Howard: A Tudor Conspiracy* (London, 2005).

[23] Examining Jane's career provides a new perspective from which to analyse the early Tudor queens, as mistress of the household, surrounded by the men and women who served them. Henry VIII's queens remain intensely popular for biographical study, yet rarely do such accounts provide any insight into their households. E. W. Ives, Elizabeth Norton, Giles Tremlett, Retha Warnicke, Lacey Baldwin Smith and many more have uncovered the lives of women who served as queens consort from 1509 to 1547. E. W. Ives, *The Life and Death of Anne Boleyn: 'The Most Happy'* (Oxford, 2004); Elizabeth Norton, *Catherine Parr* (Gloucestershire, 2010); *Jane Seymour: Henry VIII's True Love* (Gloucestershire, 2009); Giles Tremlett, *Catherine of Aragon: Henry's*

Spanish Queen (London, 2010). Retha Warnicke, *The Marrying of Anne of Cleves: Royal Protocol in Early Modern England* (Cambridge, 2000); Lacey Baldwin Smith, *A Tudor Tragedy: The Life and Times of Catherine Howard* (London, 1962). Few historians have attempted to integrate the queen's servants into the narrative in any meaningful way. Exceptions to this are Gareth Russell, who situated Katherine Howard's brief tenure as queen in the context of her household, and Susan James, who has shown that there was a core affinity in Katherine Parr's household comprised of friends, relatives and well-wishers. Gareth Russell, *Young and Damned and Fair: The Life and Tragedy of Catherine Howard at the Court of Henry VIII* (London, 2017); Susan James, *Catherine Parr: Henry VIII's Last Love* (Gloucester, 2008).

[24] Our understanding of royal service is predicated on the king's men, and the English royal household and wider court is often reconstructed as if it were 'exclusively male': the court, we are told, was a male-dominated society, the archetypal 'courtier' is male, and its politics were strictly a *masculine* preserve. (Barbara J. Harris, 'Women and Politics in Early Tudor England', *The Historical Journal*, 33, 2 (1990), pp. 259-281). Women must be integrated more fully into the master narrative of court studies. Natalie Mears, 'Courts, Courtiers, and Culture in Tudor England', *Historical Journal*, 46 (2003), pp. 703-722 (p. 722).

Chapter 2: 'Mistres Parker': Finding a foothold

[1] TNA LC 9/50, ff. 182v-216r.

[2] Cavendish, *Visions*, pp. 71-74.

[3] Her name is recorded in several extant lists of attendees, all of which are similar with only slight variations or corrections: 1) 'mistres Parker' in J. G. Nichols (ed.) *The Chronicle of Calais in the Reigns of Henry VII and Henry VIII to the year 1540* (1838), pp. 19-25 (p. 25); 2) 'Mastres Perker' in the William Jerdan (ed.), *Rutland papers: Original documents illustrative of the courts and times of Henry VII. and Henry VIII. Selected from the private archives of His Grace the Duke of Rutland* (London, 1842), p. 38; 3) 'Mistress Parker' in Bodleian MS Ashmole 1116, f. 99v, printed in Glenn Richardson, *The Field of Cloth of Gold* (New Haven, 2013), Appendix A; 4) 'Ms Parker' in LPL MS 285, f. 19. Jane is absent, however, from the list contained in the State Papers (TNA SP 1/19, f. 269r (*LP*III 704). We know that Anne, 'mistres Browne' who is also absent from this list, was certainly in attendance, suggesting that this is likely to have been an earlier draft before numbers swelled, and perhaps, before Jane was appointed to serve the queen.

[4] *LP*III, pp. 1548-1599.

[5] 'Officers, servants and scholars in Lady Margaret's household, c. 1499-1509', in Michael K. Jones and Malcolm G. Underwood, *The King's Mother: Lady Margaret Beaufort, Countess of Richmond and Derby* (Cambridge, 1993), pp. 268-287.

[6] AMB, pp. 197, 215, 382, 502, 547.

[7] AMB, pp. 289, 337, 382, 425, 446, 492, 544, 597.

[8] AMB, pp. 520, 537, 544, 574, 590.

[9] AMB, pp. 445, 503, 509, 521, 531, 534, 538, 554-555, 562, 570, 577, 587, 592, 638, etc.

[10] AMB, pp. 521-522.

[11] AMB, pp. 233, 332, 504, 507, 522, 536, 552, 559, 588, 616.

[12] AMB, pp. 216, 618.

[13] AMB, p. 25.

[14] James P. Carley, 'Henry Parker, tenth Baron Morley' (1480/81–1556), in ODNB (2004), notes that the names of two more sisters, Elizabeth and Frances, are in a manuscript (BL Harley MS, 4775) previously owned by Jane's father.

[15] AMB, p. 346.

[16] AMB, p. 281.

[17] AMB, pp. 344, 347, 360, 372, 475, 527, 567. AMB, pp. 304, 340, 556.

[18] AMB, p. 571.

[19] AMB, p. 444.

[20] AMB, pp. 422, 582.

[21] AMB, p. 534.

[22] AMB, pp. 527, 568, 571, 622.

[23] AMB, p. 306.

[24] AMB, p. 555.

[25] AMB, pp. 578, 351, 612.

[26] AMB, pp. 521-522.

[27] AMB, p. 583.

[28] AMB, pp. 534, 582, 592, 612.

[29] *HC*, p. 703. Castiglione, p. 182. Elizabeth Blount was a maid-of-honour to Catherine of Aragon.

[30] Maria Dowling, *Humanism in the Age of Henry VIII* (Kent, 1986), pp. 221, 229-30.

[31] James Daybell, *Women Letter-Writers in Tudor England* (Oxford, 2006), p. 2. Barbara J. Harris, *English Aristocratic Women, 1450-1550: Marriage and Family, Property and Careers* (Oxford, 2002), pp. 27-43.

[32] Ellis, vol. 2, pp. 67-8. Rowley-Williams, 'Image and Reality', pp. 164-5.

[33] AMB, p. 254.

[34] *Lisle*, III, p. 25. *HO*, p. 146; *BB*, pp. 105-6.

[35] *Lisle*, IV, 887, pp. 150-152 (*LP* XII, ii., 271); *Lisle*, IV, 895, pp. 163-5 (*LP* XII, ii., 711).

[36] Castiglione, pp. 175-6.

[37] Juan Luis Vives, *The Education of a Christian Woman: A Sixteenth-Century Manual*, ed. and trans. by Charles Fantazzi (Chicago, 2007), p. 71.

[38] Cavendish, *Visions*, pp. 71-74.

[39] Castiglione, pp. 174-176.

[40] *CSP* Sp, I, 268.

[41] *LP* XV 229.

⁴² There is a sketch portrait by Hans Holbein the Younger, inscribed in an eighteenth-century hand with the words 'The Lady Parker', which is often thought to be Jane. Its identification as 'The Lady Parker' may be attributed to John Cheke, Edward VI's tutor in 1544. It can be dated to Holbein's second visit to England, in around 1531 or 1532, by which time Jane was not so much a young lady as she was a mature woman, and although her maiden name was Parker, her marriage to George Boleyn predates Holbein's earliest association with the Tudor court. She would have been known to her contemporaries in the 1530s as Lady Rochford, not Lady Parker. We can only speculate but Jane is more likely to have been one of the many unnamed women in Holbein's court sketches: perhaps the 'Unidentified woman' from the late 1530s and early 1540s with a tired but shrewd expression wearing all black, as we know Jane, in her later years, following the death of her husband, dressed as a 'wydowe in blake'. Hans Holbein the Younger, 'The Lady Parker', c. 1540-1543. RCIN 912230; 'An unidentified woman', c. 1532-43, Royal Collection Trust / © His Majesty King Charles III 2023.

⁴³ *HO*, pp. 31-32; *BB*, pp. 105-6.

⁴⁴ Smith, *Catherine*, p. 137.

⁴⁵ *LP* XVI 1395; *LP* XVI 1470.

⁴⁶ *Statutes*, III, pp. 857-8 (*LP* XVII 28).

⁴⁷ BL Cotton MS, Caligula, E, IV, f. 55. (*LP* XIX, ii., 201).

⁴⁸ Fiona Kisby, 'Officers and Office-Holding at the English Court: A Study of the Chapel Royal, 1485-1547', *Royal Musical Association Research Chronicle*, 32 (1999), pp. 1-61. (pp. 5-6).

⁴⁹ TNA SP 1/161, f. 85 (*LP* XV 875). Joan Bulmer was described as Katherine's 'bedfellow' before she became queen (*LP* XVI 1321).

⁵⁰ TNA SP 1/76, f. 121 (*LP* VI 559).

⁵¹ TNA SP 1/78, f. 50 (*LP* VI 917). This Vaughan reiterated on 3 August 1533. TNA SP 1/78, f. 75 (*LP* VI 934).

Chapter 3: 'When she list to spit or do otherwise at her pleasure': Maid-of-Honour

¹ James Taffe, 'Reconstructing the queen's household: a study in royal service, 1485-1547' (Durham University, Unpublished Ph.D. thesis, 2022) for a full account of the early Tudor queen's household.

² Starkey, 'Representation through intimacy: A study in the symbolism of monarchy and Court office in early modern England' in John Guy (ed.), *The Tudor Monarchy* (London, 1997), pp. 42-77 (pp. 51-2, 59).

³ David Starkey, 'The King's Privy Chamber, 1485-1547' (University of Cambridge, Unpublished Ph.D. thesis, 1973), p. 24; Starkey, 'Representation through intimacy' in Guy (ed.), *Monarchy*, p. 59.

⁴ For architectural developments in royal palaces accommodating the queen's side, see Simon Thurley, *The Royal Palaces of Tudor England: Architecture and Court Life, 1460-1547* (London, 1993) p. 19.

⁵ Cavendish, *Wolsey*, pp. 227-231.

[6] *HO*, pp. 146. 152.

[7] *BB*, pp. 92-93.

[8] *HO*, pp. 340-351.

[9] Pam Wright has argued that 'despite the unsuitability of the Henrician regulations for female staff no new household ordinances were drawn up at the beginning of the reign', and takes this as evidence of 'the domestic, uncontentious nature of the Privy Chamber'. Pam Wright, 'A Change in Direction: the Ramifications of a Female Household, 1558-1603', in David Starkey (ed.), *The English Court: from the Wars of the Roses to the Civil War* (Essex, 2002), pp. 147-72 (pp. 147-148). However it appears that these regulations were deemed to be wholly suitable by contemporaries, as they did not revise them for a female establishment.

[10] *HO*, p. 156.

[11] *HO*, p. 118.

[12] *HO*, p. 155; *LP* IV 1939 [7].

[13] *HO*, p. 156.

[14] TNA E101/414/16, f. 3v, TNA E36/214, f. 5r. 68r. Starkey, 'Privy Chamber', pp. 29-35, 359. Starkey, 'Representations', in Guy (ed.), *Monarchy*, p. 60.

[15] The privy purse accounts for Elizabeth of York demonstrate that money was conveyed 'to the quenes purs by thandes of' her ladies and gentlewomen servants. TNA E36/210, ff. 14, 31, 35, 40, 41, 50.

[16] When Katherine Parr was queen, her sister Anne served as Keeper of the Queen's Jewels (TNA E315/161, f. 26 for Anne handling 'ladies yrings'). Her chamberers Susan Norwich and Maude Lovekyn, regularly conveyed items to the queen, including medicinal supplies, probably for the king, such as lozenges, liqorice, cinnamon comfits, sponges and plasters; they also carried fennell and rosewater and 'fyne perfumes', presumably for keeping her chambers sensually pleasing (TNA E315/161, ff. 22-31).

[17] *HO*, p. 45; *Arundell*, pp. 185-186; Starkey, 'Privy Chamber', pp. 22-23. *BB*, pp. 111, 129, 201.

[18] *HO*, p. 341.

[19] BL Add. MS. 21116, f. 8v.

[20] *HO*, p. 347.

[21] *HO*, p. 144.

[22] *Arundell*, pp. 186-193. *HO*, pp. 38, 340-342. BL Add MS 71009, f. 10v-11r.

[23] *HO*, pp. 144, 152-153; *Arundell*, pp. 199-201.

[24] *HO*, pp. 41, 155.

[25] *HO*, p. 147.

[26] *HO*, p. 41.

[27] *HO*, pp. 48-49. *Arundell*, pp. 205-206.

[28] Her meals were frequently taken in public, either in her Presence chamber, or the Great Hall, but occasionally they would be served in private. *Arundell*, pp. 197-198; *HO*, p. 341.

[29] *HO*, p. 156.

[30] *HO*, pp. 42-3.

[31] *HO*, p. 35.

[32] *HO*, p. 35.

[33] The queen's master of the horse and her receiver-general were not strictly 'Chamber' servants, but ate and drank in the queen's chambers and often liaised with her directly.

[34] BL Harleian MS, 41 f. 10 (*LP* VI 601).

Chapter 4: 'A glorified boudoir'?: Queenship

[1] Steven Gunn, *Henry VII's New Men and the Making of Tudor England* (Oxford, 2016), p. 39; G. W. Bernard, 'The rise of Sir William Compton, early Tudor courtier', *English Historical Review*, 96, 381 (1981), pp. 754-777; E. W. Ives, 'Court and County Palatine in the Reign of Henry VIII: The Career of William Brereton of Malpas', *Transactions of the Historic Society of Lancashire and Cheshire*, 123 (1971), pp. 1-38; E. W. Ives, 'Patronage at the Court of Henry VIII: The Case of Sir Ralph Egerton of Ridley', *Bulletin of the John Rylands Library*, 52 (1969-70), pp. 346-74; R. C. Braddock, 'The Royal Household, 1540-1560: A Study of Officeholding in Tudor England' (Northwestern University, Unpublished PhD thesis, 1971); R. C. Braddock, 'The Rewards of Office-holding in Tudor England', *The Journal of British Studies* (1975), pp. 29-47; Narasingha Prosad Sil, *Tudor Placemen and Statesmen: Select Case Studies* (New Jersey, 2001); Richard Egbert Brock, 'The Courtier in Early Tudor Society, Illustrated from Selected Examples' (University of London, Unpublished Ph.D. thesis, 1963).

[2] David Starkey, 'Intimacy and innovation: the rise of the Privy Chamber, 1485-1547', in Starkey (ed.), *Court*, pp. 1-24, 71-118; G. R. Elton, 'Tudor Government', a review of *The English Court* in *The Historical Journal*, 31, 2 (1988), pp. 425-434.

[3] David Loades, *Power in Tudor England* (Hampshire, 1997), p. 41 for Mary I's Privy Chamber. Women were 'limited by their sex to a purely domestic role', whereas, for Edward VI, who was a minor, power was situated in the Privy council rather than the Privy chamber, which was staffed by childhood companions. Starkey, 'Privy Chamber', p. 293; Starkey, 'Representation', in Guy (ed.) *Monarchy*, p. 52. Steven Gunn, 'The Courtiers of Henry VII', *English Historical Review*, 108 (1993), pp. 23-49 (p. 29); *Early Tudor Government, 1485-1558* (Hampshire, 1995), p. 36.

[4] John Murphy, 'The illusion of decline: the Privy Chamber, 1547-1558', in Starkey (ed.), *Court*, pp. 119-146 (p. 140).

[5] Wright, 'Ramifications', in Starkey (ed.), *Court*, pp. 147-72 (p. 150).

[6] *HO*, p. 156.

[7] TCD, pp. 383-395.

[8] CSP Sp, II, 23.

[9] CSP Sp, II, 43.

[10] CSP Sp, Supp to I and II, 7.

[11] CSP Sp, Supp to I and II, 8.

[12] CSP Sp, Supp to I and II, 8.

[13] CSP Sp, Supp to I and II, 7.

[14] HC, p. 584.
[15] BL Harleian MS, 3504, ff. 232r-233v.
[16] TNA SP 1/13, f. 38 (*LP* II 1622).
[17] TNA SP 1/78, f. 27 (*LP* VI 890).
[18] BL Add MS 4712, f. 15r (*AR*, vol. 1, pp. 304-305, 333).
[19] BL Add MS 4712, f. 15r. (*AR*, vol. 1, p. 305).
[20] TNA SP 1/26, f. 31 (*LP* XII, ii., 1004).
[21] Steven Gunn and Antheun Janse (eds), *The Court as a Stage: England and the Low Countries in the Late Middle Ages* (Suffolk, 2006).
[22] James Taffe, "Pleasaunt Pastime', or Drunken Diplomacy? Ladies and Gentlewomen at the Field of Cloth of Gold', in Anthony Musson and J. P. D. Cooper (eds), *Royal Journeys in Early Modern Europe: Progresses, Palaces and Panache* (Abingdon, 2022), pp. 127-138. Glenn Richardson, *The Field of Cloth of Gold* (New Haven, 2013); Joycelyne G. Russell, *Field of Cloth of Gold: Men and Manners in 1520* (London, 1969).
[23] 'A Memoriall of such things as be requisite', hereafter 'Memoriall', in 'Two papers relating to the interview between Henry the Eighth of England and Francis the First of France', ed. John Caley, *Archaeologia*, 21 (1827), pp. 176–91 (pp. 184, 190).
[24] It was ordained that 'neyther of theym shall bryng with theyme a mor nombre of Noblemen and women servants and horsis than is conteyned in a bill indented'. 'Memoriall', p. 184.
[25] TNA SP 1/20 f. 41 (*LP* III 806).
[26] *LP* III 698. *HC*, pp. 600-601.
[27] *HC*, pp. 600-601.
[28] Maria Hayward, *Dress at the Court of Henry VIII* (Abington, 2007), pp. 301-316 for dressing the households of Henry VIII's queens.
[29] TNA E 315/242/3, fos. 22v-31r (*LP* III 852). Michelle Beer, *Queenship at the Renaissance Courts of Britain: Catherine of Aragon and Margaret Tudor, 1503-1533* (Suffolk, 2018), p. 60.
[30] CSP Ven, III, 68.
[31] Bodleian MS Ashmole 1116, f. 101r.
[32] *HC*, pp. 615, 618.
[33] CSP Ven, III, 81.
[34] CSP Ven, III, 50.
[35] CSP Ven, III, 84.
[36] *The Anglica Historia of Polydore Vergil, A. D. 1485-1537*, ed. and trans. Denys Hay, *Royal Historical Society*, Camden Series, vol. 74 (London, 1950), p. 269.
[37] CSP Ven III 69.
[38] Castiglione, p. 175.
[39] *HC*, p. 516.
[40] Giustinian, *Four Years*, vol. 2, pp. 97-8 (*LP* II 3455).
[41] *LP* II 3462.
[42] *HC*, p. 62.

[43] *LP* III 869.
[44] Bodleian MS Ashmole 1116, f. 101r.
[45] Bodleian MS Ashmole 1116, f. 102v; 'Memoriall', pp. 182-183.
[46] *LP* III 869.
[47] 'Memoriall', p. 190; *HC*, p. 603.
[48] CSP Ven, III, 50.
[49] CSP Ven, III, 83.
[50] CSP Ven, III, 94.
[51] CSP Ven, III, 81.
[52] *HC*, p. 618.
[53] 'Here after ensueth two fruytfull sermons, made [and] compyled by the right reverende father in God John Fyssher, Doctour of dyvynyte and Bysshop of Rochester', in Cecilia A. Hatt (ed.), *English Works of John Fisher, Bishop of Rochester: Sermons and Other Writings, 1520-1535* (Oxford, 2002), pp. 212-254.
[54] Harris, *English Aristocratic Women*, p. 234.
[55] Castiglione, pp. 174-176.
[56] BL Add MS, 29549, f. 1 (*LP* I 2620).
[57] Ives, *Anne,* pp. 20, 68-69 for the 'courtly love' tradition.
[58] *HC*, pp. 533-4.
[59] *HC*, pp. 533-4.
[60] 'Memoriall', p. 177.
[61] CSP Ven, III, 84.
[62] CSP Ven, III, 84.
[63] CSP Ven, III, 90.
[64] *HC*, p. 614.
[65] CSP Ven, III, 69.
[66] Russell, *Cloth of Gold*, p. 132.
[67] *HC*, pp. 513-14.
[68] *HC*, pp. 516-9.
[69] *HC*, pp. 594-5; Giustinian, *Four Years*, vol. 2, pp. 225-228.
[70] *LP* III pp.1548-1599.
[71] *HC*, pp. 630-1.
[72] Ultimately, the evidence is insufficient to cast any one of the ladies in attendance in any one particular role.
[73] Castiglione, pp. 174-176.
[74] *HC*, p. 784.
[75] Ives, *Anne,* p. 20.

Chapter 5: 'For the establishment of good order': Ordinances and Perquisites

[1] *HO*, p. 137.
[2] HO, p. 137,
[3] *HO*, p. 161.
[4] BL Harleian MS, 6807, f. 11.

[5] BL Harleian MS, 6807, ff. 10-12.
[6] BL Lansdowne MS, 21, f. 142r.
[7] *HO*, pp. 139, 147, 229-230; BL Harleian MS 6807, f. 12.
[8] PPE, Hen. VIII, pp. 76, 195, 209, etc.
[9] CSP Sp Supp I and II, 8 (*LP*I 474).
[10] Ellis, vol. 1, pp. 88-89.
[11] CSP Sp, V, i, 97.
[12] For the household of Catherine of Aragon, see TNA LC 9/50, ff. 182v-216r for her coronation in 1509; TNA E179/70/116 for a subsidy list assessing the queen's Chamber in 1512; BL Add MS 21116, f. 40 (*LP*II 3446) for a banquet held at Greenwich in 1517; HMC Rutland, pp. 21-22 for 'Ordinaunces and appoynmentes' of 1517; TNA SP 1/19, f. 267r-269v and Bodl. MS Ashmole 1116, f. 99r, for the Field of Cloth of Gold in 1520; TNA SP 1/73 f. 70 (*LP*V 1711) for a list of plate, with the names of recipients of the gifts of plate and those who delivered them, c. 1520; *LP* Addenda I, 367 for a similar record in 1522; BL Cotton MS Vespasian C XIV ff. 269-70 for the Eltham Ordinances of 1526; TNA E101/420/4 for the New Year gift roll of 1528, and BL Cotton MS, Otho, C, X, ff. 216-217 for Catherine's will.
[13] *HO*, p. 146.
[14] *HC*, p. 592; Giustinian, *Four Years*, vol. 2, p. 136.
[15] *LP*I 709 [44]; *LP*I 3324 [36]; *LP*I 3324 [14]; *LP*I 3324 [39]; *LP*I 784 [11]; *LP*I 3324 [12].
[16] For the household of Elizabeth of York, see BL Add MS 21481, ff.15r-20r; *PPE*, Eliz, pp. 11, 13, 17, 21, 23, 38, 40, 49, 51, 52, 59, 62, 64, 70, 98-99, 181, 214; William Campbell (ed.), *Materials for a History of the Reign of Henry the Seventh*, 2 vols. (London, 1873-77), pp. 118, 294.
[17] *Statutes*, III, p. 480.
[18] *Lisle*, IV, 887.
[19] *Lisle*, IV, 894. My italics, for emphasis: this may have been some remark by Husee acknowledging that her wages as a servant of the queen would be meagre.
[20] BL Cotton MS, Appendix, LXV; *LP*IV 6121; TNA E101/417/2.
[21] TNA E101/422/15; TNA E179/69/44; Dakota L. Hamilton, 'The Household of Queen Katherine Parr' (University of Oxford, Unpublished Ph.D. thesis, 1992), p. 34; Harris, *English Aristocratic Women*, p. 225.
[22] *HO*, p. 199.
[23] PPE, Mary, p. 65.
[24] BL Add MS 45716A, f. 3v.
[25] *HO*, p. 146.
[26] *HO*, p. 153.
[27] *HO*, p. 164.
[28] *LP*III 361.
[29] *LP*II 470.
[30] *LP*II 123; *LP*III 524.
[31] BL Arundel MS 97, f. 100r.

[32] Hayward, *Dress*, p. 246.
[33] BL Add MS 71009, ff. 57v-59r.
[34] COA MS, M6, f. 17r-17v. Hayward, *Dress*, pp. 64-65.
[35] COA MS, M6, ff. 1v, 2v, 5v. Hayward, *Dress*, p. 65. *LP* XII, ii., 1060; *WC*, vol. 1, pp. 70-72 for Jane Seymour. All the ladies in Jane's procession were ordered to ride to Windsor for the burial. *Lisle*, IV, 903, p. 182. Katherine Parr's servants were issued yards of black cloth for Henry VIII's funeral on 16 February 1547. TNA LC 2/2.
[36] TNA E101/418/6, ff. 8r, 20v, 22v.
[37] *LP* I 908.
[38] TNA E101/418/6, f. 9r; Katherine Parr's ladies and gentlewomen wore the queen's badge on their caps displaying the head of St Katherine. James, *Parr*, p. 123.
[39] CSP Ven, IV, 923; Ives, *Anne*, p. 142.
[40] *Lisle*, IV, 887, pp.150-152 (*LP* XII, ii., 271).
[41] *Lisle*, IV, 887 (*LP* XII, ii., 271).
[42] *Lisle*, IV, 895 (*LP* XII, ii., 711).
[43] *Lisle*, IV, 896 (*LP* XII, ii., 808); *Lisle*, IV, 887 (*LP* XII, ii., 271).
[44] *Lisle*, V, 1102, pp. 36-7.
[45] *Lisle*, V, 1117, pp. 58-9.
[46] *Lisle*, V, 1126, pp. 70-2.
[47] *Lisle*, V, 1136, pp. 92-4.
[48] *Lisle*, V, 1137, pp. 95-6.
[49] In 1535, Anne Owen, in a petition to the king for the money, jewels and plate left by her husband Sir David Owen, remarked that she had spent as much as £113 19s. 8d. 'on his apparel' while he was in the king's service. *LP* IX 1135.
[50] Braddock, 'Household', pp. 32-33.
[51] LP III, pp. 1548-9.
[52] *HC*, vol. 1, pp. 630-1.
[53] LP III, pp. 1548-9.
[54] TNA E 315/160, ff. 104-105.
[55] BL Add MS 71009, f. 19r.
[56] BL Harleian MS 1419A, f. 257; Hamilton, 'Parr' p. 12.
[57] Giustinian, *Four Years*, vol. 2, pp. 97-8; *LP* II 3446; *LP* II 3455.
[58] *HC*, p. 599.
[59] BL Cotton MS, Caligula, D, VI, f. 152 (*LP* I 3387).
[60] Barbara J. Harris, 'The View from My Lady's Chamber: New Perspectives on the Early Tudor Monarchy', *Huntingdon Library Quarterly*, 60, 3 (1997), pp. 215-247 (p. 237).
[61] *HC*, pp. 630-1.

Chapter 6: 'The wicked wife': Marriage
[1] Alison Weir, *Henry VIII: King and Court* (London, 2008), p. 365.
[2] Rowley-Williams, 'Image and Reality', p. 160.

[3] Retha M. Warnicke, *The Rise and Fall of Anne Boleyn: Family politics at the court of Henry VIII* (Cambridge, 2000), pp. 215-8.

[4] Wood (ed.), *Letters*, vol. 2, pp. 195-7.

[5] Cavendish, *Visions*, pp. 20-24.

[6] *LP* II, Revels, 7 (George was 'Master Bollyn', one of the participants).

[7] *LP* III 2214 (29). For the life and career of George Boleyn, see Lauren Mackay, *Among the Wolves of Court: The Untold Story of Thomas and George Boleyn* (London, 2020).

[8] Carley, 'Henry Parker', in ODNB.

[9] *LP* IV Appendix, 99.

[10] CSP Sp II, 20 (*LP* I 128).

[11] Harris, 'Chamber', pp. 240-241.

[12] Beer, 'Queenship', p. 229.

[13] Wood, vol. 1, pp. 260-261 (*LP* IV 1032).

[14] TNA AR/19/37/1-2.

[15] BL Cotton MS, Galba, B, VIII, f. 150 (*LP* IV 882).

[16] *LP* IV 546 [1].

[17] David Starkey, 'An Attendant Lord? Henry Parker, Lord Morley', in Marie Axton et al. (eds), Triumphs of English : Henry Parker, Lord Morley, Translator to the Tudor Court : New Essays in Interpretation (London, 2000), p. 12 for Morley's income according to his assessment for the subsidy, and the conversion of 2000 marks to pounds, shillings and pence.

[18] Ellis, vol. 2, pp. 67-8. Carley, 'Henry Parker', in ODNB.

[19] Harris, *English Aristocratic Women*, pp. 62, 75.

[20] *LP* IV 1939 [14].

[21] Stanford Lehmberg, 'George Boleyn' (d. 1603) in ODNB (2004). David Loades, *The Boleyns: The Rise & Fall of a Tudor Family* (Gloucestershire, 2011), p. 140.

[22] Harris, *English Aristocratic Women*, p. 61.

[23] Lehmberg, 'George Boleyn', in ODNB.

[24] *LP* VI 613.

[25] Warnicke, *Anne*, p. 219.

[26] Fox, *Jane Boleyn*, p. 47.

[27] Warnicke, *Anne*, p. 216.

[28] Starkey, 'Attendant Lord?' in Axton et al (eds), 'Triumphs', p. 14. Ives, *Anne*, p. 331.

[29] Warnicke, *Anne*, p. 219.

[30] Norton, *Fatale*, p. 195 for a discussion on identifying 'Marc S.'

[31] *Excerpta Historica*, pp. 261-5.

[32] Warnicke, *Anne*, p. 218.

[33] Cavendish, *Visions*, pp. 20-4.

[34] His entry in *Athenae Oxonienses* describes him as a man who 'was much adored' at court, 'especially by the female sex, for his admirable discourse and symmetry of body'. Anthony Wood, *Athenae Oxonienses: An Exact History of All the Writers and*

Bishops Who Have Had Their Education in the University of Oxford (1691), vol. 1, p. 98.

[35] Wyatt, *Boleigne*, pp. 442-7.

[36] BL Cotton MS, Otho, C, X, f. 222 (*LP* X 798).

[37] An alternative reading of the source is made by E. W. Ives, who has suggested that 'we may, if we choose, smell malice, for the message was brought with Henry's express permission and by Carew and Bryan in his newly turned coat'. Ives, *Anne*, p. 332.

[38] BL Cotton MS, Otho, C, X, f. 222 (*LP* X 798).

[39] Harris, *English Aristocratic Women*, p. 18.

[40] Cavendish, *Visions*, p. 71. TNA SP 1/167, f. 163r-163v (*LP* XVI 1340). Norton, *Fatale*, p. 193.

Chapter 7: 'None but God can get him out of it': The Boleyn Ascendancy

[1] *LP* IV 546 (1).

[2] Harris, *English Aristocratic Women*, p. 68.

[3] *Lisle*, IV, 865, p. 117; *Lisle*, IV, 864, pp. 111-112; *Lisle*, IV, 891, pp. 156-7.

[4] *LP* IV 1939 (14). This sum may have been promised to them upon their marriage. In 1537, Jane Ashley, maid-of-honour to the queen, intended to marry Peter Mewtas, of the king's Privy Chamber, but it remained 'as yet uncertain' because 'it dependeth on the King's goodness to look towards their living'. *Lisle*, IV, 870, pp. 125-6 (*LP* XII, i., 586).

[5] *LP* IV 1939 (14).

[6] *LP* IV 1939 (4) and (5).

[7] David Starkey, *Six Wives: The Queens of Henry VIII* (London, 2004), p. 278.

[8] *LP* IV 4539.

[9] LP IV 4649.

[10] *LP* IV 4779. *LP* IV 4993 (15). *LP* IV 5248.

[11] PPE, Hen. VIII, pp. 34, 37, 68, 72, 128, 144, 156, 189, 195, 209, 210, 226, 232, 263.

[12] TNA E101/420/4 (*LP* IV 3738).

[13] *HC*, p. 754; CSP Ven, IV, 584.

[14] CSP Sp, III, ii., 541.

[15] *LP* IV 4648.

[16] *LP* IV 5016.

[17] *HC*, p. 759.

[18] James Gairdner, 'New Lights on the Divorce of Henry VIII', *The English Historical Review*, 11, 44 (1896), pp. 673-702 (p. 685).

[19] *LP* IV 4251.

[20] Ives, *Anne*, pp. 199-202, 293-295. The most vociferous reviled and slandered her as a 'whore' (*LP* VI 1254; *LP* VIII 196) and a 'harlot of her living' (*LP* VII 840). Eustace Chapuys referred to Anne as 'the concubine'. CSP Sp V, ii., 43.

[21] My italics, for emphasis. *LP* IV 5016.

[22] CSP Sp IV, ii., 1061 (*LP* V 351).

[23] CSP Sp, IV, ii., 786 (*LP* V 401); CSP Sp IV, ii., 765 (*LP* V 340).
[24] Cavendish, *Wolsey*, p. 240.
[25] CSP Sp IV, ii., 880 (*LP* V 696).
[26] *LP* IV 5016.
[27] *Lisle*, I, p. 332, p. 518; *Lisle*, II, pp. 331, 373-4; Harris, 'Women and Politics', pp. 265-266.
[28] *LP* IV 6026; *LP* IV 6199; CSP Sp IV ii., 765 (*LP* V 340).
[29] *HC*, pp. 781-782; *LP* V 375; *LP* V 594.
[30] BL Cotton MS, Otho, C, X, f. 276r.
[31] CSP, Ven, IV, 682.
[32] BL Cotton MS, Otho, C, X, f. 177 (*LP* VI 352).
[33] *Lisle*, II, 113, pp. 28-29. It was felt by some that the lives of Catherine and Mary were in danger. *Lisle*, II, p. 28.
[34] TNA E101/420/15 (*LP* V 686) for the gift roll of 1532.
[35] CSP Sp IV ii., 880 (*LP* V 696). Chapuys 'had acute political antennae and watched the rituals of New Year for signals of favour and disfavour'. Felicity Heal, *The Power of Gifts: Gift Exchange in Early Modern England* (Oxford, 2014), pp. 93-5.
[36] CSP Sp IV ii., 880 (*LP* V 696). *Lisle*, II, 302, pp. 373-374 (*LP* VIII 15).
[37] TNA E101/420/15 (*LP* V 686).
[38] TNA E101/421/13.
[39] *HC*, pp. 793-4.
[40] *LP* V 1274.
[41] *LP* V 1376.
[42] *LP* V 1377; CSP Sp IV, ii., 1003.
[43] 'The Maner of the tryumphe of Caleys and Bulleyn' in A. F. Pollard (ed.), Tudor Tracts: 1532-1588 (New York, 1903), p. 4.
[44] Pollard (ed.), *Tudor Tracts*, p. 6.
[45] *HC*, pp. 793-4.
[46] *LP* V 1484. Pollard (ed.), *Tudor Tracts*, p. 7.
[47] CSP Sp, IV, ii., 1047 (*LP* VI 142).
[48] *HC*, p. 795.
[49] *HC*, p. 795.
[50] *HC*, p. 795.
[51] CSP IV, ii,, 1073 (LP VI 508); CSP Sp IV, ii., 1077 (*LP* VI 556).
[52] *Lisle*, IV, 830 (*LP* VIII 378).
[53] *Lisle*, IV, 833 (*LP* VIII 545).
[54] *Lisle*, II, 502a (*LP* IX 1004).
[55] *Lisle*, III, 658 (*LP* X 499).
[56] Matthew Hefferan, 'Family, Loyalty and the Royal Household in Fourteenth-Century England', in D. Green and C. Given-Wilson (eds), *Fourteenth Century England*, XI, pp. 129-154 (p. 146).
[57] Harris, *English Aristocratic Women*, pp. 101-121.

[58] For the household of Anne Boleyn, see BL Add MS, 71009, ff. 57v-59r for her coronation; TNA E179/69/28 for a subsidy list assessing the queen's Chamber in c. 1535; *LP* V 1484 for Anne's visit to Calais in 1532; and TNA E101/420/15 for New Year gift roll for 1532; TNA E101/421/13 for 1534; BL Cotton MS, Otho, C, X, ff. 209-225 for letters from Sir William Kingston to Thomas Cromwell, and TNA SP 1/103 ff. 318-320, TNA SP 1/104 f. 1, and TNA SP 1/104, f. 257 for various accounts of the queen's debts.

[59] Sir John Shelton and Lady Shelton were appointed to serve in the households of the king's daughters: John was Elizabeth's lord steward, and his wife was Mary's governess.

[60] For the household of Henry VIII, see TNA LC 9/50, ff. 182v-216r for his coronation; TNA E101/417/3, f. 33 (*LP* I 228), f. 57 (*LP* I 640), TNA E101/417/6, f. 54, (*LP* I 1015), TNA E101/418/5, f. 27 for various warrants for the king's Chamber; HMC Rutland, vol. 1, p.22, for 'Ordinaunces and appoyntmentes to the Kinges' syde', BL Harleian MS 433, ff. 294v-295r (*LP* II 4409) for the visiting French embassy in 1518; TNA SP 1/18, f. 65 (*LP* III 151) for 'Names of certain personnes put owt of their Rowmes by the king's grace and other by his grace in there Rowmes appointed' in 1519; TNA SP 1/19 f. 269 and Bodleian MS Ashmole 1116, f. 99r for the Field of Cloth of Gold in 1520; BL Cotton MS Vespasian C XIV ff. 267-8 for the Eltham ordinances of 1526; BL Egerton MS 2604 for wages of the king's household c. 1525-6; BL Royal MS 7 F XIV, f. 100 (*LP* II 2735) for a book of the king's servants, c. 1536; BL Add MS 45716A, ff.4v – 8v for The Ordynary of the King's Syde, 1540; *LP* XVI 394 [6] for the king's Privy Chamber, 1540; BL Lansdowne 2, ff. 33-38 for the king's 'ordinary' from 1544-45; BL Cotton Vespasian C XIV 1 ff. 107-107v (*LP* XXI, i., 969) and BL Royal MS App. 89 f. 105 (*LP* XXI, i, 1384) for the visiting French embassy in 1546; TNA LC 2/2 for his funeral in 1547, and TNA E179/69/27, 29, 32, 45, 56 for various subsidy lists assessing the king's Chamber and Privy Chamber throughout his reign.

Chapter 8: 'She would not damn her own soul on any consideration': Oath

[1] For an oath sworn by the king, Henry VIII's servants, see BL Cotton MS Vespasian, C, XIV, f. 438v. For an oath sworn by the queen, Katherine Parr's servants, see TNA SP 1/196, f. 32.

[2] Thea Cervone, *Sworn Bond in Tudor England: Oaths, Vows and Covenants in Civil Life and Literature* (London, 2011), p. 6.

[3] *LP* XII, ii., 704; *LP* XII, ii., 711.

[4] TNA STAC 2/2, f. 134.

[5] *HC*, pp. 599-600.

[6] BL Cotton MS, Vespasian, C, XIV, ff. 144r-144v; BL Add MS 71009, ff. 60-61.

[7] BL Cotton MS, Otho, C, X, f. 213 (*LP* VI 1253). Bedyll was a clerk of the king's council.

[8] BL Cotton MS, Vitellius, C, I, f. 7r, quoted in McIntosh, 'Sovereign Princesses', p. 119.

[9] McIntosh, 'Sovereign Princesses', p. 119.

[10] My italics. TNA SP 1/196, f. 32.

[11] Lacey Baldwin Smith, 'English Treason Trials and Confessions in the Sixteenth Century', *Journal of the History of Ideas*, 15, 4 (1954), pp. 471-498 (p. 488).

[12] CSP Sp IV, ii., 1061 (*LP* VI 351); BL Cotton MS, Otho, C, X, f. 213 (*LP* VI 1253); *HC*, p. 794.

[13] BL Cotton MS, Otho, C, X, f. 199 (*LP* VI 760); CSP Sp IV, ii., 1061 (*LP* VI 351).

[14] CSP Ven, IV, 933.

[15] CSP Sp IV, ii., 1041 (*LP* VI 19).

[16] TNA SP 1/77, f. 139 (*LP* VI 759).

[17] CSP Sp IV, ii., 1061. (*LP* VI 351).

[18] CSP Sp IV, ii., 808 (*LP* V 478).

[19] BL Cotton MS, Otho, C, X, f. 177 (*LP* VI 352).

[20] CSP Sp IV, ii., 1061 (*LP* VI 351).

[21] CSP Sp IV, ii., 1061 (*LP* VI 351).

[22] BL Cotton MS, Otho, C, X, f. 199 (*LP* VI 760); CSP Sp IV, ii., 1165 (*LP* VI 1571).

[23] BL Cotton MS, Otho, C, X, f. 177 (*LP* VI 352).

[24] BL Cotton MS, Otho, C, X, f. 213 (*LP* VI 1253).

[25] TNA SP 1/79, f. 158 (*LP* VI 1252).

[26] BL Cotton MS, Otho, C, X, f. 210 (*LP* VI 1541).

[27] TNA SP 1/81, f. 3 (*LP* VI 1543).

[28] BL Cotton MS, Otho, C, X, f. 210 (*LP* VI 1541).

[29] TNA SP 1/81, f. 1 (*LP* VI 1542); CSP Sp IV, ii., 1165 (*LP* VI 1571).

[30] CSP Sp IV, ii., 1164 (*LP* VI 1558); CSP Sp IV, ii., 1158 (*LP* VI 1510). Another report a few days later reiterated that 'they took away almost all her femmes de chambre'. CSP Sp IV, ii., 1165 (*LP* VI 1571).

[31] TNA SP 1/82 f. 127 (*LP* VII 135).

[32] CSP Sp V, i., 60 (*LP* VII 726).

[33] CSP Sp V, i., 68 (*LP* VII 871).

[34] David Grummitt, 'Household, politics and political morality in the reign of Henry VII', *Historical Research*, 82, 217 (2009), pp. 393-411 (pp. 410-411).

[35] BL Cotton MS, Otho, C, X, f. 213 (*LP* VI 1253). Bedyll was not trusted and thus had no opportunity to read the letter himself.

[36] My italics. TNA SP 1/79, f. 158 (*LP* VI 1252). BL Cotton MS, Otho, C, X, f. 177 (*LP* VI 352).

[37] *LP* VI 805. Gray, *Oaths*, p. 212.

[38] TNA SP 1/79, f. 158 (*LP* VI 1252).

[39] TNA SP 1/79 f. 158 (*LP* VI 1252).

[40] *LP* I 3524.

[41] CSP Sp V, i., 75 (*LP* VII 1013).

[42] TNA SP 1/99, f. 163 (*LP* IX 1040).

[43] TNA SP 1/99, f. 163 (*LP* IX 1040).

[44] BL Cotton MS, Otho, C, X, f. 215 (*LP* X 28).

⁴⁵ BL Cotton MS, Otho, C, X, f. 213 (*LP* VI 1253).
⁴⁶ *LP* IV 5346.
⁴⁷ *LP* IV 5154, (i) for Catherine's letter, (ii) for Abel's instructions, which also urged the Emperor to prevent the matter being examined 'anywhere but in Rome'.
⁴⁸ CSP Sp IV i., 354.
⁴⁹ CSP Sp IV, ii., 619 (*LPV* 700).
⁵⁰ CSP, Sp IV, i, 509 (*LP* IV 6738); CSP Sp IV, ii., 720 (*LPV* 238); *LP* VI 585.
⁵¹ TNA SP 1/142, f. 201 (*LP* XIV, i., 190). This came from an unidentified servant of this queen's household, who was later examined.
⁵² TNA SP 1/81, f. 3 (*LP* VI 1543).
⁵³ BL Cotton MS, Otho, C, X, f. 210 (*LP* VI 1541); CSP Sp IV, ii., 1165 (*LP* VI 1571); *HC*, pp. 807-8.
⁵⁴ CSP Sp V, i., 4 (*LP* VII 83).
⁵⁵ CSP Sp IV, ii., 1165 (*LP* VI 1571); CSP Sp V, i., 75 (*LP* VII 1013).
⁵⁶ BL Cotton MS, Otho, C, X, f. 206 (*LP* VII 786).
⁵⁷ BL Add MS, 28588, f. 87 (*LP* IX 983).

Chapter 9: 'I loved you a great deal more than I made feign for': Intimacy

¹ *LP* VI 396.
² Ellis, vol. 2, pp. 32-33 (BL Harleian MS 283, f. 96).
³ Pollard, *Tudor Tracts*, pp. 9-28. *LP* VI 601. *WC*, vol. 1, p. 20. *HC*, p. 803.
⁴ BL Add MS 71009, f. 58r.
⁵ Ellis, vol. 2, pp. 33-40 (BL Harleian MS 6148).
⁶ Heylyn, *Restaurata*, p. 91. Hume, *Wives*, p. 234.
⁷ Starkey, 'Intimacy', in Starkey (ed.) *Court*, pp. 71-118.
⁸ Thurley, *Palaces*, pp. 135-6. In larger royal residences, between the queen's Presence and Privy chambers, there may even have been a 'withdrawing' chamber and additional 'galleries' or hallways.
⁹ *HO*, p. 157.
¹⁰ BL Cotton MS Vitellius, C, I, f. 7r., quoted in McIntosh, 'Sovereign Princesses', pp. 132-3.
¹¹ *Foxe*, V, pp. 62-63.
¹² The will of George Zouche, Gainsford's husband, was made in 1548, and mentions his second wife, Ellen, whereas Wyatt was not born until 1553. See Soberton, *Ladies-in-Waiting*.
¹³ Wyatt, *Boleigne*, p.422. George Wyatt was the grandson of poet and courtier, Sir Thomas Wyatt, who was among the gentlemen at court accused of committing adultery in 1536.
¹⁴ Thomas S. Freeman, Research, rumour and propaganda: Anne Boleyn in Foxe's 'Book of Martyrs', *Historical Journal*, 38, 4 (1995), pp. 797-819.
¹⁵ Christine de Pizan, *The treasure of the city of ladies; or, The book of the three virtues*, translated with an introduction by Sarah Lawson (London, 1985).

[16] Although it is unclear if this book was known in England, the popularity of Pizan's *Livre de la Cité des Dames*, or *The Book of the City of Ladies* (c. 1405), may have brought her other works to the attention of the queen and her household. It was translated into English in 1521 by a member of Catherine of Aragon's household, Brian Annesley, her yeoman of the cellar. Brian Annesley was in attendance at the coronation of the queen in 1509 as a yeoman of the cellar (TNA LC 9/50 ff. 198-211), and was still serving in her household when the *Livre* was translated in 1521 (TNA SP 1/73 f. 70). Christine de Pizan, *The Boke of the Cyte of Ladyes*, ed. Hope Johnston, trans. Brian Anslay, *Medieval and Renaissance Texts and Studies*, 457 (New York, 2014), p. xi; Hope Johnston, 'How the Livre de la cité des dames first came to be printed in England', in Liliane Dulac, Anne Paupert, Christine Reno and Bernard Ribémont (eds), *Desireuse de plus avant enquerre* (Paris, 2008), pp. 385-96.

[17] Latymer, *Cronickille*, ff. 22r-22v.

[18] Latymer, *Cronickille*, f. 25r.

[19] Latymer, *Cronickille*, ff. 24v-25r.

[20] Foxe, V, pp. 62-63; Wyatt, *Boleigne*, pp. 442-3; Latymer, *Cronickille*, f. 25r, ff. 26v-27r, ff. 31r-32v. 'time' here corrected from 'the'.

[21] Latymer, *Cronickille*, f. 32v. The Primer, Psalter, and the Book of Hours, were devotional literature for personal use.

[22] Latymer, *Cronickille*, f. 32v.

[23] Foxe, V, pp. 62-63.

[24] Wyatt, *Boleigne*, pp. 442-3.

[25] Latymer, Cronickille, f. 33r.

[26] Pizan, *Treasure*, 2 / 2.

[27] *HC*, pp. 798-805.

[28] Wyatt, *Boleigne*, pp. 429-30.

[29] Mueller, pp. 169-170.

[30] *LP* I 3524.

[31] CSP Sp, II, 238.

[32] Cavendish, p. 217.

[33] *LP* XV 844.

[34] BL Cotton MS, Vespasian, F, XIII, f. 198.

[35] Pizan, *Treasure*, 2 / 2.

[36] *LP* X 352.

[37] Mueller, pp. 80-81; BL Lansdowne MS 76, 81, f. 182r.

[38] Mueller, pp. 177-178.

[39] *Lancelot de Carle*, pp. 281-285 (lines 1173-1182).

[40] Latymer, *Cronickille*, f. 33r.

Chapter 10: 'Sythens I injoye their service they may have some porcion of my lyving': Advancement

[1] TNA SP 1/83, f. 185 (*LP* VII 600). *LP* VII 641. TNA SP 1/89, f. 50 (LP VIII 81), *LP* VIII 94. *LP* VII Appendix 22. Billingford reportedly 'lay hid there two or three days,

altering his name'. He also went by the alias 'Kett[ilb]ye'. TNA SP 1/83, f. 185 (*LP* VII 600).

² Latymer, *Cronickille*, f. 32v.

³ Harris, 'Chamber', p. 227.

⁴ Latymer, *Cronickille*, f. 26r. Spelt 'Mr Jaskyne' and 'Mrs. Jaskyne'. As Maria Dowling observes, there is no record of 'Jaskynes' in the queen's service. But this must surely be the Joscelyns, as Anne only had a handful of servants in her privy Chamber, and Anne Joscelyn was listed as one of her chamberers.

⁵ TNA E36/210, f. 54 for Anne Say, f. 70 for Nicholas Matthew.

⁶ TNA E36/210, f. 31 (William Paston), f. 35 (Bridget Crowmer), f. 39 (Nicholas Grey). Similarly Anne of Cleves gave John Wallys, groom of her chamber, a 10s. advance on his wages 'towards the finding of his poor daughter', and £7. 10s. to one of her footmen 'towards hys mariage'. TNA E101/422/15.

⁷ Latymer, *Cronickille*, f. 32v.

⁸ Wyatt, *Boleigne*, pp. 442-443.

⁹ TNA SP 1/103, f. 318r (*LP* X 912); TNA SP 1/104, f. 262r (*LP* X 1257); BL Royal MS, 7, C, XVI, f. 76 (*LP* XI 117).

¹⁰ TNA SP 1/129, f. 174 (*LP* XIII, i., 450).

¹¹ TNA SP 1/129, f. 174 (*LP* XIII, i., 450).

¹² TNA E36/210, f. 32, f. 39, f. 60.

¹³ *LP* IX 477.

¹⁴ BL Cotton MS, Titus, B, I, f. 493 (*LP* VI 1194).

¹⁵ See, for instance, TNA E101/422/15 for Anne of Cleves, or TNA E36/210 for Elizabeth of York.

¹⁶ Taffe, 'Reconstructing the queen's household', pp. 161-164.

¹⁷ TNA SP 1/104, f. 82 (*LP* X 1011), transcribed in Rowley-Williams, 'Image and Reality', p. 298.

¹⁸ TNA SP 1/167, ff. 163r-163v (*LP* XVI 1340), transcribed in Rowley-Williams, 'Image and Reality', p. 299.

¹⁹ Rowley-Williams, Appendix.

²⁰ TNA SP 1/49 f. 53v (*LP* IV 4449).

²¹ Latymer, *Cronickille*, f. 32v.

²² *LP* I 94 (35) and (36) for Catherine of Aragon's jointure; *LP* VII 419 (25), for Anne Boleyn's jointure; *LP* XVI 503 (25) for Katherine Howard's jointure; *LP* XIX, i., 141 (65) for Katherine Parr's jointure. Successive queens shared much of the same dower lands.

²³ BL Royal MS Appendix 89, ff. 83r-87v (*LP* VII 352); *LP* VII 419 [25] and [26].

²⁴ Latymer, *Cronickille*, f. 28v.

²⁵ BL Royal MS Appendix 89, ff. 83r-87v (*LP* VII 352).

²⁶ *LP* VI 419 [8].

²⁷ TNA SP 1/105, f. 268 (*LP* XI 253).

²⁸ *LP* I 3226 [7].

²⁹ Or 'Holywell', a nunnery located in Flintshire, northeast Wales, dissolved in 1536.

[30] BL Cotton MS Vespasian F III f.38 (*LP* XIX, i., 967). The king rewarded his queens' servants, and his queens rewarded the king's servants.

[31] Mueller, p. 189.

[32] Wood, vol. 1, pp. 260-261 (*LP* IV 1032).

[33] Latymer, *Cronickille*, f. 32v.

[34] CSP Sp, IV, ii., 1123.

[35] *HC*, p. 818; *WC*, vol. 1, pp. 32-33.

[36] BL Cotton MS, Otho, C, X, f. 216 (*LP* X 40).

[37] BL Cotton MS, Otho, C, X, f. 174 (*LP* X 1134 [4]).

[38] BL Cotton MS, Otho, C, X, f. 220 (*LP* X 128); TNA SP 1/101, f. 112 (*LP* X 151).

[39] TNA SP 1/101, f. 21 (*LP* X 37); BL Cotton MS, Otho, C, X, f. 219 (*LP* X 41).

Chapter 11: 'Preserve my courte inviolate': Piety and Pastime

[1] *HO*, pp. 188-189. Fiona Kisby, '"When the King Goeth a Procession": Chapel Ceremonies and Services, the Ritual Year, and Religious Reforms at the Early Tudor Court, 1485-1547', *Journal of British Studies*, 40, 1 (2001), pp. 51-56.

[2] CSP Sp, IV, ii., 1061.

[3] BL Harleian MS 6807, f. 10r.

[4] Latymer, *Cronickille*, f. 25r.

[5] This was probably Tyndale's New Testament (1534). Latymer, *Cronickille*, f. 23v, f. 32v.

[6] Latymer, *Cronickille*, ff. 22r-22v.

[7] *Foxe*, IV, pp. 62-63; Latymer, *Cronickille*, p. 59.

[8] These debts which were yet unpaid at her execution in 1536.

[9] BL Harleian MS 295, f. 149v; TNA SP 1/92, f. 150 (*LP* VIII 722).

[10] John Bruce and Thomas Perowne (eds.), *Correspondence of Matthew Parker*, Parker Society (1853), pp. 2-3.

[11] Burnet, *Reformation*, vol. 5, p. 545.

[12] Latymer, *Cronickille*, f. 30v.

[13] Records of her itinerary indicate that Catherine of Aragon and her servants, routinely, or, on at least four occasions, in 1515, 1517, 1519 and 1521, visited the shrine of Our Lady at Walsingham. 'The Itinerary of Henry VIII and Cardinal Wolsey 1514-1530', Appendix I in Neil Samman, 'The Henrician Court During Cardinal Wolsey's Ascendancy, c. 1514-1529' (University of Wales, Unpublished Ph.D. thesis, 1988), pp. 327-438. Account books indicate that queens and their servants regularly distributed alms. Catherine of Aragon handed out £195 7s. 7d. in alms between 1525 and 1526. *LP* IV 6121.

[14] *Foxe*, V, pp. 62-63; Wyatt, *Boleigne*, pp. 442-3.

[15] Cardinal Campeggio remarked on 3 April 1529 that, 'certain Lutheran books, in English, of an evil sort, have been circulated in the King's court'. *LP* IV 5416. The account is in both John Louthe's written memorandum, by Strype, found among the Foxe papers, and by George Wyatt, whose informant was Anne Gainsford herself. See

John Strype, *Ecclesiastical Memorials relating chiefly to religion, and the reformation of it, and the emergences of the Church of England, under King Henry VIII, King Edward VI and Queen Mary I*, 3 vols. (Oxford, 1822), vol. 1, pp. 171-3; J. G. Nichols, *Narratives of the Days of the Reformation* (London, 1859), pp. 52-7 for Louthe's account.

[16] Wyatt, *Boleigne*, pp. 438-40. The source for this account is surely Anne Gainsford herself, who told it to Wyatt.

[17] Strype, vol. 1, pp. 171-3.

[18] TNA SP 1/103, f. 259 (*LP* X 827).

[19] Freeman, 'Anne Boleyn', pp. 804-5.

[20] *Foxe*, V, p. 554.

[21] *APC*, I, pp. 400-408; *LP* XXI, i., 759.

[22] *Foxe*, V, p. 557.

[23] Robert Parsons, *A treatise of three conversions of paganisme to Christian religion*, 3 vols., by N. D. (1603-1604), vol. 2, pp. 493-494.

[24] *LP* XXI, ii, 756. *LP* XXI, i, 1181.

[25] *Foxe*, V, p. 547..

[26] *Foxe*, V, p. 547. *LP* XXI, i., 1181.

[27] *Foxe*, V, p. 554.

[28] *Foxe*, V, p. 554.

[29] *Foxe*, V, p. 553.

[30] *Foxe*, V, p. 557.

[31] *Foxe*, V, p. 556.

[32] *Foxe*, V, p. 558.

[33] Freeman, 'Katherine Parr', pp. 238-245.

[34] Loades, *Boleyns*, pp. 141-142.

[35] Elizabeth Ann Culling, 'The Impact of the Reformation on the Tudor Royal Household to 1553' (University of Durham, Unpublished Ph.D. thesis, 1986) for a broader overview.

[36] G. W. Bernard, 'Anne Boleyn's religion', *Historical Journal*, 36 (1993), pp. 1-20 (pp. 3-4).

[37] William Forrest, *The history of Grisild the Second: a narrative, in verse, of the divorce of Queen Katharine of Arragon*, ed. by W. D. Macray (London, 1875), pp. 28-29.

[38] Nicholas Harpsfield, *A Treatise on the Pretended Divorce Between Henry VIII. and Catharine of Aragon*, ed. by Nicholas Pocock, (London, 1878), p. 200. See also Thomas Freeman, 'Nicholas Harpsfield' (1519-1575) in ODNB (2004).

[39] Nicholas Sander, *The Rise and Growth of the Anglican Schism*, ed. by David Lewis (London, 1877), p. 7.

[40] Freeman, 'Anne Boleyn', pp. 808-810, 817; Maria Dowling, 'Anne Boleyn and reform', Journal of Ecclesiastical History, 35 (1984), pp. 30-46; Dowling, 'Scholarship, Politics and the Court of Henry VIII' (Unpublished Ph.D thesis, University of London, 1982), p. 155.

[41] Latymer, *Cronickille*, ff. 24r-24v.

[42] Pizan, *Treasure*, 2 / 3.

[43] Her servants were to be of such 'quiet and godly lyvinge' that they 'may be a spectacle to others'. Latymer, *Cronickille*, f. 23v.

[44] Latymer, *Cronickille*, ff. 22v-23v.

[45] Giustinian, *Four Years*, vol. 2., Appendix II, pp. 313-314.

[46] BL Cotton MS, Vitellius, B, XII, f. 68 (*LP* IV 4981).

[47] Russell, *Catherine*, p. 216.

[48] Pizan, *Treasure*, 1 / 18.

[49] Wyatt, pp. 425-8.

[50] BL Cotton MS, Caligula, E, IV, f. 55. (*LP* XIX, ii., 201).

[51] Wyatt, *Boleigne*, pp. 442-3.

[52] Cavendish, pp. 227-228.

[53] TNA E101/422/15; TNA E101/422/16.

[54] Wyatt, *Boleigne*, p. 428.

[55] *LP* III 152. *LP* III, pp. 1550-1553.

[56] *LP* X 913.

[57] TNA LC 5/31, ff. 7-8; *LP* XIX, ii., 688. In 1540, the household of Anne of Cleves was entertained by a tumbler, whom the queen rewarded with 5s., and on another occasion, Anne Stanhope, Countess of Hertford, had her minstrels play before the queen, for which they were rewarded with 45s. (TNA E101/422/15).

[58] PPE, Mary, pp. 48, 50, 64, 108, 113, 114, 119, 126, 130, 131, 159.

[59] *LP* VI 613.

[60] TNA SP 1/76, f. 168 (*LP* VI 613); Henry Percy, Earl of Northumberland, was apparently known to 'resort for his pastime unto the queen's chamber, and there would fall in dalliance among the queen's maidens'. Cavendish, *Wolsey*, p. 123. Wyatt, *Boleigne*, pp. 425-428.

[61] Ives, *Anne*, pp. 20-22, p. 70.

[62] BL Add MS 17492; Irish, 'Devonshire', pp. 82-3.

[63] *Devonshire*, p. 7.

[64] TNA E36/210, ff. 53r-55v, f. 65r. (*LP* XI 48); Irish, 'Devonshire', pp. 82-3. Both were arrested after news of their marriage surfaced, and on 9 July 1536, servants of Anne Boleyn's household were interrogated as to the nature of their relationship.

[65] Castiglione, p. 176.

[66] Ives, *Anne*, p. 69.

[67] Latymer, *Cronickille*, ff. 24r-24v.

[68] Pizan, *Treasure*, 1 / 18.

[69] Bernard, *Anne*, p. 154.

[70] Sleidan, f. cxl (f. 140).

[71] Cavendish, *Visions*, pp. 71-4.

[72] Roger Bigelow Merriman (ed.), *Life and Letters of Thomas Cromwell*, vol. 2 (1902), p. 21. Sir John Russell described Jane as 'gentle', and similarly remarked that 'the king hath come out of hell into heaven'. *Lisle*, III, 713, pp. 395-6.

[73] BL Cotton MS, Otho, C, X, f. 174 (*LP* X 1134 [4]).

[74] Besse did eventually return to court. She is later among the women who visit the king's ship in Portsmouth in 1539, and had a brief flirtation with Thomas Culpeper, gentleman of the Privy Chamber. She probably retired in the spring of 1541, when she was granted an annuity of £10 a year for her service (*LP*XVI, 678 [13]).

[75] *Lisle*, IV, 887, pp. 150-152 (*LP*XII, ii., 271).
[76] *Lisle*, IV, p. 196.
[77] *Lisle*, IV, 896, pp. 167-8 (*LP*XII, ii., 808).
[78] *Lisle*, IV, 901, p. 178 (*LP*XII, ii., 958).
[79] *Lisle*, IV, 901, p. 178 (*LP*XII, ii., 958).
[80] *Lisle*, IV, 895, pp. 163-5 (*LP*XII, ii., 711).

Chapter 12: 'Poor banished creature': Exile

[1] CSP Sp, V, i., 97 (*LP*VII 1257).
[2] CSP Sp, IV, ii., 1123 (*LP*VI 1069).
[3] CSP Sp IV, ii., 1144 (*LP*VI 1392).
[4] CSP Sp V, i., 90 (*LP*VII 1193).
[5] CSP Sp V, i., 90 (*LP*VII 1193).
[6] CSP Sp, V, i., 97 (*LP*VII 1257).
[7] *LP*VI 556.
[8] *LP*VII 1279.
[9] CSP Sp V, i., 90 (*LP*VII 1193).
[10] CSP Sp IV, ii., 1058 (*LP*VI 324).
[11] *LP*VII 171.
[12] *LP*VII 121.
[13] CSP Sp, IV, ii., 1133 (*LP*VI 1249).
[14] CSP Sp V, i., 4 (*LP*VII 83).
[15] CSP Sp V, i., 32 (*LP*VII 393).
[16] CSP Sp V, i., 97 (*LP*VII 1257).
[17] CSP Sp V, i., 102 (*LP*VII 1297).
[18] CSP Sp V, i., 102 (*LP*VII 1297).
[19] *LP*VIII 263.
[20] *LP*VIII 263. *LP*XII, ii., 1187 indicates that Madge was in Anne's service ('one Mrs. Sheltun that used to wait on queen Anne').
[21] *LP*X 908. Henry would later warn his third wife 'not to meddle with his affairs'. *LP*XI 860.
[22] CSP Sp, V, i., 97 (*LP*VII 1257).
[23] CSP Sp, V, i, 97 (*LP*VII 1257).
[24] CSP Sp V, i., 118 (*LP*VII 1554).
[25] CSP Sp V, i., 118 (*LP*VII 1554).
[26] CSP Sp V, i., 90 (*LP*VII 1193).
[27] CSP Sp V, i, 97 (*LP*VII 1257).
[28] CSP, Sp, Supplement to I and II, 8 (*LP*I 474).
[29] CSP Ven III, 1053.

³⁰ CSP Sp IV, i., 354.
³¹ CSP Sp IV, i., 160.
³² Warnicke, *Anne*, p. 177.
³³ CSP Sp V, i., 118 (*LP* VII 1554).
³⁴ CSP Sp V, i., 118 (*LP* VII 1554).
³⁵ Wood (ed.), vol. 2, pp. 195-7.
³⁶ Fox, *Jane Boleyn*, p. 159.
³⁷ CSP Sp V, i., 118 (*LP* VII 1554).
³⁸ Fox, *Jane Boleyn*, pp. 157-164.

Chapter 13: '…apon a certeyn tyme waytynge on your Grace at Honesdon': Jane and Princess Mary

¹ *LP* VIII 1012.
² *LP* IX 566.
³ Friedmann, *Anne*, vol. 2, pp. 128-9.
⁴ Starkey, 'Attendant Lord?' in Axton et al (eds), 'Triumphs', p. 14. Rowley-Williams, 'Image and Reality', p. 159.
⁵ Warnicke, *Anne*, p. 302. Nicola Clark, *Gender, Family and Politics: The Howard Women, 1485-1558* (Oxford, 2018), p. 127. *Lisle*, III, 735 (calendared in *LP* VI 728, misidentified by the editors as 1533).
⁶ Fox, *Jane Boleyn*, p. 172.
⁷ WC, vol. 1, pp. 69-72. *LP* XII, ii., 1060.
⁸ PPE, Mary, pp. 13, 17, 25, 64, 65, 82.
⁹ PPE, Mary, pp. 7, 51, 82, and 97, 143, 49, 11, 13, 17, and 25. Rowley-Williams, 'Image and Reality', p. 166.
¹⁰ Henry Parker, Lord Morley, Forty-Six Lives, Translated from Boccaccio's 'De Claris Mulieribus', ed. by Hubert G. Wright (London, 1943), pp. 168-184. Starkey, 'Attendant Lord?' in Axton et al (eds), 'Triumphs', pp. 14-16.
¹¹ PPE, Mary, p. cxxviii.
¹² PPE, Mary, p. 143.
¹³ BL, Add. MS 12060, fol. 20v, quoted in Carley, 'Henry Parker', in ODNB.
¹⁴ Starkey, 'Attendant Lord?' in Axton et al (eds), 'Triumphs', pp. 14-16.
¹⁵ Carley, 'Henry Parker', in ONDB. Hunsdon 'lay only six miles' from Great Hallingbury. Starkey, 'Attendant Lord?' in Axton et al (eds), 'Triumphs', p. 16.
¹⁶ *LP* XI 222.
¹⁷ *LP* X 908. *LP* X 968.
¹⁸ *LP* X 968, *LP* X 991. *LP* X 1108.
¹⁹ *LP* X 1021. CSP Sp V ii 70.
²⁰ *LP* XI 7.
²¹ *LP* X 1110.
²² CSP Sp V ii 70 (*LP* XI 7).

[23] CSP Sp V ii 70 (*LP* XI 7). See *LP* X 1150 and *LP* X 1134 for Sir Anthony Browne's examination, *LP* XI 222 and *LP* VII 1036 for Lady Anne Hussey's, *LP* X 1134 for Sir Francis Bryan's, and *LP* XIV i 189 and 190 for Sir Nicholas Carew.

[24] *LP* X 1134.

[25] *LP* XIV i 190 (13).

[26] CSP Sp V ii 70 (*LP* XI 7).

[27] Starkey, 'Attendant Lord?' in Axton et al (eds), 'Triumphs', p. 16.

[28] Retha M. Warnicke, 'The Fall of Anne Boleyn: A Reassessment', *History*, 70, 228 (1985), pp. 1-15 (p. 1) suggests Jane 'had hoped to return her to a favourable position in the succession'.

[29] Starkey, 'Attendant Lord?' in Axton et al (eds), 'Triumphs', p. 14.

[30] Warnicke, 'Reassessment', pp. 1-7. For factionalism at Henry VIII's court, see Mears, 'Courts', p. 709; E. W. Ives, *Faction in Tudor England*, 2nd ed. (London, 1986); Steven Gunn, 'The Structures of Politics in Early Tudor England', *Transactions of the Royal Historical Society*, 5 (1995), pp. 59-90 (p. 77).

[31] Weir, *Tower*, pp. 142-3.

Chapter 14: 'Certain other little follies': Arrest, Trial, Investigation

[1] T. Amyot, 'Transcript of an original Manuscript, containing a Memorial from George Constantyne to Thomas Lord Cromwell.' in Archaeologia, 23, pp. 50-78 (p. 64).

[2] *HC*, p. 819.

[3] Burnet, *Reformation*, vol. 1, p. 196.

[4] Amyot, 'Constantyne', p. 64.

[5] *WC*, vol 1, p.36.

[6] *LP* X 876.

[7] The fall of Anne Boleyn in 1536 is one of the most contentious debates in history. The recent historiography is structured around one focal question: was Anne guilty of committing adultery? E. W. Ives argued that Anne was the victim of a conspiracy, 'most carefully calculated' by Thomas Cromwell, the king's councillor. Cromwell remarked '*a fantasier et conspirer led affaire*' or, that he had 'set himself to arrange the plot' for Anne's fall (*LP* X 1069). G. W. Bernard, on the other hand, warns that there is the 'danger of the conspiratorial approach' to history, where often historians are driven into a 'world of speculation in which 'must have' and 'surely' do duty for evidence' (Bernard, *Anne*, p. 140). Bernard thus concludes that Anne was probably guilty of committing adultery. There is an alternative, if somewhat imaginative account by Retha M. Warnicke, stating that Anne was not guilty, but that her miscarriage of a 'deformed foetus' triggered a 'fearful reaction' in the king, who set in motion her execution (Warnicke, *Anne*). The story of a 'deformed foetus' comes from Nicholas Sander, a Catholic polemicist writing in 1585 who alleged, obscurely enough, that Anne gave birth to 'a shapeless mass of flesh' (Sander, *Schism*). More recently, historians have concentrated not on if Anne was guilty, but on explaining how and why she was executed in 1536. Some have argued that Anne's behaviour gave credibility to the

charges, as she did not always act with the dignity, or restraint, required of a queen. None have fully or critically investigated the role of the queen's ladies and gentlewomen, who were central to the scandal.

[8] *LPX* 953.
[9] *LPX* 964.
[10] Lancelot de Carle, p. 191 (lines 370-372). This is calendared in *LPX* 1036.
[11] Lancelot de Carle, p. 197 (lines 433-436).
[12] *LPX* 873.
[13] Ives, *Anne*, p. 61. Ives, 'Reconsidered', p. 659.
[14] Bernard, *Anne*, p. 190.
[15] *Spelman*, vol. 1, p. 71.
[16] Ives, *Anne*, p. 331.
[17] A 'lady Wingfield' received a New Year gift in January 1534. TNA E101/421/13. It is worth noting that the gift rolls for 1535 and 1536 have not survived.
[18] Bernard, *Anne*, p. 218. Bernard, 'Rejoinder', p. 671n.
[19] Her husband, Robert Tyrwhitt, did not remarry until 1539-40.
[20] BL Cotton MS, C, X, f. 209v (*LPX* 799).
[21] BL Add MS, 25114, f. 160 (*LPX* 873); TNA SP 3/12, f. 57 (*LPX* 953); TNA SP 3/12, f. 37 (*LPX* 964).
[22] Bernard, *Anne*, p. 190.
[23] *LPX* 798.
[24] *LPX* 908.
[25] *LPX* 876, corroborated with *LPX* 798 for Smeaton, and *LPX* 908 for Weston.
[26] Ives, 'Reconsidered', p. 653.
[27] Ives, 'Reconsidered', p. 654.
[28] Weir, *Tower*, p. 111.
[29] Bernard, *Anne*, p. 166.
[30] BL Cotton MS, Otho, C, X, f. 222r-v.
[31] *LPX* 785.
[32] CSP Sp V, ii., 55.
[33] *WC*, vol 1, p. 38.
[34] *LPX* 848.
[35] *Spelman*, vol. 1, p. 71
[36] *WC*, vol 1, p. 38.
[37] CSP Sp V, ii., 55 (*LPX* 908).
[38] CSP Sp V, ii., 55 (*LPX* 908).
[39] *WC*, vol 1, p. 38.
[40] CSP Sp V, ii., 55 (*LPX* 908).
[41] *LP* XI 29.
[42] CSP Sp V, ii., 55 (*LPX* 908).
[43] TCD, pp. 383-395.
[44] CSP Sp V, ii., 55 (*LPX* 908).
[45] TCD, p. 421.

[46] Bernard, *Anne*, p. 181.

Chapter 15: 'Seche desyre as you have had to such tales hase browthe you to thys': The Fall of Anne Boleyn

[1] Burnet, *Reformation*, vol. 1, p. 189.

[2] Ives, *Anne*, p. 418.

[3] CSP Sp V, ii., 55 (*LPX* 908).

[4] Starkey, 'Triumphs', p. 14 suggests Anne is unlikely to have related this information to Jane 'if she had already declared her hostility', but there is no doubt this conversation could have taken place before Jane's banishment, at which time she was clearly Anne's confidante.

[5] Ives, *Anne*, p. 331.

[6] Lancelot de Carle, p. 227 (lines 695-696).

[7] *Excerpta Historica*, pp. 260-2.

[8] Burnet, *Reformation*, vol. 1, p. 189.

[9] Cavendish, *Visions*, pp. 71-4.

[10] Foxe, vol. 4, p. 462n.

[11] Amyot, 'Constantyne', p. 66.

[12] Wyatt, *Boleigne*, p. 447.

[13] Fox, *Jane Boleyn*, pp. 190-191.

[14] Fox, *Jane Boleyn*, p. 187. Loades, *Catherine*, p. 132.

[15] Fox, *Jane Boleyn*, p. 192. Loades, *Catherine*, p. 132.

[16] Fox, *Jane Boleyn*, p. 191.

[17] Fox, *Jane Boleyn*, p. 189.

[18] BL Cotton MS, Otho, C, X, f. 222r-v.

[19] Greg Walker, 'Rethinking the Fall of Anne Boleyn', *The Historical Journal*, 45, 1 (2002), pp. 1-29 (p. 18).

[20] Walker, 'Rethinking', p. 64.

[21] CSP Sp V, ii., 55 (*LPX* 908).

[22] CSP Elizabeth I, 1303.

[23] *LPX* 785.

[24] It survives in a chronicle which is notoriously inaccurate. Martin A. Sharp Hume (ed.), *Chronicle of King Henry VIII of England, Being a Contemporary Record of some of the Principal Events of the Reigns of Henry VIII and Edward VI: Written in Spanish by an Unknown Hand* (London, 1889), p. 57; It may well have been 'sheer fantasy', but could 'preserve what was essentially popular gossip'. Ives, *Anne*, p. 329.

[25] CSP Elizabeth, I, 1303.

[26] Bernard, *Anne*, p. 158. This is corroborated by the investigation into Katherine Howard's adultery.

[27] Prior to the fire at Ashburnham House in 1731, these letters had been seen and in some measure transcribed by the antiquary John Strype.

[28] James Taffe, '"But she to be a Quene, and creuely handeled as was never sene": Anne Boleyn's confinement in the Tower of London', in Hannah Yip and Thomas Clifton (eds), *Writing Early Modern Loneliness* (London, forthcoming).

[29] BL Cotton MS, Otho, C, X, f. 225r.

[30] BL Cotton MS, Otho, C, X, f. 225r.

[31] BL Cotton MS, Otho, C, X, f. 222r.

[32] *LP* X 793.

[33] BL Cotton MS, Otho, C, X, f. 222v (*LP* X 798).

[34] BL Cotton MS, Otho, C, X, f. 225r (*LP* X 793).

[35] BL Cotton MS, Otho, C, X, f. 226r.

[36] Pizan, *Treasure*, 2 / 7.

[37] BL Cotton MS, Otho, C, X, f. 224v.

[38] BL Cotton MS, Otho, C, X, f. 225r.

[39] BL Cotton MS, Otho, C, X, f. 222r.

[40] BL Cotton MS, Otho, C, X, f. 224v.

[41] *LP* X 908. CSP Sp V ii., 55.

[42] CSP Sp V ii., 54.

[43] BL Cotton MS, Otho, C, X, f. 225r.

[44] BL Cotton MS, Otho, C, X, f. 224v.

[45] BL Cotton MS, Otho, C, X, f. 223r.

[46] BL Cotton MS, Otho, C, X, f. 222r.

[47] Ellis, vol. 2, p. 61; BL Cotton MS, C, X, f. 209v. (*LP* X 799).

[48] BL Add MS 25114, f. 160 (*LP* X 873).

[49] *Lancelot de Carle*, p. 297 (lines 1278-1295). *LP* X 1036.

[50] *LP* X 911.

[51] *Excerpta Historica*, pp. 261-5 (*LP* X 991).

[52] *HC*, p. 819. See also *WC*, vol. 1, pp. 41-42.

[53] *Lancelot de Carle*, p. 297 (lines 1290-1291).

[54] *Excerpta Historica*, pp. 261-5 (*LP* X 991).

[55] *HC*, p. 819; *WC*, vol. 1, p. 42; LP X 911; Amyot, 'Constantyne', pp. 64-66. Perhaps the Venetian ambassador, or his informant, was the only one in attendance near enough to the scaffold and to her ladies to hear and record it clearly.

[56] Jane, Lady Rochford, Anne, Lady Cobham, Mary, Lady Kingston, Margaret, Lady Coffin, Isabel Stoner, and, ultimately, Margery Horsman.

Chapter 16: 'A power desolat wydow wythoute comffort': Widowhood

[1] *LP*, X, 908. CSP, Sp, V, ii., 55.

[2] PPE, Hen. VIII, pp. 76, 195, 209, etc. Upon his arrest, George was due to receive a sum of £200 for petitioning the king on behalf of a monk.

[3] Ellis, vol. 2. pp. 67-8.

[4] Ellis, vol. 2, pp. 67-8.

[5] Rowley-Williams, 'Image and Reality', p. 162.

[6] *LP* XI 17.

[7] *LP*, XI, 17.
[8] Ellis, vol. 2, pp. 67-8.
[9] TNA SP/1/104, f. 82. See Rowley-Williams, 'Image and Reality', p. 298.
[10] TNA E/315/160, ff. 104-105. Rowley-Williams, 'Image and Reality', p. 164, p. 299.
[11] *LP*, XIV, i., 867.
[12] *LP*, XV, 1032.
[13] *WC*, vol. 1, pp. 36-37.
[14] *Lisle*, III, 698, pp. 365-6 (*LP* X 919); *Lisle*, IV, 846, pp. 47-8 (*LP* X 920).
[15] *LP* X 1036.
[16] A nephew of George Gainsford.
[17] *Lisle*, IV, 846a; Shortly after George was appointed to serve as one of Henry's gentleman ushers. *LP* XIII, ii, 249 (14).
[18] *Lisle*, III, 698, pp. 365-6 (*LP* X 919); *Lisle*, IV, 846, pp. 47-8 (*LP* X 920).
[19] *Lisle*, III, 713, pp. 395-6.
[20] *WC*, vol 1., pp. 43-44. Edward Hall observed that it was 'at Whitsontyde' (4 June) that Jane was 'openlye shewed as Quene'. *HC*, p. 819.
[21] Norton, *Fatale*, pp. 219-20.
[22] Ives, *Anne*, p. 377. *Lisle*, III, pp. 380-1.
[23] It may be significant that Jane's father, Lord Morley, too was on friendly terms with Cromwell. Starkey, *Triumphs*, p. 9. Cromwell frequented acted as his patron for the baron, and in a letter addressed to the Secretary in January 1531, for example, Morley refers to him affectionately as 'my singular good friend and old acquaintance'. Shortly after the executions of Anne and George Boleyn, Morley was granted the stewardship of Hatfield Park, which had belonged to his son-in-law. *LP* X 1256 [2].
[24] Ellis, vol, 2, pp. 66-7.

Chapter 17: 'No meet suit for any man to move such matters': Politics

[1] *Lisle*, III, 658, pp. 300-1 (*LP* X 499).
[2] TNA SP 1/85, f. 43 (*LP* VII 964).
[3] *Lisle*, IV, 896, pp. 167-8 (*LP* XII, ii., 808). This was reiterated by Henry, Lord Montague, who told Lord Lisle that, although he would do his best to petition for the appointment of Lisle's daughter Anne to the queen's household, 'if you would write to my mother yourself, it would take effect sooner'. TNA SP 3/6, f. 76 (*LP* XII, i., 1229).
[4] *Lisle*, III, 717, pp. 408-9.
[5] *Lisle*, IV, 850ii, pp. 109-110.
[6] *Lisle*, IV 882, p. 146 (*LP* XII, ii., 66); *Lisle*, VI, 1649, p. 25 (*LP* XV 215) for the Countess of Rutland; *Lisle*, IV, 887, pp. 150-152 (*LP* XII, ii., 271) for Elizabeth Harleston, Lady Wallop; *Lisle*, IV, 895, pp. 163-5 (*LP* XII, ii., 711) for Sir William Coffin; *Lisle*, III, 668, pp. 315-6 (*LP* X 573). *LP* X 1165 for Margery Horsman; *Lisle*, IV, 870, pp. 125-6 for John Powes.
[7] *Lisle*, IV, 863, pp. 107-9.

[8] *Lisle*, III, 668, pp. 315-6 (*LP* X 573); *Lisle*, II, 299, p. 330. Margery Horsman also advised Lady Lisle that 'the Queen's Grace setteth much store by a pretty dog'. *Lisle*, II, 299a, p.331 (*LP* IX 991), dated 1535 in *LP* but *Lisle* shows that the correct date is 1534.

[9] Ives, *Faction*, p. 6.

[10] TNA SP 3/3, f. 136 (*LP* VII 349).

[11] TNA SP 3/13, f. 171 (*LP* VII 734).

[12] *LP* XII, ii., 273.

[13] *Lisle*, IV, 895, pp.163-5 (*LP* XII, ii., 711).

[14] *Lisle*, IV, 850ii, pp. 109-110.

[15] *Lisle*, IV, 874, pp. 136-8 (*LP* XII, i., 1069).

[16] Mary Norris, one of the queen's maids-of-honour.

[17] *Lisle*, IV, 868a, pp. 121-3.

[18] *Lisle*, IV, 875, pp. 138-9.

[19] *Lisle*, IV, 855a, pp. 71-2.

[20] Eleanor Paston, Countess of Rutland, conveyed the quails. *Lisle*, IV, 887, pp. 150-152 (*LP* XII, ii., 271). See also *Lisle*, IV, 878, p. 141.

[21] *Lisle*, IV, 887, pp. 150-152 (*LP* XII, ii., 271).

[22] *Lisle*, IV, 887, pp. 150-152 (*LP* XII, ii., 271).

[23] *Lisle*, IV, 887, pp.150-152 (*LP* XII, ii., 271).

[24] *Lisle*, IV, 850ii, pp. 109-110.

[25] Robert Beale, 'A Treatise of the Office of ... Principall Secretarie', in Conyers Read, *Mr Secretary Walsingham and the Policy of Queen Elizabeth*, 3 vols. (Cambridge, 1925), vol. 1, pp. 423-43.

[26] *Lisle*, IV, 887, pp. 150-152 (*LP* XII, ii, 271).

[27] *Lisle*, IV, 891, pp. 156-7.

[28] *Lisle*, IV, 887, pp. 150-152 (*LP* XII, ii., 271).

[29] *Lisle*, IV, 887, pp. 150-152 (*LP* XII, ii., 271).

[30] *Lisle*, IV, 894, pp. 161-2; *Lisle*, IV, 887, pp. 150-152 (*LP* XII, ii., 271).

[31] *Lisle*, IV, 895, pp. 163-5.

[32] *Lisle*, I, xxxii, pp. 332-333. Like Elizabeth I's ladies of the Privy chamber, who functioned as barometers of the queen's favour. Elizabeth's contemporaries knew well that servants could be trusted to facilitate access to and communications with the queen. Natalie Mears, 'Politics in the Elizabethan Privy Chamber: Lady Mary Sidney and Kat Ashley', in James Daybell (ed.), *Women and Politics in Early Modern England, 1450-1700* (Hampshire, 2004), pp. 67-82 (p. 73).

[33] *Lisle*, III, 753, pp. 468-9.

[34] *Lisle*, IV, 890, p. 155 (*LP* XII, ii., 318). Dauncy also thanked Lady Lisle for her 'manifold kindness'.

[35] *Lisle*, IV, 855a, pp. 71-2.

[36] *Lisle*, IV, 880, pp. 144-5.

[37] *Lisle*, IV, 882, p. 146.

[38] *Lisle*, IV, 894, pp. 161-2.

[39] See also the reports of foreign ambassadors, who often reveal or name their source within the court to be one of the queen's servants: on 9 January 1536, two days after the death of Catherine of Aragon, for example, Chapuys wrote to Charles V, anxiously awaiting news from her servants: 'I cannot relate in detail the circumstances of the Queen's decease', he remarked, '...for none of her servants has yet come'. CSP Sp, V, ii., 3 (*LP* X 59).

[40] John Husee, Lady Lisle's agent, trusted that Anne's Receiver-General, George Taylor, could get a suit (as well as gifts) to her. *Lisle*, II, 299, p. 330. *Lisle*, II, 302, pp. 373-4 (*LP* VIII 15).

[41] TNA SP 1/109 f. 198 (*LP* XI 879).

[42] TNA SP 1/106, f. 291 (*LP* XI 567).

[43] 'To be a sollicitor'. TNA SP 1/109 f. 198 (*LP* XI 879). Previously Clementhorpe was dissolved but had lately been restored by insurgents.

[44] Wood, vol. 2, pp. 184-186.

[45] TNA SP 1/109 f. 198 (*LP* XI 879).

[46] TNA SP 1/120 f. 136 (*LP* XII, i., 1225).

[47] *LP* XI 860. 'Perhaps God permitted this rebellion', Jane apparently remarked, somewhat contemptuously, 'for ruining so many churches'. *LP* XI 1250.

Chapter 18: '...sume of your speciall frendes nygh aboute the kynges highnes': Patron

[1] *LP* XII, ii., 1020; *WC*, vol. 1, pp. 69-70; *LP* XII, ii., 1060. For the household of Jane Seymour, see *Lisle*, III and IV, *The Lisle Letters* dating from 4 June 1536 to 24 October 1537, for various entries identifying her servants; TNA E179/69/27 for a subsidy list assessing the queen's Chamber in c. 1536; TNA LC 5/31 ff. 1-6 for wardrobe warrants 'for the Quenes grace', 1536-37; BL Royal MS, 7, C, XVI, ff. 18-32 (*LP* XII, ii., 973) for 'A boke of the Quenes juelles' from 1537, and BL Additional MS, 45716A, ff. 91v-92v for those in attendance for Jane's funeral in 1537.

[2] *LP* XII, ii., 1060.

[3] TNA SP 1/126, f. 124 (*LP* XII, ii., 1084).

[4] Rowley-Williams, 'Image and Reality', p. 165.

[5] LP Addenda II 1593; LP Addenda II 1594.

[6] TNA SP 1/127, f. 49 (*LP* XII, ii., 1209); *Lisle*, V, 1249, pp. 250-1 (*LP* XIII, ii., 591). As for her 'finding', or 'board', the king 'will recompense it one way or other', Husee was told. TNA SP 3/12, f. 94 (*LP* XIV, i., 1120).

[7] TNA SP 3/1, f. 83 (*LP* XIV, ii., 284). For the household of Anne of Cleves, see TNA SP 1/155 ff. 36-37 (*LP* XIV, ii, 572 (4)) for the names of those appointed to receive Anne at Dover; TNA E101/422/15 for an account book of her expenses; TNA E101/422/16 for a similar book, with payments made to her receiver-general concerning her lands; BL Add MS 45716A, ff.15v-18r for 'Ordynary of the Quene's Syde' of 1540, and TNA SP 1/161 f. 81 (*LP* XV 872), *LP* XV 850 [14] for the proceedings of the annulment of her marriage with the king.

[8] TNA E101/422/15; TNA E101/422/16.

[9] *LP* XIII, ii., 884.

[10] *PPE*, Hen., pp. 4, 36, 42, 48, 50, 91, 92, 149.

[11] Perhaps the 'Henri Grâce à Dieu', or 'Great Harry', the flagship of Henry VIII's fleet, an English carrack which had been completely rebuilt between 1536 and 1539.

[12] Ellis, vol. 2, pp. 126-7. *Lisle*, V, 1513a, p. 616.

[13] TNA SP 1/154, f. 5 (LP XIV, ii., 297).

[14] *Lisle*, VI, 1636, p. 12. *WC*, vol. 1, pp. 109-111; *HC*, pp. 832-838.

[15] *LP* XV 22; *LP* XV 23.

[16] TNA SP 1/155 f. 85.

[17] *Lisle*, VI, 1649, p. 25 (*LP* XV 215).

[18] *Lisle*, V, 1574, pp. 681-2 (*LP* XIV, ii., 436); *Lisle*, VI, 1649, p. 25 (*LP* XV 215).

[19] *Lisle*, VI, 1653, pp.33-34 (*LP* XV 229). Arthur Plantagenet, Lord Lisle, Katherine's father, was informed that 'the ladies of the privy chamber were appointed before the coming of Madame'. Lisle's patron in this suit, Henry Olisleger, vice-chancellor of the Duchy of Cleves, had 'begged that an exception be made in her favor', but regrettably informed him that 'it has been of no avail'. *LP* XV 22; *LP* XV 23; *LP* XV 33.

[20] *Lisle*, V, 1593, pp. 701-703.

[21] *HO*, p. 146.

[22] Amanda Richardson, 'Gender and Space in English Royal Palaces c. 1160—c. 1547: A Study in Access Analysis and Imagery', Medieval Archaeology, 47, 1 (2003), pp. 131-165 (pp. 132, 163).

[23] BL Add MS 71009, f. 20r.

[24] See, for instance, *Foxe*, vol. V, p. 555; Giustinian, *Four Years*, pp. 312-313.

[25] Sebastian Giustinian, having resided at the king's court as an ambassador, described Henry VIII as 'affable, gracious' and 'harms no one'. Giustinian, *Four Years*, pp. 313-5.

[26] Cavendish, *Wolsey*, p. 12; *LP* VIII 1018.

[27] *LP* VI 212; CSP Sp IV, ii. 1055. For ceremony, banquets, or pastime in the queen's Presence chamber, see also CSP Ven, IV, 105; *LP* IV 1704.

[28] *LP* X 1069.

[29] CSP Sp, V, ii, 43.

[30] *WC*, vol. 1, p. 173.

[31] Sir Thomas Wyatt, *Collected Poems*, ed. by J. Daalder (Oxford, 1975) CVII, p. 112.

[32] *HO*, p. 157.

[33] *PCP*, Nicolas (ed.), VII, pp. 51-52.

[34] *Lisle*, V, 1620, pp. 730-1 (*LP* XIV, ii., 718).

[35] *LP* XV 954.

[36] *Lisle*, V, 1620, pp. 730-1 (*LP* XIV, ii., 718).

[37] *Lisle*, V, 1620, pp. 730-1 (*LP* XIV, ii., 718).

[38] *Lisle*, VI, 1653, p. 33-4 (*LP* XV 229).

[39] *Lisle*, VI, 1653, p. 33-4 (*LP* XV 229).

[40] *LP* III 2356 (20).

[41] BL Harleian MS 6148, ff. 44r-44v; Clark, *Gender*, pp. 41-63 for more on Agnes, Dowager Duchess of Norfolk as a patron.

[42] TNA SP 1/104, f. 282. Rowley-Williams, 'Image and Reality', p. 165.

Chapter 19: 'Those with the queen are guards and spies, not servants': Spy

[1] Ellis, vol. 2, pp. 67-8.

[2] Loades, *Catherine*, p. 133.

[3] TNA SP 3/11, f. 99 (*LP* XI 467); *LP* Addenda I 1144.

[4] Henry Ellis, *Original Letters of eminent literary men of the Sixteenth, Seventeenth, and Eighteenth Centuries* (London, 1843), p. 14.

[5] Culling, 'Impact', p. 27. George Boleyn, Lord Rochford, warned 'every man to beware of the flattering of the Court'. TNA SP 3/11, f. 99 (*LP* XI 467).

[6] TNA SP 1/138, f. 177 (*LP* XIII, ii, 804 [7]).

[7] TNA SP 1/45, f. 246 (*LP* IV 3693). Wolsey was forced to dismiss early murmurs at court of the annulment as 'false', and 'entirely without foundation, yet not altogether causeless'.

[8] TNA SP 1/42, f. 252 (*LP* IV 3327).

[9] BL Cotton MS, Vespasian, F, I, f. 77 (*LP* IV 3265). *LP* IV 3312; TNA SP 1/45, f. 237 (*LP* IV 3687).

[10] BL Cotton MS, Vespasian, F, I, f. 77 (*LP* IV 3265).

[11] TNA SP 1/42, ff. 202-203 (*LP* IV 3278).

[12] *LP* VIII 189.

[13] *LP* IV 4685.

[14] It is clear Shorton was conflicted as, a year later, Wolsey asked Shorton 'to dissuade her from making any further pursuit', but 'had no word' back from him. *LP* IV 5865.

[15] *LP* IV 4685.

[16] Strype, *Ecclesiastical Memorials*, vol. 1, p. 189; Thomas Russell (ed.), *The Works of the English Reformers: William Tyndale and John Frith*, 3 vols., vol. 1, pp. 453-4.

[17] William Tyndale, 'Practice of Prelates', in Henry Walter (ed.), *Expositions and Notes on Sundry Portions of the Holy Scriptures: Together with The Practice of Prelates*, vol. 43 (1849), pp. 308-309.

[18] Peter Gwyn, *The King's Cardinal: The Rise and Fall of Thomas Wolsey* (1990), p. 506.

[19] My italics, for emphasis. TNA SP 1/54, f. 250 (*LP* IV 5750).

[20] Strype, *Ecclesiastical Memorials*, vol. 1, p. 190.

[21] TNA SP 1/18, f. 66 (*LP* III 151).

[22] Tyndale, *Practice of Prelates*, pp. 308-309.

[23] TNA SP 1/16, f. 200 (*LP* II 4045).

[24] My italics, for emphasis. Rosemary Horrox, *Richard III: A Study of Service* (Cambridge, 1989), p. 18.

[25] BL Add MS 19398, f. 644.

[26] BL Cotton MS Vitellius, B, XII, f. 173.

[27] *LP* XV 954.

²⁸ Pizan, *Treasure*, 2 / 7.
²⁹ *LP* IV 5255. CSP Sp, III, ii., 224 for further reports by Mendoza of the cardinal's 'numerous' spies at court.
³⁰ *LP* V 1059.
³¹ *LP* IX 983; CSP, Sp, IV, i, 509. Even Anne Boleyn apparently saw the advantage of this, as Chapuys reported on 5 September 1530, the rival 'placed some women about her to spy and report anything she may say or do', although it is difficult to see exactly how she would have manoeuvred them into the queen's chamber. CSP Sp IV, i., 422.
³² CSP Sp V, i., 75 (*LP* VII 1013).
³³ CSP Sp V, i., 75 (*LP* VII 1013).
³⁴ *LP* VIII 684.
³⁵ BL Cotton MS, Otho, C, X, f. 215 (*LP* X 28).
³⁶ CSP Sp, V, ii., 3 (*LP* X 59).
³⁷ TNA SP 1/162, f. 66 (*LP* XV 991).
³⁸ TNA SP 1/162, f. 66 (*LP* XV 991).
³⁹ TNA SP 1/26, f. 31 (*LP* XII, ii., 1004).
⁴⁰ *HC*, pp. 832-8.
⁴¹ *LP* XV 850.
⁴² *LP* XV 823.
⁴³ *LP* XV 850; Strype, *Ecclesiastical Memorials*, vol. 1, part 2, pp. 462-3.
⁴⁴ Warnicke, *Cleves*, pp. 234-236.
⁴⁵ TNA SP/157/13-17; HMC, Rutland, I, 27, dated 9 July but *LP* XV 844 has 6 July.
⁴⁶ *LP* XV 844.
⁴⁷ *LP* XV 872.
⁴⁸ TNA SP 1/151, f. 116 (*LP* XV 925).
⁴⁹ *HC*, p. 839; *WC*, vol. 1., pp. 119-20; *LP* XV 901; TNA SP 1/161, f. 203 (*LP* XV 930).
⁵⁰ BL Cotton MS, Otho, C, X, f. 248 (*LP* XV 874).
⁵¹ TNA SP 1/168, f. 50 (*LP* XVI 1407). The deposition of Jane Rattsey names 'Elizabeth Basset', but all of the evidence indicates that the Basset daughter who was appointed to attend upon Anne was Katharine.
⁵² *WC*, vol. 1, pp. 130-131.
⁵³ TNA SP 1/168, f. 50 (*LP* XVI 1407).
⁵⁴ Bentley (ed.), *Excerpta Historica*, pp. 96-98.

Chapter 20: '...you wyll com whan my lade Rochforthe ys here': Bawd

¹ *LP* XVI 12. *LP* XV 901.
² *LP* XVI 578.
³ For the household of Katherine Howard, see TNA SP 1/157, ff. 13-17 (*LP* XV 21) for 'A book of certain of the Queen's Ordinary' of 1540; BL Stowe MS 559, ff. 55r-68r for a book of the queen's jewels from 1540-41; TNA SP 1/167 ff. 120-140 for a series of

letters, ambassadorial reports, indictments and, most importantly, depositions concerning Katherine's fall dating from 5 November 1541 to 13 February 1542.

[4] *LP* XVI 1366.

[5] Loades, *Boleyns*, p. 144.

[6] TNA SP 1/157, f. 15.

[7] BL Cotton MS, Vitellius, B, XXI, f. 203 (*LP* XIV, ii., 33).

[8] *Lisle*, V, 1620, pp. 730-1 (*LP* XIV, ii., 718).

[9] This report was dated 29 January 1542, after Katherine had been moved to Syon, shortly after her indiscretions had been uncovered by the king's Privy council. *LP* XVII 63; *LP* XVII Appendix B, 4; CSP Sp VI, i., 223. TNA SP 1/167, f. 133.

[10] *LP* Addenda, I, ii, 1513.

[11] BL Cotton MS, Vitellius, B, XXI, f. 203 (*LP* XIV, ii., 33). *LP* XVI 1332. We must take these assessments of queens and their character cautiously, as they are often inconsistent. The French ambassador Charles de Marillac observed that, shortly after the annulment of her marriage with the king, Anne of Cleves would take 'all the recreation she can in diversity of dress and pastime' (*LP* XVI 11).

[12] *PCP*, VII, p. 39 (*LP* XVI 62).

[13] *LP* XIII, i, 1.

[14] *LP* IX 612.

[15] *LP* XV 831 (33).

[16] Smith, *Catherine*, p. 152 and Josephine Wilkinson, *Katherine Howard: The Tragic Story of Henry VIII's Fifth Queen* (London, 2016), p. 65.

[17] *LP* XVII Appendix, 10, and 'Letter from Richard Hilles to Henry Bullinger' in Original Letters of the Reformation, vol. 1, pp226-7, Smith, *Catherine*, p. 153.

[18] Cavendish, *Visions*, pp. 68-70.

[19] *LP* XII, ii., 1150 (31); *LP* XV 831 (33); *LP* XIV, ii., 781 and *LP* XVI 380. In particular, note the inventory of his goods taken at his arrest. *LP* XVI 1343.

[20] TNA SP 1/167, ff. 140-142 (*LP* XVI 1339).

[21] TNA SP 1/167, ff. 140-142 (*LP* XVI 1339).

[22] HMC Bath, vol. 2, pp. 9-10; 'instans' – urgent solicitation or entreaty.

[23] HMC Bath, vol. 2, pp. 9-10.

[24] TNA SP 1/167, ff. 140-142 (*LP* XVI 1339).

[25] TNA SP 1/167, ff. 140-142 (*LP* XVI 1339).

[26] 'At Greenwich', Culpeper recalled in his deposition, '[she] sent to him, being sick, at diverse times flesh or the fish dinner by Morres the Page'. TNA SP 1/167, ff. 140-142 (*LP* XVI 1339). Probably Morris Ludlow, later groom of the chamber to Katherine Parr.

[27] TNA SP 1/167 f. 14 (*LP* XVI 1134).

[28] TNA SP 1/167 f. 14 (*LP* XVI 1134).

[29] James Daybell (ed.), *Early Modern Women's Letter Writing, 1450-1700* (Hampshire, 2001), pp. 6-7.

[30] Russell, *Catherine*, p. 248.

[31] TNA SP 1/167, ff. 140-142 (*LP* XVI 1339).

[32] Audrey M. Thorstad, *The Culture of Castles in Tudor England and Wales* (Suffolk, 2019), p. 155.

[33] *HO*, p. 156.

[34] BL Cotton MS, Cleopatra, E, IV, f. 99 (*LP* VI 923).

[35] There is an entry in the accounts of Elizabeth of York on 5 September 1502 when she laid out 14d. 'for cariage of the quenes Stole', the responsibility of which was reserved for the groom of the stool, yet no name is given as to who received this reward.

[36] TNA SP 1/167, ff. 140-142 (*LP* XVI 1339).

[37] TNA SP 1/167, ff. 140-142 (*LP* XVI 1339).

[38] TNA SP 1/167, ff. 142-143 (*LP* XVI 1339).

[39] TNA SP 1/167, ff. 140-142 (*LP* XVI 1339).

[40] TNA SP 1/167, ff. 142-143 (*LP* XVI 1339).

[41] TNA SP 1/167, ff. 140-142 (*LP* XVI 1339).

[42] TNA SP 1/167, ff. 140-142 (*LP* XVI 1339).

[43] TNA SP 1/167, f. 131 (*LP* XVI 1337).

[44] TNA SP 1/167, f. 131 (*LP* XVI 1337).

[45] TNA SP 1/167, ff. 142-143 (*LP* XVI 1339).

[46] TNA SP 1/167, ff. 133-134 (*LP* XVI 1338).

[47] TNA SP 1/167, f. 131 (*LP* XVI 1337). Tylney also spoke of 'strange messages' that were given to her from the queen to be handed to Jane. So strange were they that she 'knew not how to utter them'.

[48] TNA SP 1/167, ff. 140-142 (*LP* XVI 1339).

[49] TNA SP 1/167, ff. 140-142 (*LP* XVI 1339).

[50] TNA SP 1/167, ff. 140-142 (*LP* XVI 1339).

[51] TNA SP 1/167, ff. 140-142 (*LP* XVI 1339). Starkey, *Six Wives*, p. 677.

[52] TNA SP 1/167, ff. 133-134 (*LP* XVI 1338).

[53] TNA SP 1/167, ff. 133-134 (*LP* XVI 1338).

[54] HMC Bath, vol. 2, pp. 9-10; TNA SP 1/167, ff. 140-142 (*LP* XVI 1339).

[55] TNA SP 1/167, ff. 140-142 (*LP* XVI 1339).

[56] HMC Bath, vol. 2, pp. 9-10.

[57] HMC Bath, vol. 2, pp. 9-10.

[58] HMC Bath, vol. 2, pp. 9-10.

[59] Starkey, *Six Wives*, pp. 679-80.

[60] Irish, 'Devonshire', p. 92.

[61] Latymer, f. 32v.

[62] Pizan, *Treasure*, 2 / 7.

[63] HMC Bath, vol. 2, pp. 9-10

[64] Starkey, 'Privy Chamber', p. 63. The king's affairs could be carried out with the utmost discretion. Starkey, 'Representation' in Guy (ed.), *Monarchy*, p. 61.

[65] *LP* XVI 1334.

[66] TNA SP 1/167, f. 140 for Dereham, f. 144 for Mannox (*LP* XVI 1339).

[67] *LP* XVI 1334.

[68] *LP* XVI 1332.

[69] Weir, *Court*, p. 454 and Starkey, *Six Wives*, p. 671. Smith, *Catherine*, p. 165.
[70] HMC Bath, vol. 2, pp. 8-9.
[71] *LP* XVI 1334.
[72] *LP* XVI 1469; *LP* XVI 1470. The crime 'misprision of treason' was committed by someone who knows of an act of treason being committed or about to be committed without reporting it. *LP* XVI 1430; *LP* XVI 1470; *LP* XVII 28; *LP* XVI 1422; *LP* XVI 1483.
[73] *LP* XVI 1331.
[74] *LP* XVI 1359.
[75] WC, vol. 1, pp. 130-1.
[76] *LP* XVII 92.
[77] TNA SP 1/167, ff. 142-143 (*LP* XVI 1339).
[78] HMC Bath, vol. 2, pp. 8-9.
[79] HMC Bath, vol. 2, pp. 8-9.
[80] *LP* XVI 1334.
[81] *LP* XVI 1333.
[82] *LP* XVI 1366.
[83] WC, vol. 1, pp. 130-131.

Chapter 21: 'My lady of Rochford was the principal occasion of the queen's folly': The Fall of Katherine Howard

[1] TNA SP 1/167, ff. 140-142 (*LP* XVI 1339).
[2] *LP* XVI 1401. CSP Sp VI, i., 209.
[3] HMC Bath, vol. 2, pp. 8-9.
[4] Russell, *Catherine*, p. 290.
[5] *LP* XVI 1333. If a second, more satisfactory deposition was extracted from Katherine, it is no longer extant.
[6] Ives, *Anne*, pp. 20-22 for a discussion on the nature of courtly love.
[7] Wilkinson, *Katherine*, p. 190.
[8] Conor Byrne, *Katherine Howard: A New History* (2014), p. 160.
[9] Wilkinson, *Katherine*, pp. 125-6, 246.
[10] Retha M. Warnicke, 'Katherine Howard' (1518/1524-1542) in ODNB (2004). Byrne, *Katherine*, pp. 170, 192. Warnicke, 'Queenship', p. 209.
[11] Retha M. Warnicke, *Wicked Women of Tudor England: Queens, Aristocrats, Commoners* (London, 2012), p. 76.
[12] Byrne, *Katherine*, p. 163. Wilkinson, *Katherine*, p. 169.
[13] TNA SP 1/167, f. 131 (*LP* XVI 1337).
[14] TNA SP 1/167, f. 131 (*LP* XVI 1337).
[15] TNA SP 1/167, ff. 133-134 (*LP* XVI 1338).
[16] TNA SP 1/167, f. 131 (*LP* XVI 1337).
[17] *LP* XVI 1395.
[18] *LP* XVI 1438.

[19] *LP* XVI 1430. In the drafting of the indictment against the accused, it was urged by the Council that it must 'clearly leave out Mary Lasselles'. *LP* XVI 1437; *LP* XVI 1440.

[20] TCD, p. 430.

[21] TNA SP 1/167, ff. 142-143 (*LP* XVI 1339).

[22] TNA SP 1/167, ff. 142-143 (*LP* XVI 1339).

[23] TNA SP 1/167, ff. 142-143 (*LP* XVI 1339).

[24] Hume, *Six Wives*, p. 379.

[25] HMC Bath, vol. 2, pp. 8-9.

[26] *LP* XVI 1426. TNA SP 1/167, ff. 140-142 (*LP* XVI 1339).

[27] Russell also suggests that it is possible she was telling the truth. Russell, *Catherine*, p. 330.

[28] Fraser, *Six Wives*, p. 427.

[29] Alison Plowden, *Tudor Women: Queens and Commoners* (New York, 2003), p. 103.

[30] Loades, *Catherine*, pp. 123, 168.

[31] LP XIII, ii., 702.

[32] TNA SP 1/167, ff. 140-142 (*LP* XVI 1339).

[33] TNA SP 1/167, ff. 133-134 (*LP* XVI 1338).

[34] TNA SP 1/167, ff. 140-142 (*LP* XVI 1339).

[35] HMC Bath, vol. 2, pp. 8-9. Wilkinson, *Katherine*, p. 122.

[36] Cavendish, *Visions*, pp. 71-4.

[37] Starkey, *Six Wives*, p. 675; Weir, *Court*, p. 455; Smith, *Catherine*, p. 154.

[38] Loades, *Boleyns*, p. 145; Wilkinson, *Katherine*, p. 196.

[39] Norton, *Fatale*, p. 225; Russell, *Catherine*, pp. 223-4.

[40] Loades, *Queens*, p. 144; Loades, *Catherine*, p. 138. Rowley-Williams, 'Image and Reality', pp. 171-2.

[41] Maritenssen, *Parr*, pp. 141-2.

[42] Warnicke, 'Katherine Howard' in ODNB.

[43] Fox, *Jane Boleyn*, p. 361.

[44] Fox, *Jane Boleyn*, pp. 288-90, 361-2.

[45] Smith, *Catherine*, pp. 155-7.

[46] Rowley-Williams, 'Image and Reality', pp. 184-5.

[47] TNA SP 1/167, ff. 133-134 (*LP* XVI 1338).

[48] TNA SP 1/167, ff. 133-134 (*LP* XVI 1338).

[49] As suggested by Gareth Russell, 'she inflamed the household's volatile atmosphere by favouring Lady Rochford over other women of the privy chamber'. Russell, *Catherine*, p. 237.

[50] Pizan, *Treasure*, 2 / 5.

[51] *LP* XVI 1470.

[52] TNA SP 1/167, f. 144 (*LP* XVI 1339).

[53] TNA SP 1/167, f. 144 (*LP* XVI 1339).

[54] TNA SP 1/167, ff. 142-143 (*LP* XVI 1339).

Chapter 22: 'wt goodly wordes and stedfast contenance': Execution

[1] *LP* XVI 1426.
[2] *LP* XVI 1426.
[3] TCD, p. 388.
[4] *LP* XVI 1426.
[5] HC, p. 842.
[6] *LP* XVI 1395; *LP* XVI 1342.
[7] Bradley J. Irish, "The Secret Chamber and Other Suspect Places": Materiality, Space, and the Fall of Catherine Howard, *Early Modern Women*, 4 (2009), pp. 169-173 (pp. 171-172).
[8] WC, vol. 1, pp. 131-132.
[9] LP XVI 1426; CSP Sp VI, i., 209 (*LP* XVI 1401).
[10] LP XVI 1395.
[11] *LP* XVI 1395.
[12] WC, vol 1, p. 132. Starkey, *Six Wives*, p. 680.
[13] *LP* XVI 1395. See also 'The Third Report of the Deputy Keeper of Public Records' (1842), Appendix II, pp. 263-4.
[14] CSP Sp VI, i., 209 (*LP* XVI 1401).
[15] CSP Sp VI, i., 209 (*LP* XVI 1401).
[16] WC, vol. 1, p. 131 for 14th November 1541 and p133 for 9th February 1542.
[17] Miller, *Nobility*, p. 157
[18] SOTR, III, 33 Hen. VIII. c. 21. pp. 857-8. See also *LP* XVII 28.
[19] *LP* XVII 124. Norton, *Fatale*, p. 230.
[20] CSP Sp VI, i., 209 (*LP* XVI 1401).
[21] Rowley-Williams, 'Image and Reality', p. 182.
[22] CSP Sp VI, i., 209 (*LP* XVI 1401). Chapuys reported that Jane had 'been seized with a fit of madness (frenesi) by which her brain is affected'.
[23] CSP Sp VI, i., 232.
[24] BL Cotton MS, Otho, C, X, f. 251 (Ellis, *Letters*, vol. 2, pp. 128-9).
[25] *LP* XVII 100.
[26] Katherine apparently requested that the executioner's block be brought to her room so that she could rehearse positioning herself on it correctly. CSP Sp VI, i., 232.
[27] Hume, *Chronicle*, p. 86.
[28] Gregorio Leti, *Vita di Elisabetta* (Amsterdam, 1692). Alison Weir acknowledges that Leti was 'not always a reliable source' but suggests that 'there may be some truth in this'. Weir, *Tower*, pp. 368-9, 498.
[29] *LP* XVII 100.
[30] HC, p. 843.
[31] BL Cotton MS, Otho, C, X, f. 251 (Ellis, *Letters*, vol. 2, pp. 128-9).
[32] *LP* XVII 119.
[33] TNA E315/160, ff. 104-105, transcribed in Rowley-Williams, 'Image and Reality', pp. 299-300.

[34] *LP* XVIII, i., 623 [66].

[35] James Simpson, "The Sacrifice of Lady Rochford': Henry Parker, Lord Morley's Translation of De Claris mulierbus', in Axton et al. (eds), *Triumphs of English*, pp. 153-170 (p. 155).

[36] Simpson, 'De Claris mulierbus', p. 155.

[37] Simpson, 'De Claris mulierbus', p. 159.

[38] James P. Carley, 'The Writings of Henry Parker, Lord Morley: A Bibliographical Survey', in Axton et al. (eds), *Triumphs of English*, pp. 27-68 (p. 43)

[39] Fox, *Jane Boleyn*, p. 314.

[40] D. C. Bell, *Notices of the historic persons buried in the Chapel of St. Peter ad Vincula, in the Tower of London* (London, 1877), p. 23.

[41] Bell, *Notices*, p. 27.

[42] Bell, *Notices*, p. 23.

[43] Bell, *Notices*, p. 25.

Chapter 23: The Infamous Lady Rochford

[1] Smith, *Catherine*, p. 10.

[2] *LP* XVI 1331.

[3] For the household of Katherine Parr, see *HO*, pp.162-170, TNA LC 5/178, ff. 23-26 for 'The Queen's ordinary' of 1544-45; TNA E179/69/40, 41, 47, 48, 55, 56, for various subsidy lists assessing the queen's Chamber from 1543 to 1547; TNA E315/161 for an account book, BL Cotton Vespasian C XIV 1 ff. 107-107v (*LP* XXI, i., 969) and BL Royal MS App. 89 f. 105 (*LP* XXI, i, 1384) for two lists drawn up of the queen's household for the visiting French embassy in 1546; Foxe, vol. IV, pp. 547-561 for an account of the conspiracy against Katherine in 1546, in John Foxe's *Actes and Monuments*; TNA LC 2/2 for those in attendance for the funeral of Henry VIII in 1547, and TNA E101/426/2 for Katherine's household as queen dowager.

BIBLIOGRAPHY

Primary Sources

AMB	Powell, Susan (ed.), *The Household Accounts of Lady Margaret Beaufort (1443-1509): From the Archives of St John's College, Cambridge* (Oxford, 2022)
APC	Dasent, John Roche (ed.), *Acts of the Privy Council of England*, vol. 1, 1542-1547 (London, 1890)
Arundell	Grose, Francis, Astle, Thomas, Jefferey, Edward (eds), 'The Booke of Henrie Erle of Arundell, Lord Chamberleyn to King Henrie Theighte', in *The Antiquarian repertory*, vol. 2, (London, 1808)
BB	Myers, A. R., (ed.), *The household of Edward IV, the Black Book and the Ordinance of 1478* (Manchester, 1959)
BL	British Library, London Additional Manuscripts (Add) Cottonian Manuscripts (Cotton) Harleian Manuscripts (Harleian) Stowe Manuscripts (Stowe) Royal Manuscripts (Royal) Arundel Manuscripts (Arundel) Lansdowne Manuscripts (Lansdowne)
Bodleian	Bodleian Library, Oxford
Castiglione	Castiglione, Baldassare, *The Book of the Courtier*, ed. and trans. by Opdycke, Leonard Eckstein (New York, 1903)
Cavendish, *Visions*	C. Whittingham (ed.) *The Life of Cardinal Wolsey: And Metrical Visions from the Original Autograph Manuscript*, 2 vols. (1825)
Cavendish, *Wolsey*	Cavendish, George, *The Life of Cardinal Wolsey*, ed. by Singer, Samuel Weller (London 1827)
CC	Nichols, J. G. (ed.) *The Chronicle of Calais in the Reigns of Henry VII and Henry VIII to the year 1540* (1838)

COA	College of Arms MS
CPR	Black J. G., and Brodie, Robert Henry (eds), *Calendar of the Patent rolls preserved in the Public record office: Henry VII, 1485-1509*, 2 vols. (London, 1914)
CSP Elizabeth	Stephenson, Joseph (ed.), *Calendar of State Papers, Foreign, Elizabeth I*, 28 vols. (1863)
CSP Sp	Gayangos, Pascual de, et al. (eds), *Calendar of State Papers, Spanish*, 13 vols. (1888-1954)
CSP Ven	Brown, Rawdon, et al. (eds), *Calendar of State Papers, Venetian*, 38 vols. (1867-1947)
Devonshire	Heale, Elizabeth (ed.), *The Devonshire Manuscript: A Women's Book of Courtly Poetry* (Toronto, 2012)
Ellis	Ellis, Henry (ed.), *Original Letters illustrative of English History*, 2 vols. (London, 1825)
Excerpta Historica	Bentley, Samuel (ed.), *Excerpta Historica, or, Illustrations of English History* (London, 1831)
Foxe	Foxe, John, 'Actes and Monuments', in Cattley, Stephen Reed (ed.), *The Acts and Monuments of John Foxe: A New and Complete Edition*, 8 vols. (London, 1837-41)
Giustinian	Giustinian, Sebastian, *Four Years at the Court of Henry VIII*, ed. and trans. by Rawdon Lubbock Brown (London, 1854), 2 vols.
HC	Hall, Edward, *Hall's Chronicle: containing the history of England, during the reign of Henry the Fourth, and the succeeding monarchs, to the end of the reign of Henry the Eighth*, 2 vols. (1809)
HMC Rutland	Historical Manuscripts Commission, *The Manuscripts of His Grace, The Duke of Rutland, Preserved at Belvoir Castle*, 4 vols. (London, 1888-1905)

HMC Bath	Historical Manuscripts Commission, *Calendar of the Manuscripts of the Marquis of Bath preserved at Longleat, Wiltshire*, 5 vols. (Dublin, 1907)
HO	*A collection of ordinances and regulations for the government of the royal household, made in divers reigns: from King Edward III to King William and Queen Mary, also receipts in ancient cookery* (London, 1790)
Lancelot de Carle	Lancelot de Carle, 'Épistre Contenant le Procès Criminel Faict à l'Encontre de la Royne Anne Boullant d'Angleterre', trans. in JoAnn DellaNeva (ed.), *The Story of the Death of Anne Boleyn: A Poem by Lancelot de Carle*, Medieval & Renaissance Text Studies (Arizona, 2021)
Latymer	Latymer, William, 'A briefe treatise or cronickille of the moste vertuous ladye Anne Bulleyne late quene of England', in Bodleian MS Don., C, 42, ff. 21r-33v transcribed in Dowling, Maria, 'William Latymer's Chronickille of Anne Bulleyne', *Camden Fourth Series*, 39 (1990), pp. 23-65.
Lisle	Byrne, Muriel St. Clare (ed.), *The Lisle Letters*, 6 vols. (London, 1981)
LP	Brewer, J. S., et al. (eds), *Letters and Papers, Foreign and Domestic, of the Reign of Henry VIII, 1509-47*, 21 vols. and addenda (1920)
LPL MS	Lambeth Palace Library, London
Mueller	Mueller, Janel (ed.), *Katherine Parr: Complete Works and Correspondence* (London, 2011)
ODNB	Oxford Dictionary of National Biography
PCP	Nicolas, Sir Nicholas Harris (ed.), *Privy Council of England, Proceedings and Ordinances (1386-1542)*, 7 vols. (1834-1837)
PPE, Eliz	Nicolas, Sir Nicholas Harris (ed.), *The Privy Purse Expenses of Elizabeth of York and Wardrobe Accounts of*

	Edward the Fourth. With a Memoir of Elizabeth of York, and Notes (London, 1830)
PPE, Hen	Nicolas, Sir Nicholas Harris (ed.), *The Privy Purse Expenses of King Henry VIII from Nov. 1529 to Dec. 1532* (London, 1827)
PPE, Mary	Madden, Frederick, *Privy purse expenses of the Princess Mary, daughter of King Henry the Eighth, afterwards Queen Mary* (London, 1831)
Pizan	Pizan, Christine de, *The treasure of the city of ladies; or, The book of the three virtues*, edited and translated with an introduction by Sarah Lawson (London, 1985)
SC	Hume, Martin A. Sharp (ed.) *Chronicle of King Henry VIII: Being a Contemporary Record of some of the Principal Events of the Reigns of Henry VIII. and Edward VI. Written in Spanish By An Unknown Hand* (London, 1889)
Sleidan	*De Statu Religionis et Reipublicae Carolo Quinto Caesare Commentarii* (1555), trans. into English by John Daus in 1560. John Daus, *A Famouse Cronicle of oure Time, called Sleidanes Commentaries* (London, 1560).
Spelman	Baker, John Hamilton (ed.), *The reports of Sir John Spelman* (London, 1977)
Statutes	Luders, A., et al. (eds), *The Statutes of the Realm: Printed by command of his Majesty King George the Third in pursuance of an address of The House of Commons of Great Britain, from Original Records and Authentic Manuscripts*, 10 vols. (1831)
TCD	Tanner, J. R. (ed.), *Tudor Constitutional Documents: A.D 1485-1603* (Cambridge, 1922)
TNA	The National Archives, Kew State Papers, Foreign (SP) State Papers, Domestic (SP) Lord Chamberlain (LC) Chancery (C)

	Exchequer (E)
	Wills and probates (PROB)
WC	Wriothesley, Charles, *A Chronicle of England during the Reigns of the Tudors, From A.D 1485 to 1559*, ed. William Douglas Hamilton, 2 vols. (1838)
Wood	Wood, Mary Anne Everett (ed.), *Letters of Royal and Illustrious Ladies of Great Britain, from the commencement of the twelfth century to the close of the reign of Queen Mary*, 3 vols. (London, 1846)
Wyatt, *Boleigne*	Wyatt, George, 'Life of The Virtuous Christian and Renowned Queen Anne Boleigne' in 'Appendix' Samuel Weller Singer (ed.), *The Life of Cardinal Wolsey* (London, 1827)

Printed primary sources

Amyot, T, 'Transcript of an original Manuscript, containing a Memorial from George Constantyne to Thomas Lord Cromwell.' in *Archaeologia*, 23 (1831), pp. 50-78.

Beale, Robert, 'A Treatise of the Office of ... Principall Secretarie', in Conyers Read, *Mr Secretary Walsingham and the Policy of Queen Elizabeth*, 3 vols. (Cambridge, 1925), vol. 1, pp. 423-43.

Bruce, John, and Perowne, Thomas (eds.), *Correspondence of Matthew Parker*, Parker Society (1853)

Burnet, Gilbert, *The History of the Reformation of the Church of England*, 3 vols. (1679)

Caley, John (ed.), 'Two papers relating to the interview between Henry the Eighth of England and Francis the First of France', *Archaeologia*, 21 (1827), pp. 176–91.

Campbell, William (ed.), *Materials for a History of the Reign of Henry the Seventh*, 2 vols. (London, 1873-77)

Forrest, William, *The history of Grisild the Second: a narrative, in verse, of the divorce of Queen Katharine of Arragon*, ed. by Macray, W. D. (London, 1875)

Furnivall, Frederick J (ed.), *Early English Meals and Manners: John Russell's Boke of Nurture* (London, 1868).

Grafton, *Grafton's chronicle : or, History of England. To which is added his table of the bailiffs, sherrifs, and mayors, of the city of London. From the year 1189 to 1558, inclusive.* 2 vols. (London, 1809)

Harpsfield, Nicholas, *A Treatise on the Pretended Divorce Between Henry VIII. and Catharine of Aragon*, ed. by Pocock, Nicholas (London, 1878)

Hatt, Cecilia A. (ed.), *English Works of John Fisher, Bishop of Rochester: Sermons and Other Writings, 1520-1535* (Oxford, 2002), pp. 212-254.

Hay, Denys (ed.) *The Anglica Historia of Polydore Vergil, A. D. 1485-1537, Royal Historical Society*, Camden Series, vol. 74 (London, 1950)

Hayward, Maria, ed., *The Great Wardrobe Accounts of Henry VII and Henry VIII* (Suffolk, 2012)

Hume, Martin A. Sharp (ed.) *Chronicle of King Henry VIII: Being a Contemporary Record of some of the Principal Events of the Reigns of Henry VIII. and Edward VI. Written in Spanish By An Unknown Hand* (London, 1889)

Jerdan, William (ed.), *Rutland papers: Original documents illustrative of the courts and times of Henry VII. and Henry VIII. Selected from the private archives of His Grace the Duke of Rutland* (London, 1842)

Jones, Michael K., and Underwood, Malcolm G., 'Officers, servants and scholars in Lady Margaret's household, c. 1499-1509', in *The King's Mother: Lady Margaret Beaufort, Countess of Richmond and Derby* (Cambridge, 1993), pp. 268-287.

Leti, Gregorio, *Vita di Elisabetta* (Amsterdam, 1692)

Merriman, Roger Bigelow (ed.), *Life and Letters of Thomas Cromwell*, 2 vols. (1902)

Nichols, J. G. (ed.), *Narratives of the Days of the Reformation* (London, 1859)

Parker, Henry, Lord Morley, *Forty-Six Lives*, Translated from Boccaccio's 'De Claris Mulieribus', ed. by Hubert G. Wright (London, 1943), pp. 168-184.

Parsons, Robert, *A treatise of three conversions of paganisme to Christian religion*, 3 vols., ed. by N. D. (1603-1604)

Pizan, Christine de, *The Boke of the Cyte of Ladyes*, ed. by Hope Johnston, trans. by Brian Anslay, *Medieval and Renaissance Texts and Studies*, 457 (New York, 2014)

Pollard, A. F. (ed.), *Tudor Tracts: 1532-1588* (New York, 1903)

Russell, Thomas (ed.), *The Works of the English Reformers: William Tyndale and John Frith*, 3 vols (1831)

Sander, Nicholas, *The Rise and Growth of the Anglican Schism*, ed. by David Lewis (London, 1877)

Schmid, Susan Walters (ed.), *Anne Boleyn, Lancelot de Carle, and the uses of documentary evidence* (Arizona State University, Unpublished Ph.D. thesis, 2009)

Stephenson, Joseph (ed.), *Calendar of State Papers, Foreign, Elizabeth I*, 28 vols. (1863)

Stevenson, Joseph (ed.) *The Life of Jane Dormer, Duchess of Feria by Henry Clifford, Transcribed from the Ancient Manuscript in the possession of Lord Dormer* (London 1887)

Strype, John, *Ecclesiastical Memorials relating chiefly to religion, and the reformation of it, and the emergences of the Church of England, under King Henry VIII, King Edward VI and Queen Mary I*, 3 vols. (Oxford, 1822)

Tanner, J. R. (ed.), *Tudor Constitutional Documents: A.D 1485-1603* (Cambridge, 1922)

Tyndale, William, 'Practice of Prelates', in Henry Walter (ed.), *Expositions and Notes on Sundry Portions of the Holy Scriptures: Together with The Practice of Prelates*, vol. 43 (1849)

Vives, Juan Luis, *The Education of a Christian Woman: A Sixteenth-Century Manual*, ed. and trans. by Charles Fantazzi (Chicago, 2007)

Wood, Anthony, *Athenae Oxonienses: An Exact History of All the Writers and Bishops Who Have Had Their Education in the University of Oxford* (1691)

Wyatt, Sir Thomas, *Collected Poems*, ed. by J. Daalder (Oxford, 1975)

Secondary sources

Akkerman, Nadine and Houben, Birgit (eds), *The Politics of Female Households: Ladies-in-Waiting across Early Modern Europe* (Boston, 2013)

Asch, Ronald G. and Birke, Adophe M. (eds), *Princes, Patronage and the Nobility: The Court at the Beginning of the Modern Age c.1450-1650* (Oxford, 1991)

Beer, Michelle, *Queenship at the Renaissance Courts of Britain: Catherine of Aragon and Margaret Tudor, 1503-1533* (Suffolk, 2018)

Bell, D. C., *Notices of the historic persons buried in the Chapel of St. Peter ad Vincula, in the Tower of London* (London, 1877)

Bernard, G. W., 'Anne Boleyn's religion', *Historical Journal*, 36 (1993), pp. 1-20.

Bernard, G. W., *Anne Boleyn: Fatal Attractions* (London, 2010)

Bernard, G. W., 'The rise of Sir William Compton, early Tudor courtier', *English Historical Review*, 96, 381 (1981), pp. 754-777.

Betteridge, Thomas, and Lipscomb, Suzannah (eds), *Henry VIII and his Court: Art, Politics and Performance* (London, 2013)

Birch, Thomas, *The Heads of Illustrious Persons of Great Britain* (London, 1747)

Braddock, Robert C., 'The Rewards of Office-holding in Tudor England', *The Journal of British Studies* (1975), pp. 29-47.

Braddock, Robert Cook, 'The Royal Household, 1540-1560: A Study of Officeholding in Tudor England' (Northwestern University, Unpublished Ph.D. thesis, 1971)

Brock, Richard Egbert, 'The Courtier in Early Tudor Society, Illustrated from Selected Examples' (University of London, Unpublished Ph.D. thesis, 1963)

Burke, S. Hubert, *Historical Portraits of the Tudor Dynasty and the Reformation Period* (London, 1880)

Burnet, Gilbert, *The History of the Reformation of the Church of England*, 3 vols. (1679)

Byrne, Conor, *Katherine Howard: A New History* (2014)

Carley, James P., 'The Writings of Henry Parker, Lord Morley: A Bibliographical Survey', in Axton et al. (eds), *Triumphs of English*, pp. 27-68.

Carte, Thomas, *A General History of England*, 4 vols. (London, 1752)

Cervone, Thea, *Sworn Bond in Tudor England: Oaths, Vows and Covenants in Civil Life and Literature* (London, 2011)

Cherry, Clare, and Ridgeway, Claire, *George Boleyn: Tudor Poet, Courtier & Diplomat* (2014).

Clark, Nicola, *Gender, Family and Politics: The Howard Women, 1485-1558* (Oxford, 2018)

Coote, Charles, *The History of England*, 9 vols. (London, 1791)

Culling, Elizabeth Ann, 'The Impact of the Reformation on the Tudor Royal Household to 1553' (University of Durham, Unpublished Ph.D. thesis, 1986)

Daybell, James (ed.), *Early Modern Women's Letter Writing, 1450-1700* (Hampshire, 2001)

Daybell, James, *Women Letter-Writers in Tudor England* (Oxford, 2006)

Denny, Joanna, *Katherine Howard: A Tudor Conspiracy* (London, 2005)

Dowling, Maria, 'Anne Boleyn and Reform', *The Journal of Ecclesiastical History*, 35, 1 (1984), pp. 30-46.

Dowling, Maria, *Humanism in the Age of Henry VIII* (Kent, 1986)

Dowling, Maria, 'Scholarship, Politics and the Court of Henry VIII' (University of London, Unpublished Ph.D thesis, 1982)

Elton, G. R., *The Tudor Revolution in Government: Administrative Changes in the Reign of Henry VIII* (Cambridge, 1953)

Elton, G. R., 'Tudor Government: The Points of Contact. III. The Court', *Transactions of the Royal Historical Society*, 26 (1976), pp. 211-228.

Fenton, Charlie, *Jane Parker: The Downfall of Two Tudor Queens?* (Hampshire, 2021).

Fox, Julia, *Jane Boleyn: The Infamous Lady Rochford* (London, 2009)

Fraser, Antonia, *The Six Wives of Henry VIII* (London, 2002)

Freeman, Thomas S., 'One Survived: The Account of Katherine Parr in Foxe's 'Book of Martyrs', in Betteridge, Thomas and Lipscomb, Suzannah (eds), *Henry VIII and his Court: Art, Politics and Performance* (London, 2013), pp. 235-252.

Freeman, Thomas S., 'Research, rumour and propaganda: Anne Boleyn in Foxe's 'Book of Martyrs'', *The Historical Journal*, 38, 4 (1995), pp. 797-819.

Granville, Charles, *A Synopsis of the Troubles and Miseries of England, during the Space of 1800 Years*, 4 vols. (London, c. 1747)

Grummitt, David, 'Household, politics and political morality in the reign of Henry VII', *Historical Research*, 82, 217 (2009), pp. 393-411.

Gunn, S. J., *Early Tudor Government, 1485-1558* (Hampshire, 1995)

Gunn, Steven, *Henry VII's New Men and the Making of Tudor England* (Oxford, 2016)

Gunn, Steven, and Janse, Antheun (eds), *The Court as a Stage: England and the Low Countries in the Late Middle Ages* (Suffolk, 2006)

Gunn, Steven, 'The Courtiers of Henry VII', *English Historical Review*, 108 (1993), pp. 23-49.

Gunn, Steven, 'The Structures of Politics in Early Tudor England', *Transactions of the Royal Historical Society*, 5 (1995), pp. 59-90.

Guth, D. J., and McKenna, J. W. (eds), *Tudor Rule and Revolution* (Cambridge, 1982)

Guy, John (ed.), *The Tudor Monarchy* (London, 1997)

Guy, John, Review of Alison Weir, *The Lady in the Tower*, The Sunday Times, 1 November 2009

Gwyn, Peter, *The King's Cardinal: The Rise and Fall of Thomas Wolsey* (1990)

Hamilton, Dakota L., 'The Household of Queen Katherine Parr' (University of Oxford, Unpublished Ph.D. thesis, 1992)

Hamilton, Dakota L., Review of Jane Boleyn: The True Story of the Infamous Lady Rochford by Julia Fox, *The Sixteenth Century Journal*, 40, 3 (2009), pp. 828-829.

Harris, Barbara J., *English Aristocratic Women, 1450-1550: Marriage and Family, Property and Careers* (Oxford, 2002)

Harris, Barbara J, 'The View from My Lady's Chamber: New Perspectives on the Early Tudor Monarchy', *Huntingdon Library Quarterly*, 60, 3 (1997), pp. 215-247.

Harris, Barbara J., 'Women and Politics in Early Tudor England', *The Historical Journal*, 33:2 (1990), pp.259-281.

Hayward, Maria, *Dress at the Court of Henry VIII* (Abington, 2007)

Heal, Felicity, *The Power of Gifts: Gift Exchange in Early Modern England* (Oxford, 2014)

Hefferan, Matthew 'Family, Loyalty and the Royal Household in Fourteenth-Century England', in Green, D., and Given-Wilson, C. (eds), *Fourteenth Century England*, XI, pp. 129-154.

Herbert of Cherbury, Edward, *The Life and Raigne of King Henry the Eighth* (London, 1649)

Heylyn, Peter, *Ecclesiae Restaurata, or the History of the Reformation of the Church of England* (1660)

Horrox, Rosemary, *Richard III: A Study of Service* (Cambridge, 1989)

Hume, David, *The History of England, from the Invasion of Julius Caesar to the Revolution in 1688*, 5 vols. (London, 1789)

Hume, Martin, *The Wives of Henry the Eighth, and the Parts they Played in History* (London, 1905)

Irish, Bradley J., "The Secret Chamber and Other Suspect Places": Materiality, Space, and the Fall of Catherine Howard, *Early Modern Women*, 4 (2009), pp.169-173.

Ives, E. W., 'Court and County Palatine in the Reign of Henry VIII: The Career of William Brereton of Malpas', *Transactions of the Historic Society of Lancashire and Cheshire*, 123 (1971), pp. 1-38.

Ives, E. W. *Faction in Tudor England*, 2nd ed. (London, 1986)

Ives, E. W., *Lady Jane Grey: A Tudor Mystery* (Oxford, 2011)

Ives, E. W., 'Patronage at the Court of Henry VIII: The Case of Sir Ralph Egerton of Ridley', *Bulletin of the John Rylands Library*, 52 (1969-70), pp. 346-74.

Ives, E. W., 'The Fall of Anne Boleyn Reconsidered', *English Historical Review*, CVII (1992), pp. 651-664.

Ives, E. W., *The Life and Death of Anne Boleyn: 'The Most Happy'* (Oxford, 2004)

James, Susan, *Catherine Parr: Henry VIII's Last Love* (Gloucestershire, 2008)

Johnston, Hope, 'How the Livre de la cité des dames first came to be printed in England', in Dulac, Liliane, Paupert, Anne, Reno, Christine and Ribémont, Bernard (eds), *Desireuse de plus avant enquerre* (Paris, 2008), pp. 385-96.

Kisby, Fiona, 'Officers and Office-Holding at the English Court: A Study of the Chapel Royal, 1485-1547', *Royal Musical Association Research Chronicle*, 32 (1999), pp.1-61.

Kisby, Fiona, '"When the King Goeth a Procession": Chapel Ceremonies and Services, the Ritual Year, and Religious Reforms at the Early Tudor Court, 1485-1547', *Journal of British Studies*, 40:1 (2001), pp.44-75.

Levine, Mortimer, 'The Place of Women in Tudor Government', in Guth, Delloyd J., and McKenna, John (eds), *Tudor Rule and Tudor Revolution, Essays for G.R. Elton from his American Friends* (Cambridge, 1982) pp. 109-123.

Loades, David, *Power in Tudor England* (Hampshire, 1997)

Loades, David, *The Boleyns: The Rise & Fall of a Tudor Family* (Gloucestershire, 2011)

Loades, David, *Tudor Queens of England* (London, 2009)

Mackay, Lauren, *Among the Wolves of Court: The Untold Story of Thomas and George Boleyn* (London, 2020)

Malcolmson, Cristina, 'Christine de Pizan's *City of Ladies* in Early Modern England', in Malcolmson, Cristina and Mihoko, Suzuki (eds), *Debating Gender in Early Modern England, 1500–1700* (New York, 2002), pp. 15-36.

Mantel, Hilary, 'Frocks and Shocks', Review of Jane Boleyn: The Infamous Lady Rochford by Julia Fox, London Review of Books, 30, 8 (2008)

Martienssen, Anthony, *Queen Katherine Parr* (London, 1975)

McFarlane, K. B., *The Nobility of Later Medieval England* (Oxford, 1973)

McIntosh, J. L., 'Sovereign Princesses: Mary and Elizabeth Tudor as Heads of Princely Households and the Accomplishment of the Female Succession in Tudor England, 1516-1558' (John Hopkins University, Unpublished Ph.D thesis, 2002)

Mears, Natalie, 'Courts, Courtiers, and Culture in Tudor England', *Historical Journal*, 46 (2003), pp. 703-722.

Mears, Natalie, 'Politics in the Elizabethan Privy Chamber: Lady Mary Sidney and Kat Ashley', in Daybell, James (ed.), *Women and Politics in Early Modern England, 1450-1700* (Hampshire, 2004), pp. 67-82.

Mears, Natalie, *Queenship and Political Discourse in the Elizabethan Realms* (Cambridge, 2005)

Merton, Charlotte Isabelle, 'The Women Who Served Queen Mary and Queen Elizabeth: Ladies, Gentlewomen and Maids of the Privy Chamber, 1553-1603' (University of Cambridge, Unpublished Ph.D. thesis, 1990)

Miller, Helen, *Henry VIII and the English Nobility* (Oxford, 1986)

Murphy, John, 'The illusion of decline: the Privy Chamber, 1547-1558' in Starkey, David (ed.), *The English Court: from the Wars of the Roses to the Civil War* (Essex, 2002), pp.119-146.

Norton, Elizabeth, *Catherine Parr* (Gloucestershire, 2010)

Norton, Elizabeth, *Jane Seymour: Henry VIII's True Love* (Gloucestershire, 2009)

Norton, Elizabeth, *The Boleyn Women: The Tudor femmes fatales who changed English history* (Gloucestershire, 2009)

Plowden, Alison, *Tudor Women: Queens and Commoners* (New York, 2003)

Richardson, Amanda, 'Gender and Space in English Royal Palaces c. 1160—c. 1547: A Study in Access Analysis and Imagery', *Medieval Archaeology*, 47, 1 (2003), pp. 131-165.

Richardson, Glenn, *The Field of Cloth of Gold* (New Haven, 2013).

Richardson, W. C., *Tudor Chamber Administration, 1485-1547* (Louisiana, 1952)

Rowley-Williams, Jennifer Ann, 'Image and Reality: the Lives of Aristocratic Women in Early Tudor England' (University of Wales, Unpublished Ph.D. thesis, 1998)

Russell, Gareth *Young and Damned and Fair: The Life and Tragedy of Catherine Howard at the Court of Henry VIII* (London, 2017)

Russell, Joycelyne G., *Field of Cloth of Gold: Men and Manners in 1520* (London, 1969)

Samman, Neil, 'The Henrician Court during Cardinal Wolsey's Ascendancy, c. 1514-1529 (University of Wales, Unpublished Ph.D. thesis, 1988)

Sil, Narasingha Prosad, *Tudor Placemen and Statesmen: Select Case Studies* (New Jersey, 2001)

Simpson, James, "The Sacrifice of Lady Rochford': Henry Parker, Lord Morley's Translation of De Claris mulierbus', in Axton et al. (eds), *Triumphs of English*, pp. 153-170.

Smith, Lacey Baldwin, *A Tudor Tragedy: The Life and Times of Catherine Howard* (London: 1962)

Smollett, T. G., *A Complete History of England, from the Descent of Julius Caesar, to the Treaty of Aix la Chapelle*, 11 vols. (London, 1758-1760)

Soberton, Sylvia Barbara, *Ladies-in-Waiting: Women Who Served Anne Boleyn* (2022)

Starkey, David, 'An Attendant Lord? Henry Parker, Lord Morley', in Marie Axton et al. (eds), *Triumphs of English : Henry Parker, Lord Morley, Translator to the Tudor Court : New Essays in Interpretation* (London, 2000).

Starkey, David, 'Court and Government', in Christopher Coleman and David Starkey (eds), *Revolution Reassessed: Revisions in the History of Tudor Government and Administration* (Oxford, 1986), pp. 29-58.

Starkey, David, 'Representation through intimacy: A study in the symbolism of monarchy and Court office in early modern England', in Guy, John (ed.), *The Tudor Monarchy* (London, 1997), pp. 42-77.

Starkey, David, *Six Wives: The Queens of Henry VIII* (London, 2004)

Starkey, David (ed.), *The English Court: from the Wars of the Roses to the Civil War* (Essex, 2002)

Starkey, David, 'The King's Privy Chamber, 1485-1547' (University of Cambridge, Unpublished Ph.D. thesis, 1973)

Stone, Edward, *Remarks upon the History of the Life of Reginald Pole*, 2nd edition (Oxford, 1766)

Strickland, Agnes, *Lives of the Queens of England,* 8 vols. (1851)

Taffe, James, '"But she to be a Quene, and creuely handeled as was never sene": Anne Boleyn's confinement in the Tower of London', in Yip, Hannah, and Clifton, Thomas (eds), *Writing Early Modern Loneliness* (London, forthcoming)

Taffe, James, '"Pleasaunt Pastime', or Drunken Diplomacy? Ladies and Gentlewomen at the Field of Cloth of Gold', in Musson, Anthony, and Cooper, and J. P. D. (eds), *Royal Journeys in Early Modern Europe: Progresses, Palaces and Panache* (Abingdon, 2022), pp. 127-138.

Taffe, James, 'Reconstructing the queen's household: a study in royal service, 1485-1547' (Durham University, Unpublished Ph.D. thesis, 2022)

Thorstad, Audrey M., *The Culture of Castles in Tudor England and Wales* (Suffolk, 2019)

Thoyras, P. Rapin de, *The History of England, as well Ecclesiastical as Civil*, 2nd edition (London, 1732)

Thurley, Simon, *The Royal Palaces of Tudor England: Architecture and Court Life, 1460-1547* (London, 1993)

Tout, T. F., *Chapters in the Administrative History of Mediaeval England*, 6 vols. (Manchester, 1920-33)

Tremlett, Giles, *Catherine of Aragon: Henry's Spanish Queen* (London, 2010)

Turner, Sharon, *The History of England, From the Earliest Period to the Death of Elizabeth*, 12 vols. (London, 1839)

Walker, Greg, 'Rethinking the Fall of Anne Boleyn', *The Historical Journal*, 45, 1 (2002), pp. 1-29.

Warnicke, Retha M., 'The Fall of Anne Boleyn: A Reassessment', *History*, 70, 228 (1985), pp. 1-15.

Warnicke, Retha M., *The Marrying of Anne of Cleves: Royal Protocol in Early Modern England* (Cambridge, 2000)

Warnicke, Retha M., *The Rise and Fall of Anne Boleyn: Family politics at the court of Henry VIII* (Cambridge, 2000)

Warnicke, Retha M., *Wicked Women of Tudor England: Queens, Aristocrats, Commoners* (London, 2012)

Weir, Alison, *Henry VIII: King and Court* (London, 2008)

Weir, Alison, *The Lady in the Tower: The Fall of Anne Boleyn* (London, 2000)

Wilkinson, Josephine, *Katherine Howard: The Tragic Story of Henry VIII's Fifth Queen* (London, 2016)

Wright, Pam, 'A Change in Direction: the Ramifications of a Female Household, 1558-1603' in Starkey, David (ed.), *The English Court: from the Wars of the Roses to the Civil War* (Essex, 2002), pp. 147-72.

Printed in Great Britain
by Amazon